sittin' in

JAZZ CLUBS OF THE 1940s AND 1950s

JEFF GOLD

HARPER
DESIGN

An Imprint of HarperCollins Publishers

↑ ABOVE Photograph folder, the Royal Chicken Roost, 1948.

For my dear departed friends Eric Miller, Gary Stewart, and Hal Willner.

CONTENTS

← OPPOSITE **Fans at an unknown club, circa 1940s.**

New
CLUB ★ DeLiSA
4 SHOWS NIGHTLY

BUY
WAR BONDS

V

AND STAMPS

BUY
WAR BONDS

V

AND STAMPS

BREAKFAST DANCE
EVERY MONDAY MORNING

AIR CONDITIONED

NO COVER
OR MINIMUM CHARGE

↑ ABOVE An integrated group at Chicago's Club DeLisa, mid-1940s. At left, one of the four DeLisa brothers.

Introduction

In my work as a music executive, historian, collector, and dealer I've had my fair share of crazy adventures, so sorting through the contents of a jazz collector's safe-deposit boxes in a closet-size room in a bank didn't strike me as particularly unusual. In the four hours I was there, I discovered many treasures that I coveted and eventually bought: concert tickets and handbills, autographs, contracts, letters, and other documents. But most interesting were the souvenir photographs from jazz clubs of the 1940s and 1950s. Each was in its own custom folder; the graphics were fantastic and so evocative of that classic era of jazz.

As I went through the boxes, I kept finding more photos—twenty-five, fifty, one hundred, and, eventually, more than two hundred—all mixed in with the rest of the collection. Some were well photographed, some were amateurish. But each had something to offer. Even before I finished, the thought struck me that the photographs would make a great book. If I hadn't seen pictures like these, I doubted many others had.

I bought all of them. Though the images were primarily of African Americans, some pictured white fans, and some showed mixed groups or white and Black people seated next to each other. There were couples on double dates, mothers and fathers with grown children, enlisted men and women in uniform, and even a picture of the Harriet Tubman Social Club. In a few, famous musicians—Dizzy Gillespie, Charlie Parker, Duke Ellington, Art Blakey, Oscar Peterson, and Louis Armstrong—posed with audience members. There was plenty of alcohol, which wasn't surprising.

These quick snapshots were taken by each club's in-house photographer, developed on-site, and ready to be taken home at the end of an evening for a dollar, a cheap souvenir of a night out. Collectively, though, they are something altogether different, something important today—a visual record of a rarely seen and poorly documented world. An accidental history.

These pictures turn the camera around. We've seen photographs of these clubs before, of the performers onstage, the marquees, the lines outside. But rarely, if ever, have we seen the audiences, the fans, as we do here. And they are a critical part of what jazz pianist, composer, and educator Jason Moran calls the "ecosystem" of jazz. Sonny Rollins told me that in small clubs like these, the audiences "sort of played with you. They're like part of the band."

If you're looking for a comprehensive history of jazz, this isn't it. The focus here is on something that hasn't been properly explored: American jazz clubs of the 1940s and 1950s—what some call the golden age—as seen through the lens of these audience photographs and related memorabilia. Moran says, "Seeing these images is powerful because we never document the jazz audience." The Library of Congress, for example, is home to more than 1,600 images taken by legendary jazz photographer William Gottlieb, only a tiny fraction of which picture audience members.

Almost all the souvenir photographs in this book date from the 1940s and 1950s. It doesn't seem many clubs had in-house photographers before 1940, and by the end of the 1950s, most of these clubs were out of business. As New York City was already well established as the jazz center of the world, the majority of the images here are from the city's clubs. But there were hundreds of other clubs in cities across America, and we are fortunate to have a representative sampling from many of them.

These photographs were made at a time when discrimination and segregation were the norm in the United States, and some of them document how "jazz was really where the racial barriers were broken down heavily," according to Rollins.

I am incredibly fortunate that Quincy Jones and Sonny Rollins, who played these clubs, agreed to speak with me about the culture, the fans, and so much more. I'm grateful to Jason Moran, who looked at these photographs through the eyes of a contemporary jazz musician and historian and shared his insights. Dan Morgenstern, a jazz historian without peer, shared his experiences as a patron of some of these clubs beginning in the late 1940s. And writer and cultural critic Robin Givhan graciously shared her insights on the photographs themselves. This book would have been a much lesser work without them.

I've included whatever information I could find about the clubs, musicians, photographers, and mostly anonymous fans. But in some cases, we have only the photos. As I study them, they continue to reveal layers of information. It is my sincere hope they do the same for you.

—JEFF GOLD

PART ONE

Bop City

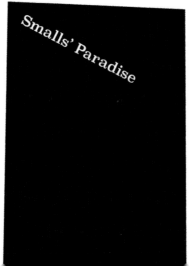

Smalls' Paradise

Harlem Club

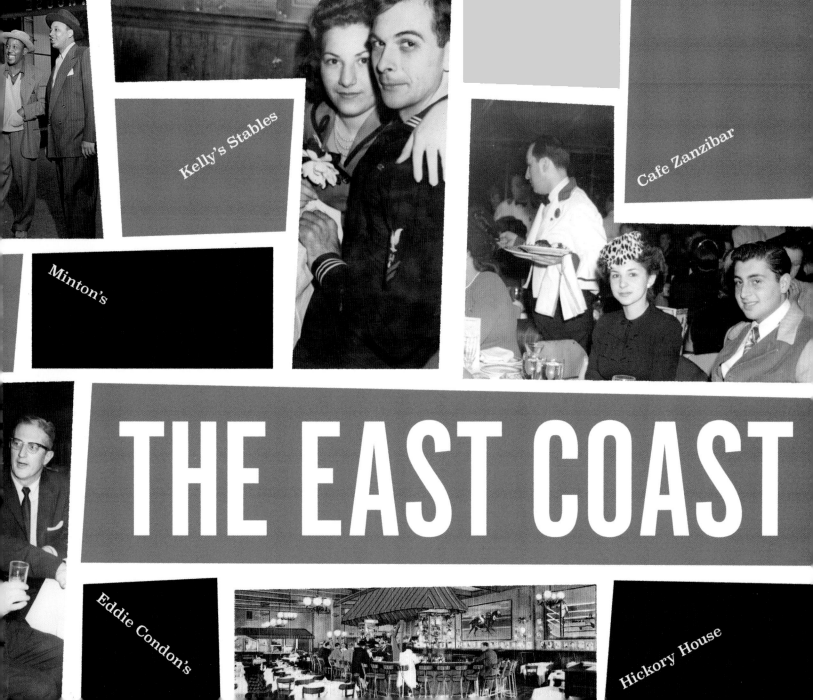

Kelly's Stables

Cafe Zanzibar

Minton's

THE EAST COAST

Eddie Condon's

Hickory House

NEW YORK City

New York City wasn't always the jazz capital of the world. Jazz was born in New Orleans at the turn of the twentieth century, predominantly in the city's red-light district, Storyville, where bar owners and brothel keepers hired ragtime and blues musicians and members of the city's dance and marching bands to entertain customers. Legendary musicians like cornetist Buddy Bolden, who pioneered a looser, more improvised version of ragtime and added blues, and pianist Jelly Roll Morton, writer of "Jelly Roll Blues," the first published jazz composition, helped shape the emerging sounds into what we today recognize as jazz.

But the development of jazz was driven both by the music and, just as often, by unrelated external circumstances. The first was in 1917, when the United States entered World War I. Concerned that troops were being distracted by the abundant sin on offer in Storyville, Secretary of War Newton Baker instituted orders prohibiting prostitution within five miles of military sites. The army and navy demanded that New Orleans close down Storyville, and the city complied.

When Storyville closed, many out-of-work musicians joined other job seekers headed north, as part of the beginnings of the Great Migration. The war had created jobs in America's industrial centers, and hundreds of thousands of African Americans left their homes in the South in search of better employment and a less racially oppressive environment.

Chicago, the railroad center of the country, was a logical destina-tion. Its economy was humming, and its clubs had abundant jobs for players. In the 1920s, Chicago became America's second major jazz hub.

But things were happening in New York City too. In 1915, the Original Creole Band, featuring cornetist Freddie Keppard, performed at the Winter Garden, alongside comedians, jugglers, and various other performers. In 1917, the Original Dixieland Jass Band, a New Orleans via Chicago group, played a wildly successful engagement at Reisenweber's Café on Columbus Circle and was recorded by the Victor label, resulting in the release that year of "Livery Stable Blues," the first jazz record ever and an almost instant hit, eventually selling more than one million copies.

In 1920, another external force began to impact jazz in a major way: Prohibition. Passage of the Eighteenth Amendment to the U.S. Constitution, establishing the prohibition of "intoxicating liquors," resulted in the closure of tens of thousands of bars across the country. But in their place, thousands of speakeasies selling bootleg liquor opened, and many of them offered live music—often jazz. These clubs were also often owned or controlled by mob-sters. At the biggest clubs, competition became stiff for the top musicians, and the careers of many artists, including Duke Ellington, Fletcher Henderson, Louis Armstrong, and Fats Waller, received a major boost as a result.

While some clubs were segregated, a culture of "Black and tan" clubs soon emerged, where Black and white people mixed—an extremely unusual phenomenon at a time when segregation was common and often

During the early years of Prohibition, New York City played along, but that all changed in 1926, when Jimmy Walker was elected mayor. Walker was strongly opposed to the alcohol ban. Under his rule, the speakeasy scene flourished; reportedly there were more than five thousand of them in the city. The situation was similar in Chicago, with thousands of illegal speakeasies and a flourishing jazz scene, but again, external circumstances were about to change everything.

In 1929, the stock market crash and ensuing Great Depression put pressure on clubs everywhere. That same year, Chicago's violent Saint Valentine's Day Massacre focused unwanted attention on mobster Al Capone and his illegal empire. In 1931, the government was finally able to send Capone to prison—for income tax evasion. With Chicago's biggest bootlegger in jail, the music business, media, and broadcasting increasingly centralized in New York, and a growing club and ballroom scene in the city caused many Chicago musicians to leave for the abundant opportunities in the Big Apple, soon to become the next hub of jazz.

The first original jazz style to develop in New York was "Harlem stride," a highly rhythmic, almost orchestral piano style. Stride originated during the 1920s and was pioneered by James P. Johnson and Willie "the Lion" Smith, but its most famous exponent was New Yorker Fats Waller.

Another critical moment for jazz in New York came in 1923, when Duke Ellington moved from Washington, D.C., to Harlem. Inspired by the city's new piano sounds, Ellington chose New York over Chicago for the next stage of his career, and soon other important musicians followed. In 1924, Louis Armstrong came to the city to join Fletcher Henderson's band, and though that move was short-lived, in 1929 he relocated to New York for good. In 1928, singer and bandleader Ben Pollack brought his jazz orchestra to New York; his Chicago-born clarinetist Benny Goodman soon left the band to become a sought-after musician for Broadway shows, recording sessions, and radio broadcasts.

New York City's jazz venues were centered on three areas: Harlem, Fifty-Second Street and midtown, and Greenwich Village.

→ RIGHT **Dizzy Gillespie on Fifty-Second Street, circa 1946–1948.**

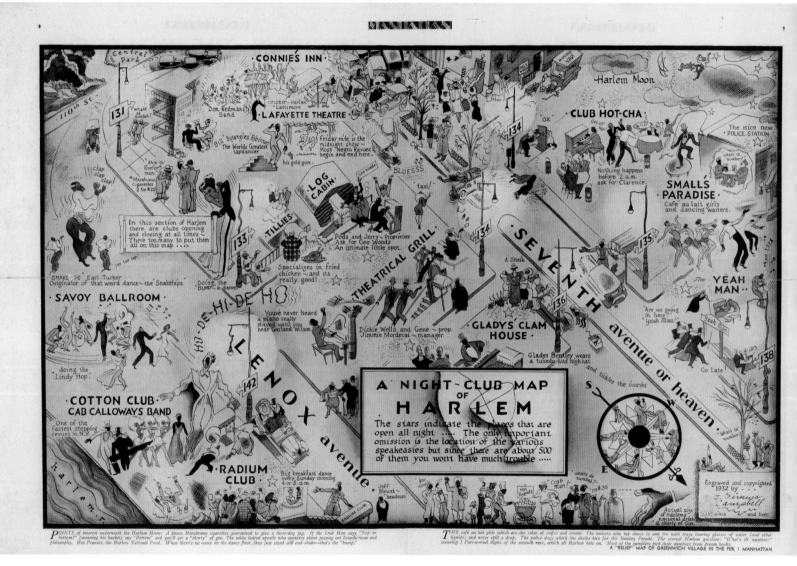

↑ ABOVE *A Night-Club Map of Harlem*, E. Simms Campbell, 1932.

Harlem

During the 1920s and 1930s, most of the musicians who moved to New York settled in Harlem, the city's predominant African American neighborhood. Like Storyville and Chicago's South Side, it was a hotbed of live music, filled with clubs, ballrooms, theaters, and, during Prohibition, more than five hundred speakeasies, many located along Seventh Avenue in the 130s and Lenox Avenue in the 140s.

During the Jazz Age, many rich white midtown and downtown denizens headed uptown to the dance halls and nightclubs of Harlem, seeking exotic entertainment. Club owners were happy to oblige, though what they presented was often a highly romanticized and racist view of Black culture. But amid the dancing girls, floor shows, and comedians was some extraordinary music.

Harlem's three dominant nightclubs at the time were the Cotton Club, Smalls' Paradise, and Connie's Inn. The block-long Savoy Ballroom was the area's main dance hall. The Cotton Club was segregated, featuring exclusively African American entertainers but admitting only white patrons, while the other clubs featured mostly African American performers and admitted both Black and white people. Smaller clubs could be found all over Harlem, with at least twenty on a stretch of 133rd Street, which Billie Holiday called "the real swing street."[1]

After the bigger clubs closed at two A.M., venues like the Lenox Club and the Rhythm Club hosted all-night jam sessions where bandleaders like Fletcher Henderson and Chick Webb and musicians like saxophonist Johnny Hodges went to unwind and play for themselves.

By the end of the 1920s, coast-to-coast radio broadcasts from the Cotton Club and other Harlem nightspots brought the music of Duke Ellington, Louis Armstrong, and others into homes across America, spreading their fame and boosting their record sales. The stock market crash and the long depression that followed affected business at the clubs, but radio—it's estimated that ten million households had radio sets by that time—played an outsize role in promoting jazz, bringing free entertainment to those who couldn't afford to go out. The newly emerging "talkies"—films with synchronized sound—brought jazz to yet another audience, with Ellington and Armstrong both starring in short films in 1932.

The music had been evolving too. Swing—an exciting, danceable music with clear melodies, a strong beat, and soloists often playing call-and-response riffs—began taking hold in the Harlem big bands of Ellington, Jimmie Lunceford, and Cab Calloway. During the 1920s and 1930s, touring groups known as "territory bands" brought jazz and swing to smaller cities across the United States.

Though Black and white people may have been able to enjoy the music together in some New York City clubs, things were different elsewhere. In 1934, the year after a triumphant European tour, Ellington and his band hit the road for a twelve-week tour of the Jim Crow South. Wishing to avoid the indignities of segregation, the group traveled in its own private rail cars, where band members could eat and sleep. When asked how he felt about not being able to stay in many of the hotels he performed in, Ellington replied, "I merely took the energy it takes to pout and wrote some blues."[2]

After race riots in 1935, Harlem was considered unsafe for white clubgoers, and many clubs were forced to either close or move downtown.

COTTON CLUB
644 LENOX AVENUE AT 142ND STREET

Upon his release from prison in 1923, gangster and bootlegger Owney Madden bought the Club Deluxe from boxer Jack Johnson and rechristened it the Cotton Club. Madden's vision was to present the finest Black entertainers in New York to Manhattan's elite caviar-and-martini crowd in an elegant showplace—while selling them his bootleg liquor. The Cotton Club was segregated; while all the performers were African American, only white audience members were allowed. Cultural historian Steven Watson wrote, "The division between the performers and the audience was more carefully maintained than in any other club in Harlem."[3] "It isn't necessary to mix with colored people if you don't feel like it," offered the unevolved singer Jimmy Durante.[4]

The club presented musical revues featuring singers, dancers, comedians, variety acts, and, perhaps most important, an African American house band playing jazz. From 1927 to 1931, Duke Ellington led the club's band, a residency that gave him critical national exposure through weekly radio broadcasts from the club. Having a regular gig also gave him the time and forum to experiment with his music; while at the club he wrote music for dancing, overtures, and transitions and recorded more than one hundred of his compositions.

The club later employed orchestras led by Cab Calloway and Jimmie Lunceford, and headliners included Louis Armstrong, singer Ethel Waters, dancers Bill "Bojangles" Robinson and the Nicholas Brothers, the Will Mastin Trio (with a young Sammy Davis Jr.), and actress-singer-dancer Dorothy Dandridge.

During its heyday, the club featured Sunday "Celebrity Nights," with guest stars including George Gershwin, Eddie Cantor, Mae West, Sophie Tucker, and Al Jolson. White writer Carl Van Vechten once arrived at the club as part of a racially mixed group and was turned away by the bouncer; he vowed to boycott the club until Black patrons could hear Ethel Waters singing on its stage.

Following Harlem's race riots in 1935, the Cotton Club was forced to close. The next year it reopened on Broadway and Forty-Eighth Street, with a revue headlined by Calloway and Robinson, who was paid $3,500 a week, reportedly the most ever paid to a nightclub performer. In 1940, the Cotton Club closed permanently as a result of increasing rent, changing tastes, and a government inquiry into tax evasion.

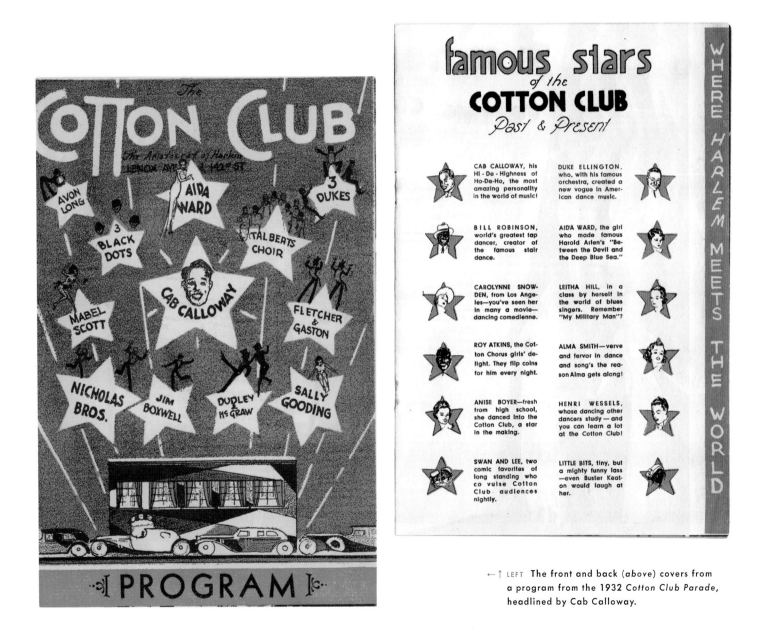

← ↑ LEFT The front and back (*above*) covers from a program from the 1932 *Cotton Club Parade*, headlined by Cab Calloway.

The Famous
COTTON CLUB
PROGRAM

COTTON CLUB PARADE

MUSIC & LYRICS by
TED KOEHLER
HAROLD ARLEN

PRODUCED by
DAN HEALY

DANCES STAGED by
ELIDA WEBB

COSTUMES by
GENE

OPENING.."CALLOWAY FOR PRESIDENT"
(NOTE: With apologies to Mr. Sam Harris, the authors of "Of Thee I Sing" and Mr.
George Gershwin, whose "Wintergreen for President" theme inspired this opening.)
"HARLEM HOLIDAY"
  a. Specialty ....Cab Calloway & Entire Company
                                                                    Elmer Turner
2. "THAT'S WHAT I HATE ABOUT LOVE"........Aida Ward, Carolynn Snowden and
                                                                   Lethia Hill
  a. Specialty ....Roy Atkins
  b. Specialty ....Four Blazers
3. "BILL ROBINSON STOMP"......................Harold Nicholas and Girls
  a. Specialty ....Necodemus
  b. Specialty ....Henri Wessels and Anice Boyer
  c. Specialty ....Alma Smith
4. "FLAT TIRE PAPA"..........................Lethia Hill, Swan and Lee
5. "I'VE GOT THE WORLD ON A STRING".......Aida Ward, Cab Calloway,
                                                     Boys and Girls
  a. Specialty ....Carolynn Snowden
  b. Specialty ....Brown and McGraw
6. "THE TRIAL ON MINNIE THE MOOCHER"......Cab Calloway, Lethia Hill,
           Swan and Lee, Alma Smith, Roy Atkins, Little Bits,
                              Cotton Club Trio and Girls
  a. Specialty ....Nicholas Bros.
7. "RAISIN' HADES IN GREEN PASTURES".........Carolynn Snowden
8. FINALE ....Entire Company

SECOND SHOW
1. "THE WAIL OF THE REEFER MAN"..................Cab Calloway,
    Four Blazers, Henri Wessels, Roy Atkins, Little Bits and Girls
  a. Specialty ....Nicholas Brothers
  b. Specialty ....Aida Ward
  c. Specialty ....Henri Wessels
  d. Specialty ....Carolynn Snowden
2. "JUNGLE ON MANHATTAN"....................Alma Smith and Girls
  a. Specialty ....Roy Atkins, Phil Scott
                            and Elmer Turner
  b. Specialty ....Lethia Hill
  c. Specialty ....Four Blazers
  d. Specialty ....Swan and Lee
3. "THAT'S HOW DARKIES KEEP WARM"....Alma Smith,
                    Roy Atkins and Phil Scott
4. FINALE ....Entire Company

↑ ABOVE **The 1932 *Cotton Club Parade* featured songs by legendary composer Harold Arlen and lyricist Ted Koehler,
including the standard "I've Got the World on a String," written specifically for the revue.**

↑ ABOVE **Cab Calloway leads the band at the midtown Cotton Club's New Year's Eve Celebration, 1937.**

DRINK LIST

•

MINERAL WATERS

POLAND WATER, SPLITS	1.00
WHITE ROCK, SPLITS	1.00
APPOLLANARIS, SPLITS	1.00
FRENCH VICHY, SPLITS	1.00

GINGER ALE

DRY GINGER ALE, SPLITS	1.00
SARSAPARILLA, SPLITS	1.00
LEMONADE	1.00
ORANGEADE	1.00
GRAPE JUICE	1.00
HORSE'S NECK	1.25
PURE ORANGE JUICE, GLASS	1.25
PURE LEMON JUICE, GLASS	1.25

When you've experienced the pure enjoyment of America Dry Ginger Ale, you, too, will join the enormous fraternity of America Dry enthusiasts.

You'll appreciate supreme satisfaction when you try a bottle of America Dry. A perfect mixer!

AMERICA'S DRINK
The Ultra of Ginger Ale

CONNIE'S INN **MENU**

CHIN[ESE]

PORK OR BEEF

Pepper Steak w. Onions	1.00
Pepper Steak w. Mushrooms	1.25
Pork and Tomatoes	1.00
Egg Foo Yung Dan	1.00
Shrimp Foo Yung Dan	1.25
Pepper Pork w. Onions	1.00
Pepper Pork w. Mushrooms	1.25
Hot Roast Pork	.75
Chicken Foo Yung Dan	1.25

Chicken
Chicken
Subgum
Chicken
Shrimp

Chicken
Chicken
Subgum
Chicken
Chicken
Moo G[ow]
Beef Ch[ow]
Plain C[how]

AMERICAN DISHES

SANDWICHES

Imported Russian Caviar	1.75
Steak, Beefsteak style	1.50
Club 1.00 Steak	1.25
Tongue .60 Chicken	.75
Sardine .50 Ham	.50
Western	.50
American or Swiss Cheese	.50

SALADS

Chicken Salad	1.25
Crab Meat	1.25
Shrimp 1.25 Lobster	1.25
Combination	1.00
Fruit Salad	1.00
Lettuce and Tomato	.75
Hearts of Lettuce	.75

Stuffed Celery	.75
Canape of Anchovies	.75
Portion of Genuine Caviar	2.25

Celery		.40
Large Ripe or Queen Olives		.40
Fruit Cocktail		.50

SOUPS

Chicken Broth	.40	Onion au Gratin	.60
Cream of Tomato	.40		

STEAKS and CHOPS

Sirloin Seak, Broiled	1.75
Steak, a la Minute w. O'Brien Potatoes	1.50
Filet Mignon, Jardiniere	2.00
Broiled Tenderloin Steak	1.75
Broiled Lamb Chops on Toast, Green Peas	1.50
Ham or Bacon and Eggs	1.00
Ham and Eggs, Southern Style	1.25

CHICKEN

Half Broiled or Fried Chicken	1.50
Chicken a la King	1.50
Chicken Hashed in Cream on Toast	1.50
Chicken Mexican w. Rice	1.50
Chicken Liver Saute w. Green Peppers	1.25

POTATOES

Hashed Brown	.40
Au Gratin	.40
Lyonnaise	.40
French Fried	.25

RAREBITS

Golden Buck	1.25
Long Island	1.25
Welsh	1.00
Yorkshire Buck	1.50

CHEESE

American	.50
Camembert	.50
Swiss	.50
Roquefort	.50

COFFEE, TEA, Etc.

Pot Coffee	.25
Pot Tea	.25

We earnestly request the co-operation of all our guests in seeing that no liquors are brought into or consumed upon these premises. It is illegal to transport such prohibited beverages, and the management assumes no responsibility for any one detected doing so. THE MANAGEMENT.

← ↑ ABOVE **This Prohibition Era–menu from Connie's Inn offered non-alcoholic drinks only. Date unknown.**

"Fats" Waller

VICTOR'S EVER-POPULAR PIANO HUMORIST

CONNIE'S INN
2221 SEVENTH AVENUE AT 131ST STREET

Connie's Inn was opened in 1923 by Latvian immigrant brothers Connie, George, and Louie Immerman, bootleggers and owners of a Harlem delicatessen (a nineteen-year-old Fats Waller had handled their deliveries). From the mid-1920s to 1930s, the basement club billed itself as "Harlem's Largest" and was one of the area's "big three" clubs, along with Smalls' Paradise and the Cotton Club.

Connie's floor shows featured African American performers, but the club welcomed Black and white people alike. During 1929, the club's peak year, Louis Armstrong performed as part of Carroll Dickerson's Chicago orchestra, and that year's floor show, Fats Waller and Andy Razaf's *Hot Chocolates* (featuring "Ain't Misbehavin'"), was such a success it moved to Broadway's Hudson Theatre.

A period followed with Fletcher Henderson and His Connie's Inn Orchestra, featuring Coleman Hawkins and Rex Stewart, and then bands led by Luis Russell and Don Redman. In 1933, with Harlem's nightlife rush ebbing, the Immermans moved the club to a short-lived midtown location, presenting the revue *Stars over Broadway*, starring Billie Holiday (and when she became ill, temporary replacement Bessie Smith). But the repeal of Prohibition and the Depression hurt business, and soon Connie's was forced to close.

← LEFT **Fats Waller,** who performed at Connie's Inn and once worked for the Immerman's deli, date unknown.

SMALL'S PARADISE, 135th STREET and 7th AVE., NEW YORK CITY

SMALLS' PARADISE

2294½ SEVENTH AVENUE NEAR 135TH STREET

Smalls' Paradise, which billed itself as the "Hottest Spot in Harlem," opened in the basement of an office building on October 26, 1925, quickly becoming one of Harlem's most popular integrated nightclubs. Pianist Charlie Johnson's group was the main attraction. In the ten years it was the house band, it featured at various times saxophonist Benny Carter and trumpeters Jabbo Smith and Sidney de Paris.

During the 1920s, the integrated club—also the longest-operating nightclub in Harlem—was the only major nightspot in the area owned by an African American, Ed Smalls.

The club, renowned for its top entertainment and elaborate floor shows, stayed open all night. While most clubs closed at two, three, or four A.M., Smalls' offered a six o'clock breakfast dance and floor show. There was no cover charge, although prices for food and liquor were steep. Customers could bring in their own flasks or buy bootleg drinks from the club's dancing waiters, who did the Charleston—sometimes on roller skates—as they toted large, heavy trays. After finishing their own shows at other clubs,

musicians including future bandleaders Tommy Dorsey and Glenn Miller often dropped by Smalls' to jam with the house band. In the early 1930s, a teenage Billie Holiday had her first audition at the club. When asked what key she wanted to sing in, Holiday answered, "'I don't know, man, you just play.' They shooed me out of there so fast it wasn't even funny."[5]

The club became popular with celebrities, including actors Tallulah Bankhead and George Raft, boxing champion Joe Louis, and columnist Walter Winchell. Malcolm Little, who later became known as Malcolm X, worked at the club as a waiter in the early 1940s. In 1951, at a party sponsored by Albert Einstein, Paul Robeson, and others, civil rights activist W. E. B. DuBois celebrated his eighty-third birthday there.

In 1955, Ed Smalls sold the club to disc jockey Tommy "Dr. Jive" Smalls (no relation), who in turn sold it to basketball star Wilt Chamberlain in 1961. Chamberlain renamed the club Big Wilt-Smalls' Paradise and changed the music from jazz to more commercial rhythm and blues. Smalls' eventually became a disco club, finally closing in 1986.

← LEFT Smalls' Paradise photograph folder, 1940s.

↓ BELOW The Progressive Social Club at Smalls', late 1940s.

↖ OPPOSITE, LEFT At Smalls' Paradise, 1940s.

↖ OPPOSITE, RIGHT Smalls' postcard, 1940s. Ed Smalls is pictured at top right.

↑ ABOVE A handbill advertising a Savoy Barn Dance, late 1930s.

SAVOY BALLROOM
596 LENOX AVENUE BETWEEN 140TH AND 141ST STREETS

The "World's Most Beautiful Ballroom" opened in 1926, owned by white businessmen Jay Faggen and Moe Gale and managed by African American civic leader Charles Buchanan, who sought to operate a "luxury ballroom to accommodate the many thousands who wished to dance in an atmosphere of tasteful refinement, rather than in the small stuffy halls and the foul smelling, smoke laden cellar nightclubs."[6]

Fashioned after Faggen's midtown Roseland Ballroom, the second-floor, block-long Savoy could accommodate up to four thousand music fans and dancers. The lavish interior had mirrored walls, a sprung dance floor, and a double bandstand that held two groups, so the music could be continuous—as one group finished, the other began.

The Savoy was a hit from the very beginning; on March 20, 1926, the African American newspaper *New York Age* ran the headline "Savoy Turns 2,000 Away on Opening Night—Crowds Pack Ball Room All Week." The ballroom's regular battle of the bands was a major draw; in 1927, Chick Webb's Chicks (from New York) faced off against a group from Chicago led by Fess Williams and Joe "King" Oliver. The crowds reportedly jammed Lenox Avenue for blocks, resulting in the riot squad being called.

The Savoy hosted nearly all the era's major bands, including those led by Duke Ellington, Cab Calloway, Luis Russell, Cecil Scott, and white bandleaders Guy Lombardo and Benny Goodman. But most popular was the house band led by drummer Chick Webb, who, in 1934, added a new vocalist: seventeen-year-old Ella Fitzgerald, fresh from winning the Apollo Theater talent contest.

Equally important to the Savoy audience was dancing. Known as the "Home of Happy Feet" and "the Track" (because of its long, thin dance

SAVOY BALLROOM —— Lenox Avenue and 140th Street —— NEW YORK

floor), dancers at the Savoy created many dances, but none achieved the fame of the Lindy Hop, named after aviator Charles Lindbergh. Highly competitive Lindy Hop dancers dominated an area dubbed "the corner," awaiting their opportunity to shine, while the less serious dancers formed a horseshoe around the bandstand to watch the proceedings.

The Savoy was fully integrated, and as the African American newspaper the *Amsterdam News* reported, "At the Savoy Ballroom, social, racial and economic problems fade away to nothingness."[7] Legendary Lindy Hop dancer Frankie Manning recalled dancing skills were what mattered at the ballroom: "One night somebody came over and said, 'Hey man, *Clark Gable* just walked in the house.' Somebody else said, 'Oh, yeah, can he dance?' All they wanted to know when you came into the Savoy was, do you dance?"[8]

Admission was a reasonable thirty to eighty-five cents, and it's estimated nearly seven hundred thousand people visited each year—necessitating the replacement of the dance floor every three years. As swing began to ebb in the late 1940s, the dancing at the Savoy became more sedate and featured longer engagements with bands led by Cootie Williams, Erskine Hawkins, and others. In 1958, the Savoy was torn down and a housing complex was built where it once stood.

↗ ABOVE, RIGHT **Savoy Ballroom postcard, date unknown.**

← OPPOSITE Dizzy Gillespie and his big band at the Savoy, late 1940s.

→ RIGHT Savoy Ballroom flyer, 1939.

→ RIGHT Ubangi Club post-card advertising Erskine Hawkins' "Bama" State Collegians with "Gladys Bentley and a cast of 40," mid-1930s.

UBANGI CLUB
2221 SEVENTH AVENUE AT 131ST STREET

The Ubangi Club opened in 1934 in what had been the original location of Connie's Inn. Writer James F. Wilson noted, "With a name intended to evoke associations with Africa and 'the suggestion of voodooism,' the Ubangi Club traded on the taste for the exotic that tourists craved from Harlem."[9]

While the Ubangi had house bands led by respected leaders including Erskine Hawkins and Teddy Hill, it is best remembered as the home base for "gender-bending" African American vocalist and pianist Gladys Bentley. Dressed in her signature cream-colored tuxedo and top hat, her hair closely cropped and slicked back, Bentley was notorious throughout the city for putting her own raunchy lyrics to popular melodies of the day. A 1936 article in the *Afro American* noted: "To describe one night at the famous Ubangi Club should be sufficient to convince the most skeptical just why the playboys from Broadway and Riverside Drive desert their own sin dives and come to Harlem to bask in the muted brilliance of this popular Black and tan resort. Sunday night saw the club alive with fashionable guests, famous artists of stage, screen and radio and an unusual array of talent on hand to display their wares. The singing waiters . . . move about the floor with a portable piano plunked by blue-eyed Lea Simmons. . . . About fifty people, including the prettiest Creole chorus of twenty-five svelte lovelies . . . take part in the gala review. The drawing card of the Ubangi club is the buxom, mannish dressed Gladys Bentley, who has been a fixture there for years and still draws a crowd."[10]

But in 1937, New York passed a law prohibiting cross-dressing entertainment, and the Ubangi had to "go straight." Sometime afterward, the club relocated to midtown, to a building that was later home to Birdland. After a 1944 cabaret tax went into effect, the club stopped presenting floor shows and was forced to close a few years later.

AMERICA'S GREATEST SEPIA PIANA ARTIST

BROWN BOMBER OF SOPHISTICATED SONGS

Gladys Bentley

← LEFT Gladys Bentley, 1936–1939.

Announcing
"The Event of the Season."

The New Edition

of the

UBANGI CLUB FOLLIES

•

Acclaimed by Press and Public

"THE HOTTEST SHOW EVER PRESENTED
IN HARLEM"

•

AT THE

UBANGI CLUB

131st STREET and SEVENTH AVENUE
NEW YORK, N. Y.

PROGRAM

For Reservations Telephone TIllinghast 5-9366 - 9418

← LEFT *Ubangi Club Follies*
program, mid-1940s.

→ OPPOSITE Songs featured in
this version of the *Ubangi
Club Follies* include "Nudist
and "Reefer Smokers Ball."

..UBANGI CLUB..

131st STREET cor. 7th AVENUE

JOE SPRINGER, Mgr., PRESENTS

Who's Who

MAE JOHNSON

GLADYS BENTLEY

LEE SIMMONS

DUSTY FLETCHER

PEARL BAINES

BOBBY EVANS

EDNA MAE HOLLY

BILLIE DANIELS

BUNNY BRIGGS

VELMA MIDDLETON

BROWN & BROWN

THE THREE SPEED DEMONS

UBANGI GIRLS ENSEMBLE

Baby Simmons, Vera Bracken, Annetta Morrison, Marjorie Hubbard, Marian Egbert, Wilhelmina Gray, Julia Moses, Lucia Moses, Ethel Moses, Dorothy Malone, Emma Moorehead, Cleo Hayes.

ENTIRE PRODUCTION CONCEIVED AND STAGED

by LEONARD HARPER

PRODUCTION MUSIC AND LYRICS

by ANDY RAZAF

ADDITIONAL NUMBERS

by LOU CRAWFORD

COSTUMING

by HILDA FARNAM

NEVER A COVER CHARGE

New Edition of the Ubangi Club Follies

PART ONE

1. OPENING — "YOU BROKE IT UP WHEN YOU SAID DIXIE"
   Mae Johnson, Velma Middleton, Dusty Fletcher, Edna Mae Holly, Bunny Briggs, Ubangi Girls Ensemble and Ubangi Boys Ensemble
2. I GUESS WE'RE GONNA GET ALONG .... PEARL BAINES
   (Rhythm in Song and Dance)
3. GET RHYTHM IN YOUR FEET (Hot Puppies) .... BUNNY BRIGGS
4. LIVING IN A GREAT BIG WAY .... VELMA MIDDLETON
5. TWO SHADES OF RHYTHM PEARL BAINES, LORRAINE BROWN, and UBANGI GIRLS ENSEMBLE
6. "THE ONLY TIME YOUR OUT OF LUCK" .... BOBBY EVANS
7. A—RECKLESS
   B—NOW I'M A LADY .... MAE JOHNSON
8. A—JUST A LITTLE COMEDY .... DUSTY FLETCHER
   B—MAE GETS DUSTY TOLD DUSTY FLETCHER & MAE JOHNSON
9. ITS THE JUNGLE IN ME
   Bobby Evans, Pearl Baines, Edna Mae Holly, Billie Daniels and Ubangi Girls Ensemble
10. APACHE ALA HARLEM .... BROWN & BROWN
11. SOPHISTICATION IN SONG & DANCE .... GLADYS BENTLEY
    Assisted by CHARLES PRIME
12. TAPS & MORE TAPS .... THE THREE SPEED DEMONS
13. FINALE—TA-DA-DA-DA .... VELMA MIDDLETON & Entire Company

INTERMISSION

ERSKINE HAWKINS and the original BAMA STATE COLLEGIANS

BROADCASTING AND DANCING

PART TWO

1. OPENING—"NUDIST" .... PEARL BAINES & BOBBY EVANS
   featuring EDNA MAE HOLLY in BUBBLE DANCE with UBANGI GIRLS ENSEMBLE
2. OFF TIME (Hot Puppies) .... BUNNY BRIGGS
3. LIVING IN A GREAT BIG WAY .... VELMA MIDDLETON
4. DANCING THATS DIFFERENT .... BROWN & BROWN
5. SOPHISTICATION IN SONG AND DANCE .... GLADYS BENTLEY
   Assisted by CHARLES PRIME
6. SPEED AND MORE SPEED .... THE THREE SPEED DEMONS
7. HONEY SUCKLE ROSE .... MAE JOHNSON
8. REEFER SMOKERS BALL

Announcer .... BILLIE DANIELS	Minnie the Moocher .... LORRAINE BROWN
Sister full Bosom .. VELMA MIDDLETON	Sepia Mae Wongs .... HOLLY & BAINES
Teddy Pansy .... TEDDY EVANS	Chinkie Man .... BILLY COLE
The Carioca Kid .... DUSTY FLETCHER	Corn Bread the Viper .... CHAS. WALKER
Smokie Joe .... BOBBY EVANS	The Reefer Man .... HERBERT BROWN

and Entire Company

PROGRAM SUBJECT TO CHANGE WITHOUT NOTICE

ERSKINE

HAWKINS

and the Original

BAMA STATE COLLEGIANS

CREOLES

20 PRIZE BEAUTIES

Dancing

Singing

Waiters

AIR COOLED!

APOLLO THEATER

253 WEST 125TH STREET BETWEEN ADAM CLAYTON POWELL JR.
BOULEVARD (SEVENTH AVENUE) AND FREDERICK DOUGLASS
BOULEVARD (EIGHTH AVENUE)

The Apollo opened on January 16, 1934, during the height of the swing era. The 1,506-seat venue presented multi-act bills headlined by the era's most popular big bands, including those of Duke Ellington and Chick Webb, and filled out with dancers like Bill "Bojangles" Robinson and the Nicholas Brothers and comedians such as Jackie "Moms" Mabley and the duo Butterbeans and Susie. Occasionally the theater would book celebrities too, including boxers Joe Louis and Sugar Ray Robinson and horror film star Boris Karloff.

The Apollo was integrated: during the 1940s, white patrons accounted for an estimated 40 percent of the audience during the week and up to 75 percent on weekends. While the theater presented mostly African American entertainers, many white artists played the hall, including bands led by Buddy Rich, Woody Herman, and Charlie Barnet. As swing declined in popularity, the theater began adding blues, rhythm and blues, and, eventually, even rock and roll performers such as Buddy Holly to its lineups.

On Mondays, the Apollo hosted amateur night contests. Billed as the place "where stars are born and legends are made," the competitions, which were broadcast live on the radio, featured young aspiring talent looking for exposure. One of the first winners was seventeen-year-old Ella Fitzgerald, who had planned to dance during the contest but, unnerved by the performance of a dance duo, instead sang Hoagy Carmichael's "Judy"

and Pinky Tomlin's "The Object of My Affection" and won the twenty-five-dollar first prize. In 1942, Sarah Vaughan, just eighteen, entered the contest on a dare. She won, singing "Body and Soul," which led to her discovery by Billy Eckstine.

But perhaps the most popular part of amateur night was Porto Rico, described by David Hinkley of the *New York Daily News* as "an outlandishly dressed character whose assignment was to go onstage, at a cue from his silent partner in a side box or the audience at large, and chase faltering contestants into the wings before they further mistreated whatever song they were trying to sing. This process began with the wail of an offstage siren, followed by the arrival of Mr. Rico himself, firing a cap gun or a starter's pistol into the air while often also wielding some other instrument of banishment. That might be a pitchfork, with Porto Rico dressed as a farmer. It might be a broom, with Porto Rico as a housewife. On other nights, Porto Rico just liked to feel pretty. Old-timers recall a night when he came out in a Turkish turban with a bright yellow cone brassiere and pink tights."[11]

As music changed, the Apollo continued to thrive, particularly during the soul music explosion of the 1960s. Despite intermittent closings during the 1970s and multiple owners, the theater continues to present world-class performers today.

→ OPPOSITE **Apollo Theater marquee, circa 1946–1948.**

America's Greatest
Arranger-Composer-Conductor

DUKE ELLINGTON

His New BAND and REVUE with

AL HIBBLER

"Cat" Anderson — Ray Nance — Harry Carney — Willie Smith

Week Only
Beg.
Friday, June 1st

KING of the TENOR SAX

ILLINOIS JACQUET
And His BAND

1st LADY OF SONG **ELLA FITZGERALD**

Fun By **PATTERSON & JACKSON** The Ton

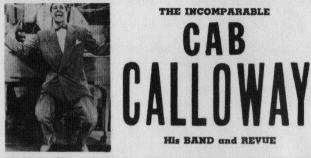

THE INCOMPARABLE

CAB CALLOWAY

His BAND and REVUE

HE'S BACK ! After an absence of several years, the incomparable CAB CALLOWAY is back in circulation . . . with a new band, a large band, a terrific band! Reports from HAVANA, where CAB is currently standing the payees in line indicate that this, the greatest of all showmen is back in circulation with a vengeance. Incidentally, this is the first time CAB has fronted a large band in about five years . . . this in place of the small combinations he's had of more recent date. Watch for this one! It'll be a humdinger!

Week Beg. Friday, June 15th

ROYAL BATTLE OF THE BLUES

MR. BLUES

WYNONIE HARRIS

Annie Laurie ★ "Sticks" McGhee

Eddie Durham ★ "Flash" Gordon
And BAND

⇆ OPPOSITE **Celebrity Club souvenir photograph and folder** (*right*)**, 1940s.**

CELEBRITY CLUB
35 EAST 125TH STREET

When it opened in the mid-1930s, the Celebrity Club was mostly a club for rent, letting out its large basement hall and ground-level room for private events. During at least some part of the 1940s and 1950s, the club didn't serve liquor but provided "setups" for those patrons who brought their own. The basement room was decorated in "old fashioned Harlem-style—artificial trees topped by bogus leaves in autumn colors."[12]

In the mid-1940s, Art Simms was the house pianist; guitarist Tiny Grimes appeared there too. Beginning in 1953, longtime Count Basie saxophonist Buddy Tate began a residency with his group, the Celebrity Club All-Stars, in the basement room. For the next nineteen years, the group played for dancers, until the club began hosting rock acts in 1974. By the 1980s, the club was presenting hip-hop, reggae, and dance acts including Madonna, who performed there in 1983. The Celebrity Club is name-checked by rapper Kurtis Blow in his 1983 song "One-Two-Five (Main Street, Harlem, USA)."

RIGHT **Club Baron** folder and souvenir photograph (*opposite*), 1940s.

CLUB BARON

437 LENOX AVENUE AT WEST 132ND STREET

The well-appointed Club Baron opened circa 1940. The club's owner, John Barone, noted, "I owed my many friends something in return for their patronage . . . that would offer every, if not more, pleasure than one finds in a Broadway club."[13] Barone booked African American artists including Ethel Waters, Boston bandleader Sabby Lewis, and Valaida Snow, a multi-instrumentalist nicknamed "Little Louis" after Louis Armstrong, who called her the world's second-best jazz trumpeter, after himself. At the Baron, the musicians played on a stage behind the bar.

Club Baron closed in 1946 but reopened in the 1950s as a community theater where the Committee for the Negro in the Arts produced plays by Black writers. In the 1960s and 1970s, the Baron again became a venue for live music, billing itself as "New York's Oldest Jazz Club."

⇆ OPPOSITE **Palm Cafe souvenir photograph and folder** (*right*)**, 1950s.**

Souvenir

PALM CAFE INC.

Most Modern
CAFE and COCKTAIL LOUNGE
in Harlem

209 WEST 125th STREET
NEW YORK . . . . . . NEW YORK

PALM CAFE
209 WEST 125TH STREET OFF ADAM CLAYTON
POWELL JR. BOULEVARD (SEVENTH AVENUE)

The Palm Cafe, the self-proclaimed "Most Modern Cafe and Cocktail Lounge in Harlem," opened in the early 1940s just down the street from the Apollo. Many of the Apollo's headliners patronized the Palm, including Cab Calloway and Nat King Cole. Former Palm manager Robert Royal remembered, "It was one of the most popular clubs in New York, and they catered to a sophisticated bourgeois."[14]

In the early 1950s, radio station WOV installed a studio in the club and broadcast programs six nights a week. The programs featured disc jockeys playing records and interviewing visiting celebrities including Sarah Vaughan and Duke Ellington. *Billboard* noted the radio shows ended each night at three o'clock with a "twelve-minute period of soft lights and sweet music discs."[15]

The Palm closed in the early 1970s.

CLUB SUDAN
644 LENOX AVENUE AT 142ND STREET

The short-lived Club Sudan opened in the former home of the Cotton Club in November 1945. At the time, *Billboard* reported that the plan "is to attract white trade to the Harlem spot, so while the hunt for acts is limited by tentative [$5,000] budget, it is ready to put it on the line if it can get names that will pull. Present line-up consists of [dancers] Pops and Louie, [singer] Ann Lewis, [singer] Babe Wallace, Steeple-chasers, [dancer and singer] Mable Lee, Leon Abbey Quartet, Andy Kirk's ork and a 12-girl [chorus] line."[16] Other performers who played the Sudan include Count Basie, Illinois Jacquet, and Billy Eckstine, who played a short stint before the club closed in 1946.

↗→ TOP **Club Sudan folder and souvenir pho-tograph** (*bottom*), **1946.** Pictured at center is legendary drummer Art Blakey, then with Billy Eckstine's big band.

CLUB BABY GRAND

319 WEST 125TH STREET

Former Cotton Club dancer Vivian Brown and her twin sister opened Club Baby Grand in the late 1940s. Future comedy star Nipsey Russell was the club's master of ceremonies, and reportedly the Baby Grand was writer and social activist Langston Hughes's favorite Harlem nightclub.

Singer Jimmy Scott, a frequent headliner, recalled: "The Baby Grand crowd was the most musically sophisticated I'd ever faced. These brothers and sisters were accustomed to hearing Ella and Billie. This was the neighborhood of Fats Waller and Willie 'The Lion' Smith. . . . The Baby Grand opened many doors. All the cats came by after their own gigs or on their nights off. Basie, Bud Powell, Oscar Pettiford. Willie Bryant, emcee at the Apollo, was always dropping in and spreading my name around."[17]

Willie Bryant, who was also a bandleader and the "unofficial mayor of Harlem," and disc jockey Ray Carroll broadcast *The After-Hour Swing Session* live from the integrated club on WHOM. Other headliners included organist Jimmy Smith, blues singers Big Maybelle and Etta James, and singer-actor Eddie Fisher. In 1955, pianist Walter Bishop Jr.'s band—with bassist Charles Mingus, drummer Kenny Clarke, and saxophonist Hank Mobley—was headlining when Bishop fell ill. Pianist Horace Silver took over, and during the engagement, legendary saxophonist Charlie Parker sat in multiple times. Silver later recalled, "Walter Bishop asked me if I wanted to play, and I told him yeah. Miles also sat in, so did Gerry Mulligan. That was a helluva set."[18]

In the mid-1950s, singer Dakota Staton was discovered at the Baby Grand by Capitol Records producer Dave Cavanaugh, who signed her to the label. Perhaps less predictably, during the early 1960s, future Velvet Underground founders Lou Reed and John Cale occasionally busked outside the club. The Baby Grand closed in the 1970s.

→ RIGHT **Club Baby Grand** postcard, date unknown.

← TOP **Club Baby Grand** souvenir photograph, 1950s.

↙→ BOTTOM **Club Baby Grand** souvenir photograph and folder (*opposite*), 1950s.

Souvenir of ...
Club Baby Grand

MUSIC

ENTERTAINMENT

The Finest FOOD and DRINKS

•

Chinese and American Dishes A Specialty

319 WEST 125th STREET, NEW YORK

The Brightest Spot On The New York Scene Uptown!

STARS OF STAGE, SCREEN AND RADIO

Always The Best In Entertainment

Comfortably Air Conditioned . . . For Reservations - UNiversity 4-6481

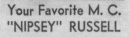

Your Favorite M. C.
"NIPSEY" RUSSELL

52nd Street and Midtown

After the repeal of Prohibition in 1933, Fifty-Second Street between Fifth and Seventh Avenues became known as the city's "Swing Street," or simply "the Street." Small-group Dixieland had been the dominant musical style in the area's speakeasies, but during the 1930s swing became all the rage, peaking during World War II. As swing began to ebb, bebop became popular in the Street's clubs.

In the early years, the Fifty-Second Street scene was segregated. But as the music evolved, a few clubs began booking African American musicians, though they generally didn't welcome Black patrons. That began to change in 1938, when jazz writer and producer John Hammond helped the not-yet-famous Count Basie band get a summer booking at the Famous Door. Hammond closed the deal by agreeing to loan the club's owners money to pay for badly needed air-conditioning. A stipulation of the loan was that Hammond be allowed to bring Black friends into the club. In Arnold Shaw's *52nd Street: The Street of Jazz* (1971), Hammond recalled, "Until then, you never saw a black face at the tables or even at the bar of the Door."[19]

Producer and writer Leonard Feather told Shaw: "After a time it became wide open. But [Fifty-Second Street] started out just as discriminatory and Jim Crow as any place in town, in spite of the number of musicians that were Black. At first if there was any tendency at all, club owners would hire white groups over Black groups. But then more and more there were mixed groups, and the lines became blurred. . . . It was not until 1943–44 that the raised eyebrows began disappearing."[20]

In 1938, "King of Swing" Benny Goodman became the first jazz bandleader to headline nearby Carnegie Hall. During the sold-out concert, Goodman's integrated group performed in various configurations, including a legendary jam session that included members of the Ellington and Basie bands. After the show, Goodman's orchestra headed uptown to the Savoy Ballroom, for a battle of the bands with Chick Webb's group. Jazz historian George T. Simon noted, "Benny's band played first and made a great impression. But then the Webb boys got into it. They blew the roof off the Savoy! The crowd screamed and whistled with delirium. The Webb band easily toppled Goodman's that night."[21] Goodman's drummer, Gene Krupa, later wrote, "I'll never forget that night. Webb cut me to ribbons!"[22]

When the United States entered World War II in 1941, the now ubiquitous swing music boosted morale at home and overseas. Bands continued to perform for radio broadcasts, and some of the musicians who joined the military organized bands to entertain the troops. Singers and musical groups that stayed behind recorded special records, called "V-Discs" (for "Victory"), to be sent abroad. And a number of all-women bands formed; until that point, most jazz players had been men, with women usually performing as vocalists or on instruments considered "more feminine," such as the piano or harp.

Gasoline and rubber rationing made touring by bus difficult, and curfews and excise taxes on entertainment made it challenging for clubs in some cities. But the Fifty-Second Street and midtown clubs thrived, with business from military members on leave supplanting the city's already large audience for jazz. By that time, the Fifty-Second Street scene was fairly well integrated, but problems occasionally arose when servicemen from the South encountered race mixing in the clubs. In Shaw's *52nd Street*, drummer Shelly Manne recalled: "I remember one night at the Onyx when a Southern soldier pulled a knife on [pianist] Argonne Thornton.

→ OPPOSITE **Fifty-Second Street, New York City, circa July 1948.**

[I] can never forget how [saxophonist] Ben Webster walked from the bandstand. You know how the tables in those joints were set one on top of the other. Well, Ben paid no attention. He just walked through them. And when he got to the bar, he grabbed this guy, lifted him off the floor with one hand, and just held him there at arm's length. The guy kept squirming until he was ready to pass out. Ben kept holding him and talking to Argonne. Then he just opened his hand, the guy dropped to the floor, and took off like a scared rabbit."[23]

In 1944, a national wartime cabaret tax was enacted, levying a 30 percent (later reduced to 20 percent) charge on the receipts of any venue that served food or drink, featured singers, or allowed dancing. The consequences were almost immediate, with the *New York Times* reporting, "The new 30 percent entertainment tax that went into effect three weeks ago has already thrown 5,000 performers out of work and it is expected that this figure will mount to 15,000 by May 1.... [T]hus far twenty-four places in the metropolitan area formerly featuring entertainment have abolished their shows."[24]

Club owners, wary of passing the additional charges on to their customers, eventually realized the law had an unintended, but potentially lifesaving, exception. Clubs that provided strictly instrumental music to which no one danced were exempt from the tax.

The cabaret tax and the war's end in 1945 spelled the end for swing. Much of the money that had fueled the boom in live music had come from workers with lucrative defense jobs. With the cost of going to clubs increasing, defense jobs drying up, and soldiers coming home, people began shifting their priorities to owning homes, starting families, and buying things that hadn't been available during the war. Declining attendance meant many clubs and ballrooms could no longer afford to meet their expenses, with some operating only on weekends. A number of top bandleaders were forced to reduce the number of musicians in their groups, with Cab Calloway, Tommy Dorsey, Woody Herman, and Charlie Barnet among the many who downsized.

Ironically, the cabaret tax helped spur the next great revolution in jazz. During the 1940s, Harlem had again become a hotspot. In regular jam sessions at Minton's Playhouse and Monroe's Uptown House, a group of adventurous young musicians, including pianist Thelonious Monk, trumpeter Dizzy Gillespie, guitarist Charlie Christian, Charlie Parker, and Kenny Clarke, was experimenting with a radical new sound that came to be known as bebop, or simply bop.

Swing was a highly arranged and composed music; these musicians were searching for something different—a way of playing that was more spontaneous, more personal, and more expressive of their individuality. Bebop, with its complex melodies and harmonies and new style of drumming, was music for listening. It was played in small groups, and ideally for club owners, bop groups didn't have singers and you couldn't dance to it. In Dizzy Gillespie's memoir *To Be, or Not ... to Bop*, bop drummer Max Roach noted, "[Clubs] couldn't have a big band because the big band played for dancing.... If somebody got up to dance, there would be 20 per cent more tax on the dollar. If someone got up there and sang a song, it would be 20 per cent more.... [I]t was a wonderful period for the development of the instrumentalist."[25]

With the Three Deuces, the Famous Door, and the Onyx all booking bop groups, Fifty-Second Street quickly became the hub of bebop. The new sounds generated fanatic followers, and while the crowds weren't as big as the swing audience, the music spread quickly, not only to cities like Chicago, Detroit, and Washington, D.C., but also to other countries. In 1949, the Festival International de Jazz in Paris played host to boppers Charlie Parker and Miles Davis, who headlined alongside traditional jazz players, including saxophonist Sidney Bechet and trumpeter Hot Lips Page.

Almost from its beginnings, bop was an integrated scene, onstage and off. During the mid-1940s, white musicians like drummer Stan Levey and pianist Al Haig played alongside Charlie Parker and Dizzy Gillespie, and Black and white fans jammed the Fifty-Second Street and midtown clubs that took a chance on the new sounds. Bop influenced non-bop players, like Dave Brubeck and Stan Kenton, and Beat generation writers, including Allen Ginsberg and Jack Kerouac.

As the popularity of bop grew, so did drug use among musicians. Martin Torgoff writes in *Bop Apocalypse*, "As reefer was associated with swing, heroin marked the transition from swing to bop."[26] Heroin took a heavy toll on many musicians, including Miles Davis, who was able to quit, and Charlie Parker, who wasn't. Numerous younger musicians who idolized Parker started using the drug, thinking it could enhance their playing, with devastating effects on the scene. Bandleader Artie Shaw famously commented, "Jazz was born in a whiskey barrel, grew up on marijuana, and is about to expire on heroin."[27]

There were other challenges for jazz too. In the postwar years, television began to exert its hold on America, and many who had previously gone out for entertainment were happy to stay home and watch TV. Swing fans, who enjoyed dancing and the romantic songs sung by big band vocalists, didn't find the same escape in the dissonant sounds of bop. Popular music began changing, with singers becoming the main attraction and the bands taking a backing group role. Former Tommy Dorsey Orchestra vocalist Frank Sinatra, a sensation during the war at New York's Paramount Theatre, became a huge recording star. Jazz singers Frankie Laine, Peggy Lee, and Nat King Cole became stars singing pop music. Radio, which had been so important to the spread of jazz, began to shift its programming from jazz groups to popular vocalists and disc jockeys playing records.

Still, jazz continued, and with it, innovation. In 1949, two leading lights of bebop took left turns. Charlie Parker fulfilled a long-held desire to record standards with a string section, resulting in the classic album *Charlie Parker with Strings* (1950). In 1949 and 1950, Miles Davis and composer-arranger Gil Evans began recording the groundbreaking *Birth of the Cool* (1957) with Davis's nine-piece group.

By the end of the 1940s, the Street began to decline. The causes were numerous: the increasing cost of talent, rising rents, a "clip-joint attitude towards customers" and, as Leonard Feather wrote in *Metronome*, April 1948, a "low-life reputation [with] its fringe of dope addicts and peddlers, pimps, prostitutes, and assorted characters."[28] New clubs had begun to open on nearby Broadway and in other midtown locations, and by the mid-1950s, the Street had six strip joints, but only one jazz club. New York's center of jazz had shifted downtown.

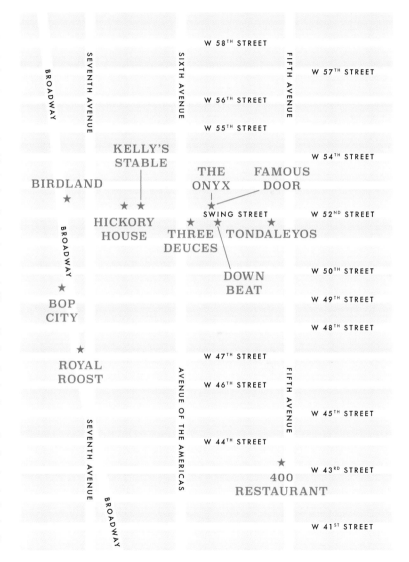

↗ RIGHT **Jazz clubs in midtown.**

BEBOP

what is it...?

BEBOP IS the new way of playing jazz!

EVERY DECADE, since the beginning in New Orleans, the jazz style has undergone marked change. Chicago jazz of the Volstead era superseded the parent New Orleans style, nurtured and in the Thirties gave way to the mighty Swing of Basie and Goodman. Now the cycle of change and growth has recurred— the bebop insurgents are eclipsing the swingmen with a burst of dynamic new emotional, rhythmic and harmonic concepts. One form spawns and is in turn devoured by the next. The art progresses.

MODERN JAZZMEN are learning their art from the two great iconoclasts of this generation: Charlie Parker and Dizzy Gillespie. The impact of these innovators on jazz thought might be compared to that of the atomic bomb on modern geopolitics. Because the new way of playing is an extension of history and of musical logic and, because emotionally the style captures the mood of these times, it is impossible to speak of going back. Jazz has spurted forward, into a new epoch of its brief and tumultuous history. The bebop men have assumed unchallenged leadership.

DIAL HAS UNDERTAKEN to hold the mirror of finely-produced phonograph records to the art and thereby reflect this evolution of musical growth. Every name prominent in the movement is featured in the DIAL catalog and the creative performances of Dizzy Gillespie and Charlie Parker in particular are afforded the latitude they demand. Parker is an exclusive DIAL artist.

AMERICAN JAZZ will doubtless undergo further modifications. When it does DIAL will be on the spot, recording these changes as they take place.

IN MUSICAL SERIOUSNESS and mechanical excellence DIAL recordings are deliberately competitive with the best in music. The DIAL catalog is permanent: all of the releases described herein are always available. Your jazz dealer maintains a complete stock of these classics of

Lasting Listening Pleasure

CHARLIE PARKER

CHARLIE PARKER— fabulous musician of the jazz Forties—is a very much - alive counterpart of such mythical geniuses as Bix Beiderbecke and Leon Rappollo. Idol of a fanatical group of admirers the "Bird's" habits are like his playing—unpredictable. Charlie turns up in places as various as dawn jam fests, first alto chair of name bands, occasionally on phonograph records. DIAL has been fortunate in assembling the larger and better half of Charlie Parker's discography.

Ecstatic is the adjective best applied to Parker's alto style which cascades notes, phrases, melodies, entire compositions forth like a golden cornucopia. Within the phrasing itself each note is articulate with meaning: bland, imperious, nostalgic, explosive, as the creative imagination moulds it. Parker's musical system, like that of any genius, is subject to few laws other than his own. Parker, more than any other single musician, has revolutionized jazz. He has made the alto sax the most articulate of instruments. Never has such an excess of jazz been contained in so tight a space. Here, without dispute, is one of the few real giants in fifty years of jazz history. His recordings on DIAL reflect many moods and stages of maturity of the artist and are requisites of all modern collections.

CHARLIE PARKER NEW STARS

CHARLIE PARKER......alto sax   BARNEY KESSEL......guitar
HOWARD McGHEE......trumpet   RED CALLENDER......bass
WARDELL GRAY......tenor sax   DODO MARMAROSA......piano
ROY PORTER......drums

DIAL 1002   ORNITHOLOGY
   A NIGHT IN TUNISIA

DIAL 1003   YARDBIRD SUITE
   MOOSE THE MOOCHE

CHARLIE PARKER ALL STARS

CHARLIE PARKER......alto sax   ARV GARRISON......guitar
MILES DAVIS......trumpet   VIC McMILLAN......bass
LUCKY THOMPSON...tenor sax   DODO MARMAROSA......piano
DON LAMOND......drums

DIAL 1012   RELAXIN' AT CAMARILLO
   BLUE SERGE (**Serge Chaloff**)

***DIAL 1013**   CHEERS
   CARVING THE BIRD

CHARLIE PARKER QUARTET

CHARLIE PARKER......alto sax   DOC WEST......drums
ERROLL GARNER......piano   RED CALLENDER......bass
EARL COLEMAN......vocal on Dark Shadows only

***DIAL 1014**   BIRD'S NEST
   DARK SHADOWS

***DIAL 1015**   COOL BLUES
   BLOWTOP BLUES

**Watch for release dates*

DIZZY GILLESPIE

DIZZY GILLESPIE, a fascinating contradiction in personalities is at once a bespectacled beret-wearing intellectual at home in a discussion of atonal harmonics, and a mad fun-poking sprite capable of fantastic zanyness. Yet his is a personality completely without pose, his many-sidedness compounded of intellectual curiosity, creative talent of the first order, and a bubbling abundance of energy manifested in the sheer love of living and playing jazz. Dizzy Gillespie fairly leaps at you through the loud speaker. His genius pervades every recording date in which he participates.

Dizzy's trumpet solos are full of mad twists, breathless flights and hoarse laughter. Impatience with banality and grasp of modern harmonics enable him to construct new jazz melodies with every effort at improvisation. The recordings listed reflect many facets of this dynamic musical personality: CONFIRMATION is moody and haunting, DIGGIN' DIZ bright and puckish, 'ROUND MIDNIGHT muted and nocturnal, DYNAMO a pyrotechnical display of dazzling vividness.

DIZZY GILLESPIE JAZZMEN

DIZZY GILLESPIE......trumpet   AL HAIG......piano
LUCKY THOMPSON...tenor sax   RAY BROWN......bass
MILT JACKSON......vibraphone   STAN LEVEY......drums

DIAL 1001   DYNAMO
   'ROUND ABOUT MIDNIGHT

DIAL 1005   DIGGIN' DIZ
   TRUMPET AT TEMPO (**McGhee**)

HOWARD McGHEE

Every art form depends not only upon the innovators, but those who organize new ideas into a unity. It is the latter role that Howard McGhee, perhaps the outstanding technician of the bebop movement, has followed with marked success.

HOWARD McGHEE may be compared to an architect whose emphasis is structure and musical logic. McGhee's technicianship permits him to play up tempos and higher registers with the ease of a clarinetist—bin tone and swing make him an emotionally persuasive soloist on ballads. With Gillespie's trend towards large bands McGhee is easily the outstanding bebop trumpet playing small band jazz.

HOWARD McGHEE SEXTET

HOWARD McGHEE......trumpet   DINGBOD KESTERSON......bass
TEDDY EDWARDS....tenor sax   DODO MARMAROSA......piano
ARV GARRISON......guitar   ROY PORTER......drums

DIAL 1010   UP IN DODO'S ROOM
   HIGH WIND IN HOLLYWOOD

DIAL 1011   DIALATED PUPILS
   MIDNIGHT AT MINTON'S

1947 BEBOP ALBUM

DURING ITS FIRST YEAR of existence DIAL carefully laid away from each of its several recording sessions one choice master ear-marked for release in album form. The album so conceived proved to be a thorough-going anthology of bebop and because readily merchandised, a powerful propagandist for the new jazz.

The talent represented was formidable and excluded no important artist of the contemporary school. Besides the leaders (see titles below) the following sidemen were to be heard: Miles Davis, Lucky Thompson, Flip Phillips, Serge Chaloff, Bill Harris, Al Haig, Jimmy Bunn, Dodo Marmarosa, Milt Jackson, Ray Brown, Dingbod Kesterson, Vic McMillan, Arv Garrison, Chuck Wayne, Roy Porter, Stan Levey, and Don Lamond. Of these sidemen, less than five (Davis, Thompson, Marmarosa, Jackson and Brown) —all featured prominently on DIAL masters recorded early 1946—won New Star awards in national polling in 1947, a remarkable testimony to the progressive character and clairvoyant insight of DIAL's recording policy.

DIAL D-1 ALBUM—Book Cover by Wally Berman and including

1006   CURBSTONE SCUFFLE—Sonny Berman Octet
   BIRD LORE—Charlie Parker New Stars

1007   BEBOP—Howard McGhee Quintet
   LOVER MAN—alto solo, Charlie Parker

1008   CONFIRMATION—Dizzy Gillespie Jazzmen
   DIAL-OGUE—Ralph Burns-Serge Chaloff

BEBOP

Bebop evolved in Harlem during the early 1940s at after-hours jam sessions at Minton's Playhouse and Clark Monroe's Uptown House. The new sound confused many listeners; this 1947 Dial Records catalog (*opposite*) attempted to explain it.

↗ TOP *From left:* **Thelonious Monk, one of the key innovators of bop, at Minton's Playhouse with bop trumpeter Howard McGhee, big band trumpeter Roy Eldridge (a major influence on many bop players), and bandleader and Minton's manager Teddy Hill.**

→ BOTTOM **Early bebop album with four 78 RPM discs featuring Charlie Parker, Fats Navarro, Kenny Clarke, Max Roach, and others, 1946.**

The Onyx   Tops in Entertainment

↑ ABOVE Onyx postcard, 1940s.

THE ONYX

35 WEST FIFTY-SECOND STREET

The first of the Onyx's four incarnations was as a speakeasy opened in 1927 by bootlegger Joe Helbock in a single-room walk-up apartment with a piano. John Hammond told Arnold Shaw the Onyx had a piano but "did not have any regular entertainment. Not during the speakeasy days anyway. Musicians would simply drop in and jam for their own amusement. . . . [Guitarist] Eddie Condon would drop in after he finished working at the Stork [Club], as would a Harlem group known as the Spirits of Rhythm."[29] The Onyx became the hangout for Helbock's friends, and artists like Jimmy and Tommy Dorsey, Art Tatum, Maxine Sullivan, and Louis Prima all played. Musician Jim Cullum noted, "This was a place where musicians could pick up phone messages or have their mail delivered, or even leave their horns for safekeeping."[30]

The Onyx moved to a larger space at 72 West Fifty-Second Street after Prohibition ended, becoming a legitimate enterprise and booking musicians including Billie Holiday and violinist Stuff Smith; Art Tatum was the intermission pianist. There were also regular jam sessions, featuring musicians like saxophonist Bud Freeman and singer and trombonist Jack Teagarden. From 1937 to 1939, the Onyx was at a third location, 62 West Fifty-Second Street, before finally closing.

In 1942, a new club opened using the Onyx name at 57 West Fifty-Second Street. Billing itself as the "Cradle of Swing," this venue offered Dixieland, swing, and bop performed by top artists including Hot Lips Page, Lester Young, Charlie Parker, Dizzy Gillespie, and Billie Holiday, who played an eighteen-month residency beginning in mid-1943. The final location thrived until about 1949, when it became a striptease club that kept the name.

→ RIGHT **Onxy postcard advertising Billie Holiday's residency, circa 1943.**

BILLIE HOLIDAY
America's Foremost Song Stylist
APPEARING AT THE ONYX CLUB NITELY

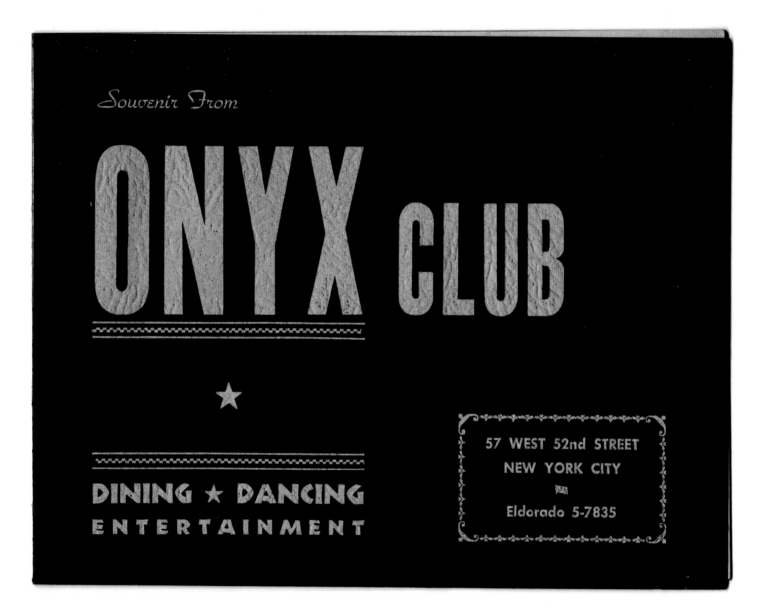

← ↑ OPPOSITE **Onyx folder and souvenir photograph of World War II servicemen** (*above*), mid-1940s.

→ RIGHT **Hickory House**
postcard, date unknown.

HICKORY HOUSE
144 WEST FIFTY-SECOND STREET

The Hickory House opened as a steak and chop restaurant in a former used-car showroom in the mid-1930s. Soon afterward, owner John Popkin decided to add live music, and the place became one of the Street's longest-running jazz venues.

The long room featured high ceilings, a forty-foot-long oval bar with a stage in the middle, stained-glass windows, and oil paintings of sports heroes such as Jack Dempsey, Babe Ruth, and golfer Bobby Jones. In the back, chefs broiled steaks over hickory logs on open grills.

House bands led by trumpeter Wingy Manone and clarinetist Joe Marsala were broadcast live from the club. Jam sessions were reserved for Sunday afternoons; in the late 1930s, Sidney Bechet and a young Billie Holiday performed as guest stars. Decades later, Holiday recalled that session, remembering she had not been paid for the appearance but that Marsala bought her a much-appreciated steak.[31]

Other musicians who played the Hickory House include vibraphonist Red Norvo and pianists Billy Taylor and Marian McPartland, who performed regularly from 1952 through 1960. In his autobiography, Taylor wrote about playing the club in the late 1950s, calling it "a place known for its casual jam sessions and free and comfortable interaction between Black and white musicians."[32]

The Hickory House closed in 1968.

The HICKORY HOUSE

144 West 52nd Street
New York

THE HICKORY SHOW BAR
IN NEW YORK

Dinner

← LEFT A menu from the Hickory House, date unknown.

↓ → RIGHT **Famous Door souvenir folder and photograph (*below*), 1940s.**

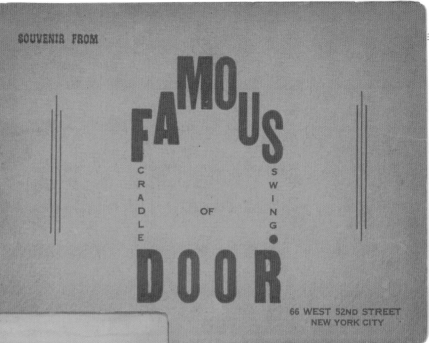

SOUVENIR FROM

FAMOUS CRADLE OF SWING **DOOR**

66 WEST 52ND STREET
NEW YORK CITY

→ OPPOSITE **Billie Holiday at the Famous Door during an engagement with saxophonist Babe Russin and his group, July 1941.**

FAMOUS DOOR
35 WEST FIFTY-SECOND STREET

At least five clubs on the Street operated at various times as the Famous Door. The first location was opened in 1935 by musicians Jimmy Dorsey, Glenn Miller, and Lenny Hayton and manager Jack Colt as a gathering place for performers playing nearby clubs. The club's name came from a wooden door set up next to the bar that was autographed by the club's founders, performers, and visiting celebrities.

Specializing in swing and Dixieland music, the Famous Door featured performers including trumpeters Bobby Hackett and Louis Prima and singers Billie Holiday and Bessie Smith. The club featured jam sessions as well, but financial problems arose and it closed after only one year.

In 1937, a second incarnation of the Famous Door opened at 66 West Fifty-Second, in a small room that held only sixty people. The house band was led by Louis Prima, with intermission sets by Art Tatum. Despite its small size, the new location played host to many top artists including Ella Fitzgerald and Count Basie, and broadcasts from the club went out over CBS Radio. During a 1942 booking at the club, bandleader Benny Carter was asked to fire trumpeter Dizzy Gillespie, who was part of the development of bop at the time. Carter said, "I was asked to get rid of him because he was playing augmented ninths, etc. They thought he was hitting bad notes." However, Carter "could see that Dizzy . . . was groping for something" and "stood up for him."[33]

The club moved twice more during the 1940s, eventually settling at 56 West Fifty-Second Street, where it continued to book swing musicians but added bebop groups to the mix. In 1950, the Famous Door closed for good, with a strip club opening in its place. Clubs in other cities including New Orleans and Los Angeles used the illustrious name, and during the 1960s, another unrelated club opened on Fifty-Second Street as the Famous Door.

THREE DEUCES
72 WEST FIFTY-SECOND STREET

The Three Deuces, which opened in 1937, became another of the Street's prime destinations for bebop. The club's small bandstand with upholstered walls played host to modern jazz innovators Dizzy Gillespie, Miles Davis, Charlie Parker, pianist Lennie Tristano, and bassist Slam Stewart, as well as more established musicians, including Ben Webster and Coleman Hawkins. In the mid-1940s, jazz disc jockey "Symphony Sid" Torin broadcast live from the club on WHOM; his show was popular in Harlem and helped boost the prospects of bop on Fifty-Second Street.

In 1944, *DownBeat* reported the club had introduced an "Hour of Silence," intended "to keep the nosier customers quiet for 60 minutes so that rabid fans of Art Tatum can hear the pianist without any clinking glasses obbligato."[34] But it was a failure, as this same article reported that "many 52d Street habitues regard it as their inalienable right to make as much noise as they please and that any musician who's worth his salt will be better for the competition." Tatum's response was to protest, "What do I have to do, perform a major operation to get you to keep quiet?"[35]

In his autobiography *Lullaby of Birdland*, George Shearing recalled one of his earliest jobs, playing intermission piano at the club during a run by Ella Fitzgerald, who was backed by Hank Jones on piano, Ray Brown on bass, and Charlie Smith on drums. "We all had to have one night off during the week, and when it was Hank's turn, I would get somebody to take over my intermission job so that I could substitute for him in Ella's band. . . . I thought I'd died and gone to heaven."[36]

Live recordings from the club featuring Charlie Parker, Roy Eldridge, and the Charlie Ventura/Bill Harris Quintet have been issued. Art Tatum can be seen performing at the Three Deuces on YouTube, in a clip from a 1943 short film that was part of *The March of Time* series that *Time* magazine produced and showed in movie theaters from the mid-1930s to the early 1950s.

The club closed in 1954.

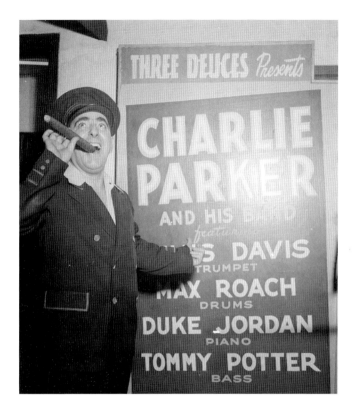

← OPPOSITE **Clockwise from top left: Tommy Potter, Max Roach (obscured), Miles Davis, Duke Jordan (obscured), and Charlie Parker.**

↑ ABOVE **Three Deuces doorman Gilbert J. Pincus, August 1947.**

Souvenir of

THREE DEUCES

72 WEST 52nd STREET ✦ NEW YORK ✦ ELdorado 5-7742

←↑ OPPOSITE **Three Deuces photo folder and souvenir photograph** (*above*), date unknown.

KELLY'S STABLE
137 WEST FIFTY-SECOND STREET

After operating a club of the same name in Chicago from 1915 to 1930, pioneering jazz banjoist and bandleader Bert Kelly opened Kelly's Stable on Fifty-First Street near Seventh Avenue in the late 1930s. Coleman Hawkins, while leading a band there, developed his version of the standard "Body and Soul," considered an early precursor of bop and one of the most important recordings in jazz history.

In March 1940, Kelly's Stable relocated to Fifty-Second Street, taking over the premises of a short-lived club called O'Leary's Barn, and was eventually sold to new owners including musician Ralph Watkins. The new location had a small stage with carriage lamps and a mural of a racehorse on the track. Hawkins returned in 1941, and other headliners included Billie Holiday, Dizzy Gillespie, and the King Cole Trio.

In about 1942, the club began hosting jam sessions organized by promoters Pete Kameron and Monte Kay. The two would go each week to Minton's Playhouse to scout talent and invite the most promising new bop musicians to join their jams, which also featured swing instrumentalists from Duke Ellington's, Count Basie's, and pianist Earl "Fatha" Hines's bands. Each player was paid ten dollars, but Dizzy Gillespie, booked in Philadelphia at the time, sometimes had to spend six dollars of that on train fare. After six months or so, the jam sessions were forced to end. Kay told Arnold Shaw, "We arrived one Sunday—the artists booked, the postcards mailed—and there was a padlock on the door.... If they gave an explanation, we received none when we began asking. There were just hints.... Naturally it had to do with the Black-white [race] thing. We drew an integrated crowd. We didn't go asking or looking for it. But the audience for jazz was then mixed."[37]

By 1943, the club had begun to book bop, first with a group led by Kenny Clarke and later a group with trumpeter Fats Navarro and pianist Bud Powell, as well as another led by Gillespie. According to *The New Grove Dictionary of Jazz*, owner Watkins's interest in the club waned in the mid-1940s, after he opened the Royal Roost with Morris Levy.[38] He sold Kelly's Stable in 1947.

↖ OPPOSITE, LEFT **Kelly's Stable postcard and photo
folder** (*opposite, right*)**, 1940s.**

↑ ABOVE **Kelly's Stable souvenir photograph, 1940s.**

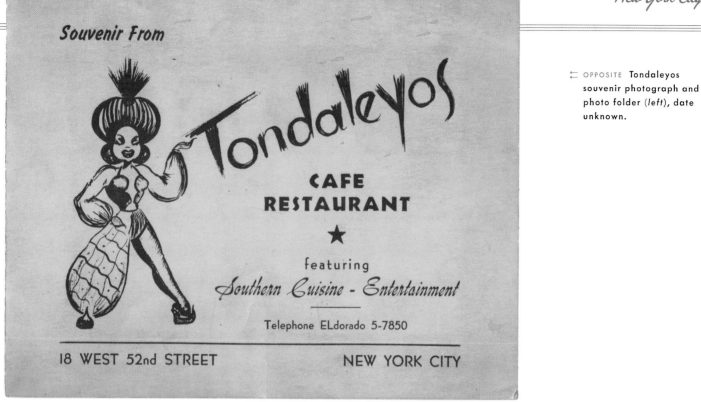

Souvenir From

Tondaleyos

CAFE RESTAURANT

★

featuring

Southern Cuisine - Entertainment

Telephone ELdorado 5-7850

18 WEST 52nd STREET   NEW YORK CITY

⇐ OPPOSITE **Tondaleyos** souvenir photograph and photo folder (*left*), date unknown.

TONDALEYOS
18 WEST FIFTY-SECOND STREET

In *Come In and Hear the Truth*, Patrick Burke writes, "Another facet of the increasing Black presence on the street was the appearance of two Black-owned clubs. The first of these was Tondaleyos, which opened around August 1944 . . . and was 'named after the Black dancer (née Wilhelmina Gray) who fronted the club with money provided by her husband, John Levy,' who was also African American."[39]

Gray had been a dancer at the Harlem Cotton Club and, in 1937, performed as a rumba and stag dancer at the original Ubangi Club in an act reviewed by *Variety* as "the last word in nitery erotica this side of a stag affair."[40] Levy was a well-respected bassist who gave Philadelphia pianist Erroll Garner his first New York shows at the club. Guitarist Tiny Grimes also played at Tondelayos, with frequent guest Charlie Parker sitting in.

It's not known when the poorly documented club closed, but in October 1953, *Jet* magazine reported, "Wilhelmina (Tondaleyo) Gray, who once owned her own 52nd St. nitery, is now a hat-check girl at the Flame Melody Room."[41]

↓ → BELOW **Downbeat photo folder
and souvenir photograph** (*right*),
mid-1940s.

Souvenir of

DOWN
BEAT
CLUB

★

**66 WEST 52nd STREET
NEW YORK CITY**

DOWNBEAT CLUB
66 WEST FIFTY-SECOND STREET

Three different Manhattan clubs used some variation of the Downbeat name. Morris Levy opened the first in 1944, at 66 West Fifty-Second Street; it quickly became one of the top jazz venues in the city, presenting artists like Sarah Vaughan, Billie Holiday, Lester Young, Coleman Hawkins, and Dizzy Gillespie.

In his autobiography, Miles Davis recalls his experience at the venue in the mid-1940s: "I started sitting in with Coleman Hawkins's band at the Downbeat Club on 52nd Street. Billie Holiday was the star singer with this group. The reason that I got to sit in a lot was because Joe Guy, Bean's [Hawkins] regular trumpet player, had just gotten married to Billie Holiday. Sometimes, they'd be so high off heroin and be fucking so good that Joe would miss his gig. So would Billie. So, Hawk would use me when Joe didn't show up. I used to check with Hawk down at the Downbeat every night to see if Joe had shown up. If he didn't, then I would play the set."[42]

In 1948, the Downbeat closed, but four years later a new venue, Le Down Beat, opened on West Fifty-Fourth Street, showcasing musicians such as pianist Mary Lou Williams and vibraphonist Terry Gibbs. During the late 1960s, a third Downbeat opened on Forty-Second and Lexington. It featured jazz by the likes of Roy Eldridge and singer Anita O'Day before becoming a rock club in 1970.

← LEFT **Dizzy Gillespie** (*right*) **watching Ella Fitzgerald perform at the Downbeat, New York City, September 1947.**

Midtown

CAFE ZANZIBAR

1634 BROADWAY

Cafe Zanzibar opened in 1943 in a space over the Winter Garden theater, just a few blocks from Fifty-Second Street. Ella Fitzgerald and Don Redman and His Orchestra were the first headliners, joined by tap-dance trio the Berry Brothers and comedy duo Moke and Poke. Later bookings included Louis Armstrong, Cab Calloway, singer Pearl Bailey, and saxophonist and bandleader Louis Jordan, all joined by the club's chorus line of skimpily attired showgirls, the Zanzibeauts.

In 1945, *Billboard* magazine published the results of a survey of newspaper and magazine reporters and editors, naming the Zanzibar "the best colored show in town." In July 1945, *New York World-Telegram* columnist Robert W. Dana wrote that the club "has an average turnover of 1500 persons weekdays and 2300 Saturdays, and [does] gross business of $2,000,000 a year."[43] Proprietor and publicist Carl Erbe told Dana, "During the war former $25-a-week men making $80 came to know and like us. Old-timers who never thought they could afford a club had to do something with money that formerly bought cars, refrigerators and washing machines, so they gave a night to us and continued to do so."[44]

Always on the lookout for a way to publicize his club, Erbe announced plans to build a landing pad on the roof, so helicopters could drop off important patrons and performers could travel easily to other shows. Though nothing came of that particular idea, Erbe was able to generate media coverage that kept the club in the headlines.

With success, the club moved one block to the former site of the Hurricane Club, on the corner of Forty-Ninth Street and Broadway. While integrated, the better tables often went to white patrons. In a September 1944 article in the *Chicago Defender*, Langston Hughes described how white patrons were seated up front and Black patrons on raised platforms on the sides, noting the club had "so many Black customers that they will have to build more sides to the room to be able to sit them all!" Hughes described being taken to a seat so far back behind the band that he complained, "Listen, man, I am not in the show! I came to see the show." Despite it all, Hughes said Cafe Zanzibar was very popular among his friends and Black people visiting the city, and that its shows were among the best on Broadway.[45]

But changing tastes and increased overhead meant the club had to downscale, and after moving once again in 1947, the club closed the next year.

→ OPPOSITE **Cafe Zanzibar**
souvenir photograph, mid-1940s.

← LEFT Cafe Zanzibar handbill, 1945.

→ RIGHT Cafe Zanzibar mailer, mid-1940s.

Joe Howard *presents The Winter Edition of* "ZANZIBARABIAN NIGHTS"

PROGRAM
(IN THE ORDER OF APPEARANCE)
Your Host - Pee Wee Marquette

OVERTURE:
LOUIS ARMSTRONG & ORCHESTRA
in a medley of Zanzibar song hits

"WEST SIDE OF TOWN"
BILL ROBINSON and THE ZANZIBEAUTS
Words and Music by BENNY DAVIS and TED MURRY

LOUIS "SATCHMO" ARMSTRONG
His Trumpet • His Orchestra
and His Vocalist

Velma Middleton

MAURICE ROCCO
"Rockin' With Rocco"

PETERS SISTERS
"A Ton of Harmony and Rhythm"

"DOIN' THE ZANZIBAR"
Buell Thomas - Leon LaMorie
and The ZANZIBEAUTS

THE STAFF
Talent Supervisor - WILLIAM KENT
Production under Direction of CLARENCE ROBINSON
Words and Music by BENNY DAVIS and TED MURRY
Musical Director - LOUIS ARMSTRONG
Costumes by MADAME BERTHA

NICHOLAS BROTHERS
Dancing Stars of Stage and Screen

DELTA RHYTHM BOYS
"Quintessence of Quintets"

BILL "BOJANGLES" ROBINSON
"America's Most Beloved Dancing Star"

FINALE:
"ONE HUNDRED MILLION STARS
IN THE STAR SPANGLED BANNER"
with The Entire Company

FOR DANCING:
LOUIS ARMSTRONG and HIS ORCHESTRA
CLAUDE HOPKINS and HIS ORCHESTRA

IF YOU WOULD LIKE TO HAVE THIS PROGRAM MAILED TO A FRIEND, ADDRESS AND GIVE TO YOUR WAITER . . . WE WILL PAY THE POSTAGE.

↑ ABOVE **A program for the** *Zanzibarabian Nights* **revue, starring Louis Armstrong and Bill "Bojangles" Robinson, mid-1940s.**

400 RESTAURANT
FIFTH AVENUE AT FORTY-THIRD STREET

The 400 was a ritzy supper club best remembered for hosting a series of live coast-to-coast radio broadcasts featuring Duke Ellington and His Orchestra in 1945. Sponsored by the U.S. Treasury Department, *Your Saturday Date with the Duke* featured live music and appealed to listeners to buy war bonds. In April 1945, the club also played host to a special Ellington broadcast in conjunction with the funeral of President Franklin D. Roosevelt, "A Tribute to F.D.R. by the American Negro."

Other than Ellington, the 400 featured bands mostly led by white bandleaders, including Gene Krupa, Woody Herman, Benny Goodman, and Tommy Dorsey. But when the club reopened after remodeling in 1946, the headlining act was African American bandleader Louis Jordan, who shared the bills with white performers: the vocal group Modernaires and trumpeter Randy Brooks's big band.

ROYAL ROOST

1580 BROADWAY AT FORTY-SEVENTH STREET

In early 1948, former Kelly's Stable partner Ralph Watkins teamed with Downbeat Club founder Morris Levy to open a chicken restaurant offering live music, the Royal Chicken Roost. When their opening night act, Jimmie Lunceford's Orchestra, failed to attract an audience, the owners became desperate. According to *DownBeat* magazine, Watkins "tried novelty bands, rhumba bands, jazz trios, cocktail trios, hot combos, piano teams, single names, vocal stars . . . and even offered [President Harry Truman's daughter] Margaret Truman a job, which got the spot a lot of publicity but no customers."[46]

Eventually Watkins gave Symphony Sid and promoter Monte Kay a shot at staging a bebop concert on a Monday night, when the Roost was normally closed; the performers included Charlie Parker, Miles Davis, Max Roach, Fats Navarro, pianist Tadd Dameron, and saxophonist Dexter Gordon.

Watkins was shocked when "such a crowd showed up that we had to call the cops."[47] Levy recalled, "We had Dexter Gordon or Charlie Parker or Miles Davis. They did two nights a week, and then it grew to three nights a week, then six and seven nights a week. . . . It was really fabulous."[48] The club, with the name abbreviated to Royal Roost, took off, drawing fans eager to experience the new sounds of modern jazz. The Roost published a free pamphlet, *What Is Bebop?*, aimed at those seeking to understand the new phenomenon, and soon the club became known as the "Metropolitan Bopera House."

Admission was only ninety-nine cents, and the Roost also welcomed underage patrons, or those who only wanted to listen, seating them in bleachers in an enclosed area next to the bar. For teetotalers, the club had a soda fountain, which Watkins said often took in more than the bar.

A spinoff record label, Royal Roost, released music by artists who appeared at the club, including Roost discovery Harry Belafonte, Bud Powell, saxophonist Stan Getz, and guitarist Johnny Smith. The label's motto was "Music of the Future."

As author Richard Carlin writes: "Things were going very well at the Royal Roost through early 1949, so well that its managers started to look for a larger space. According to Levy, his original partner (presumably the unnamed Watkins) failed to cut him into the new deal that involved opening a lavish new restaurant/nightclub . . . to be called Bop City. . . . While Watkins was moving into the big time, Levy was left to manage the Roost. Unable to compete with the better-funded Bop City enterprise to attract acts, he soon had to close the club."[49]

Also cut out were Symphony Sid and Monte Kay. According to Levy, Kay soon came to him about opening a new club, and Levy launched what became the most celebrated club in jazz history: Birdland.

→ OPPOSITE, LEFT **Royal Chicken Roost postcard, circa 1945.**

→ OPPOSITE, RIGHT **Royal Roost menu, late 1940s.**

Cocktail Lounge

Royal Chicken Roost
1580 Broadway
Bet. 47th & 48th Streets. N.Y.C.

Broadway's Most Elaborate Dining Room

BILL AND RALPH
welcome you
to the
Royal ROOST

NOW YOU'LL FRY!

OPPOSITE
STRAND THEATRE
at
1580 BROADWAY
"NEW YORK'S
GROOVIEST NEST"

Program

→ RIGHT Program for Bop City's 1950 show "The Jazz Train," featuring musicians Red Allen, Lucky Thompson, Tyree Glenn, and others.

BOP CITY

1619 BROADWAY AT WEST FORTY-NINTH STREET

In 1949, Ralph Watkins opened Bop City in Broadway's Brill Building, in a space formerly home to Cafe Zanzibar. The first headliners were Ella Fitzgerald and Artie Shaw, and the African American newspaper *New York Age* reported: "Over 300 celebrities, bop lovers, music lovers, and the generally curious were able to push, squirm and pack themselves into the huge [room] . . . but over twice that many were unable to gain admittance. . . . In keeping with the tone of the place, owner Ralph Watkins saw to it that his waiters, a big, interracial crew, were dressed exactly as you'd expect a waiter to be dressed at a palace of bop, and they looked interesting if not completely authentic in big, flowing polka dot bop bow ties. Outside of Ella Fitzgerald, the greatest performance was that put in by the audience, the greatest mixture of humanity this side of the Casbar [*sic*]. Celebs came to ogle each other, beautiful dames came to be ogled, and the rest of 'em just came to ogle, period."[50]

Subsequent headliners included Sarah Vaughan, Louis Armstrong, Fletcher Henderson, Mary Lou Williams, Nat King Cole, and Dizzy Gillespie's band. Watkins's ambitious ideas for the club included booking modern dancer Katherine Dunham, known for her African- and Caribbean-influenced performances, and franchising the Bop City concept in other cities, but competition from other clubs, including the nearby Birdland, proved too great, and Bop City was forced to close in December 1950.

→ RIGHT **A souvenir photograph of Billie Holiday at Bop City, date unknown.**

BIRDLAND

1678 BROADWAY, JUST NORTH OF WEST FIFTY-SECOND STREET

On December 15, 1949, former Royal Roost partner Morris Levy opened Birdland with his brother Irving, manager Oscar Goodstein, and six other partners. The three-hundred-seat basement club, named in honor of bebop giant Charlie "Bird" Parker, opened with *A Journey thru Jazz 1920–1950*, showcasing the history of jazz as played by some of those who had created it: trumpeters Max Kaminsky and Hot Lips Page, up-and-comers Stan Getz and Lennie Tristano, Lester Young, Harry Belafonte, and Parker.

Birdland historian Leo T. Sullivan wrote, "Many jazz clubs opened and closed over the many years, but never has there been a venue showcasing such incredible jazz greats on a nightly basis as the 'Jazz Corner of the World,' Birdland."[51]

The club featured a long bar on one side, booths on the other, and tables running down in the middle. Above the booths were portraits of jazz stars painted by Diana Dale, the club's hatcheck girl. For those too young to drink or who came only to listen, there was the "bullpen" or "peanut gallery," a section to the right of the bar separated from the rest of the club by a barrier. When the club first opened, there were birdcages with live finches hanging from the ceiling; unfortunately, the noise and smoke proved too much for the birds, who lasted only about a month.

Birdland didn't have a dance floor, and the stage was small enough that on occasion, if a large group was playing, the piano was placed on the floor. Nearby was a radio booth where Symphony Sid broadcast nightly to listeners on the East Coast, from midnight until six o'clock in the morning. Pee Wee Marquette, standing three feet, nine inches tall, was the club's notorious emcee, most famous for intentionally mispronouncing the name of any performer who refused to tip him.

Birdland booked top acts for six-night runs, with Mondays reserved for jam sessions. As one of the main bebop venues, the club played host to Parker as well as Bud Powell, Thelonious Monk, Dizzy Gillespie, and Miles Davis. Count Basie, a favorite of Morris Levy's, made Birdland his New York base of operations and signed to Levy's record label, Roulette, in the late 1950s. The club did well with women vocalists, booking Billie Holiday, Nina Simone, Ella Fitzgerald, and Dinah Washington. Other musicians who appeared included trumpeter Clifford Brown, Sonny Rollins, Art Tatum, Duke Ellington, Lester Young, Stan Getz, and Dave Brubeck. George Shearing wrote the standard "Lullaby of Birdland" after Levy asked him to compose a theme song for Symphony Sid's broadcasts.

← OPPOSITE **Birdland souvenir photograph with frequent patron Marlon Brando (*right*) posing with clubgoers, date unknown.**

↖ TOP, LEFT **Birdland postcard, 1950s.**

↓ BELOW Birdland handbill for 1954 triple-bill featuring
Dinah Washington, Dizzy Gillespie, and Charlie Parker.

→ RIGHT Birdland handbill for a 1955 engagement with Al
Hibbler, Dizzy Gillespie, and Gil Melle.

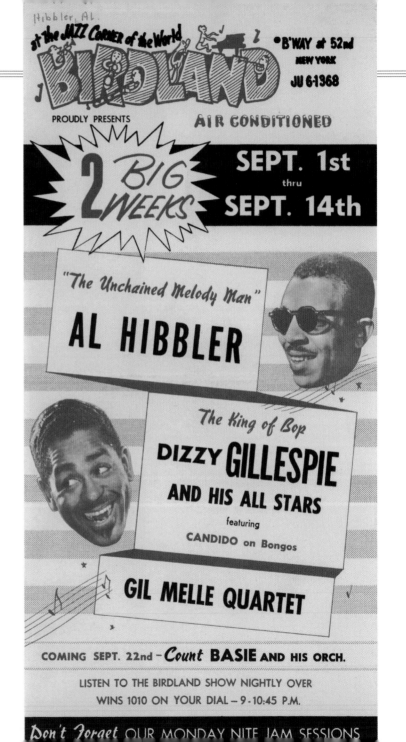

← LEFT **Handbill advertising 1956 Birdland shows with Count Basie, Johnny Smith, and Bud Powell.**

↑ ABOVE **Birdland menu, date unknown.**

As the club's popularity grew, it became a draw for celebrities; patrons included Marilyn Monroe, Marlene Dietrich, Frank Sinatra, Ava Gardner, Judy Garland, Sugar Ray Robinson, and even classical music icon Igor Stravinsky. Eventually the Birdland name gained enough cachet that the club was able to sponsor national—and, in at least one case, international—concert tours during the mid- to late 1950s.

While Levy was committed to integration and Birdland an oasis of sorts from racism, things could be different just outside the door. On August 25, 1959, Miles Davis, who was performing with his quintet at the club, stepped outside to take a break. In his autobiography, Davis recalled: "I had just walked this pretty white girl named Judy out to get a cab. She got in the cab, and I'm standing there in front of Birdland wringing wet because it's a hot, steaming, muggy night in August. This white policeman comes up to me and tells me to move on. . . . 'Move on, for what? I'm working downstairs.

That's my name up there, Miles Davis,' and I pointed to my name on the marquee all up in lights. He said, 'I don't care where you work, I said move on! If you don't move on I'm going to arrest you.' I just looked at his face real straight and hard, and I didn't move. Then he said, 'You're under arrest!'[52]

A fight ensued, with Davis badly beaten by three officers before being hauled off to jail, charged with disorderly conduct and the assault of a police officer. The story was widely reported, with photographs of a bloodied Davis, and eventually the charges were dropped, but Davis never forgot the incident. "[It] changed my whole life and my whole attitude again, made me bitter and cynical again when I was really starting to feel good about the things that had changed in this country."

Many legendary live albums were recorded at the club, including Art Blakey's two-volume *A Night at Birdland* (1954), Count Basie's *Basie at Birdland* (1961), and most of John Coltrane's *Live at Birdland* (1964). But

as rents in the area rose, running a profitable jazz club became increasingly difficult, and in June 1964, Birdland filed for Chapter 11 bankruptcy, closing for good the next year.

The club's legacy was boosted in 1977 by Josef Zawinul's song "Birdland," featured on his band Weather Report's bestselling album *Heavy Weather*. In 1980, the Manhattan Transfer's version of the song won a Grammy Award, and in 1991, Quincy Jones's version won two more. In 1986, a new club with the Birdland name opened in the midtown theater district.

✓ OPPOSITE, LEFT **Birdland souvenir photograph with Dizzy Gillespie** (*third from left*) **posing with fans, date unknown.**

✓ OPPOSITE, RIGHT **Birdland souvenir photograph, date unknown.**

↓ BELOW **Jazz DJ Symphony Sid pictured on the inside of a Birdland photo folder along with other notable jazz figures. For more on Sid, see page 203.**

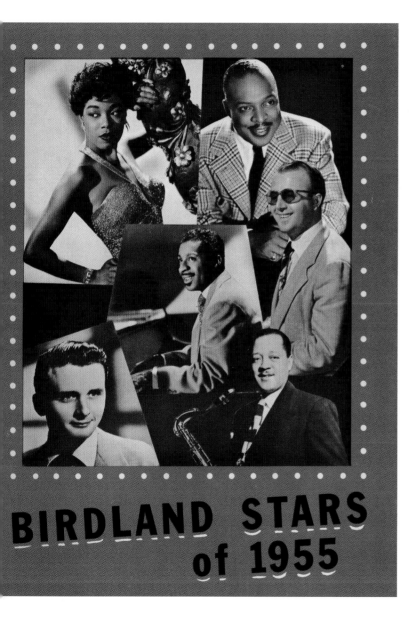

BIRDLAND STARS of 1955

← OPPOSITE AND LEFT **Birdland** concert tour programs, 1955–1957.

↑ ABOVE **Birdland** photo folder, date unknown.

A Conversation with

QUINCY JONES

Musician, composer, arranger, entertainment industry executive, and producer Quincy Jones was born in Chicago in 1933. Jones grew up in Seattle, where he was mentored by Count Basie band trumpeter Clark Terry, and while still a teen he joined Lionel Hampton's big band as a trumpeter, pianist, and arranger. In the early 1950s, he moved to New York City and was soon arranging music for Count Basie, Sarah Vaughan, Duke Ellington, Julian "Cannonball" Adderley, and childhood friend Ray Charles.

In 1961, Jones was hired by Mercury Records as vice president, becoming the first African American senior executive at a major label. In 1964, he earned his first scoring assignment for an American film, Sidney Lumet's *The Pawnbroker*, and following its success, left Mercury and moved to Los Angeles to focus on composing for film, eventually scoring nearly forty features.

Named one of the most influential jazz musicians of the twentieth century by *Time* magazine, Quincy Jones is an impresario in the broadest and most creative sense of the word. His career has encompaassed the roles of composer, record producer, artist, film producer, arranger, conductor, instrumentalist, television producer, record company executive, television station owner, magazine founder, multimedia entrepreneur, and humanitarian. Among the multitude of awards that he has received for his contributions are an Emmy Award, seven Academy Award nominations, the Academy of Motion Picture Arts and Sciences' Jean Hersholt Humanitarian Award, and twenty-eight Grammy Awards (the highest of any individual). Jones is also the all-time most Grammy-nominated artist, with a total of eighty nominations. In 2001, he was made a Commandeur de Légion d'Honneur by the Republic of France and named a Kennedy Center Honoree for his contributions to the cultural fabric of the United States of America. He was recognized by the National Endowment for the Arts as a Jazz Master—the nation's highest jazz honor—in 2008, and in 2010 was bestowed the National Medal of Arts, the nation's highest artistic honor. In 2016, he received a Tony Award for Best Revival of a Musical for the Broadway production of *The Color Purple*. The award completed the rare EGOT set for Jones, making him one of only twenty-one individuals in history who have received an Emmy, Grammy, Oscar, and Tony Award.

In 2013, Quincy Jones was inducted into the Rock & Roll Hall of Fame.

Jeff Gold (JG): You began playing jazz in Seattle clubs when you were a teenager. What was the Seattle club scene like in the 1940s?

Quincy Jones (QJ): Man, it was absolutely insane. I'm talking about bebop heaven. Everybody was there. We had Ray Charles playing jazz piano like the baddest cat out there, playing alto like Charlie Parker, and singing like Charles Brown and Nat King Cole. We also had [bassist] Buddy Catlett, [trumpeter and saxophonist] Floyd Standifer, [singer] Ernestine Anderson, you name it. It was hard to underestimate. . . . An absolutely sacred place.

JG: Which clubs did you frequent?

QJ: The Rocking Chair, the Elks Club, the Washington Educational Social Club.

JG: Ray was only a few years older than you, and I wondered if being teenage musicians was an obstacle to getting gigs—or even getting into clubs?

QJ: Hell no, that's why I had that cigarette! I didn't smoke then, I just held it in my mouth so that I looked old and cool enough to get in the clubs.

JG: What was it like to be a professional musician at such a young age?

QJ: Unbelievable. Bumps Blackwell made us [the Bumps Blackwell Jr. Band] into a real show band. Trombonist Major Pigford and I would work up a comedy routine using the names "Dexedrine" and "Benzedrine," where we put on fedoras and had empty wine bottles in our coat pockets and used raggedy "country" one-liners like this one:

Me: Say, Major, is that a diamond in your nose?
Major: No, it's snot!

We thought we were real adults back then, but we were just kids.

JG: How were you treated by the other musicians and the club owners?

QJ: With nothing but love and cooperation. It was absolutely beautiful and was almost like a bottle club. We were at home, especially at the Washington Educational Social Club. It was a space of mutual respect.

JG: Were there frightening situations?

QJ: There were occasional police busts, fistfights, and sometimes even gunfire. We'd always know to haul ass out the back door, though, and you'd always get your clothes ripped on the thickets in the backyard. But overall, the music made it a safe space for us. It was a way to get away from the more dangerous situations, like getting wrapped up in gang fights.

JG: You met a lot of important musicians when they'd come through Seattle and sometimes get to play with them. You've mentioned Billie Holiday, Thelonious Monk, Charlie Parker, Cab Calloway, Count Basie, and Billy Eckstine. I was wondering how you met these more established musicians.

QJ: It was all different, but one of my favorite stories was when Bumps marched into rehearsal one day in 1948 and announced, "Billie Holiday is coming to town and we're gonna back her up." We all freaked out in disbelief. We said, "Why us? Why the junior band? Why not the senior band?" He said, "Because y'all can sight-read better than anybody else around here." Like most singers in those days, Billie traveled with only a pianist who served as musical director and hired local musicians in the various cities. We were so excited we could barely stand it. I was only fifteen then!

JG: Were you able to just introduce yourself at gigs? Were they responsive to you, open to sharing and playing?

QJ: Absolutely. It was simply about: Can. You. Play?!

JG: Who had a big impact or influence on you?

QJ: Man, all of them. They all taught me something. But Ray Charles probably had the biggest impact overall. He was only two years older, but he seemed like he knew it all. He taught me how to read in braille, how to arrange, and so much more that I can't even put into words. Bumps Blackwell had the booking thing down and taught me so much about the business. Basie taught me about how to stay above the board, and man, Buddy Catlett and I started at the same time. The list just goes on.

JG: At eighteen, you moved to Boston to go to Berklee, where there was an active club scene. Did you play in the clubs regularly or meet other artists there?

QJ: All the time. Five clubs a night. We'd be in there from 2:00 to 6:30 A.M., then go to school right after, around 12:45 P.M. Even back in Seattle, the music teacher at Garfield [High School], Parker Cook, never scolded me because he said I'm doing what God made me to do. He let me have free rein in his band room and I am forever grateful for that.

JG: At nineteen, you got an offer to join Lionel Hampton's big band and moved to New York. You've spoken about how going to Birdland was important for you. Can you talk about Birdland?

↑ ABOVE **Charlie Parker and trumpeter Red Rodney with Chuck Wayne, Barbara Carroll, Dizzy Gillespie, and Clyde Lombardi** (*reflected in mirror*) **Downbeat Club, circa 1947.**

→ OPPOSITE **A flyer advertising records by jazz greats on Norman Granz's Clef and Norgran labels, mid-1950s.**

QJ: It had a thing about it. It was like the Vatican of bebop, where all the great stuff happened. I used to go down there every Monday to Basie's rehearsals to try to get him to play my arrangements. It was a special place.

JG: What was the midtown–Fifty-Second Street club scene like back then? Was it different from the Harlem club scene?

QJ: It was pure bebop. The land of the revolutionaries.

JG: Was race an issue in the clubs?

QJ: Not at all. Back then it wasn't about color in the clubs, it was about how good can you play, mofo. Racism would've been over in the 1950s if they listened to the jazz guys!

JG: Did people mix more easily in jazz clubs than elsewhere?

QJ: Hell yes. It was a place of community and pure love of the art. You couldn't find that anywhere else.

JG: Touring Europe with Hampton in 1953 was a pivotal experience for you, in terms of how Black American musicians were treated and how the music was embraced. How did Europe differ from the United States, in terms of audience reaction and how you were treated?

QJ: We were sanctified. We wouldn't have had jazz if it weren't for the French. I'm telling you, Paris was frightening! They were so supportive and absolutely loved the music. It was a unique place and it'll always be one of my favorite spots.

JG: Why do you think Europeans were so receptive to American jazz and the musicians who played it?

QJ: Because they have a culture that's older than ours, and they can respect the use of the twelve notes!

JG: In 1957, you moved to Paris, something a number of African American musicians did—Bud Powell, Dexter Gordon, Kenny Clarke. Why did you make that move?

QJ: I got a call from Nicole Barclay to be the musical director of her record company [Barclay], which was the hippest record company in the history of France. They were connected with [Mercury Records founder] Irving Green and had platinum records forever. [Verve Records founder and jazz impresario] Norman Granz did the distribution for Mercury, and they had the Jazz at the Philharmonic as well as the pop stuff. They had it all. So it was my time to move!

JG: You came back to New York in 1960 to work for Mercury Records as an executive while continuing to make your own music. Some of the Fifty-Second Street clubs had closed, and some very important artists had passed away, including Bird, Billie Holiday, Clifford Brown, and Lester Young. When you returned, had the New York club scene changed from the one you first encountered?

QJ: No, not at all. They all left their legacies and you could feel it emanating through the rooms. They were gone physically, but their spiritual energy remained, and there was no doubt about that. Jam sessions happened all the time. Everywhere in America, we'd find a spot to play a gig. We were all like family. When you spend most of your time with them, I guess that's natural!

JG: The photographs in this book make clear that going to see live music in a jazz club was a big deal—people got dressed up in their finest, most stylish clothes and were primed to enjoy themselves. And many were happy to pay a dollar to take home a photo as a souvenir of a special evening, and the clubs happily obliged. What did going out to see live music mean to audiences during that era, especially African Americans?

QJ: Live music is always important. Jazz clubs were huge in New York because of the human connection. You'd walk in one of those clubs and it felt almost as if you had not a care in the world. It was a dark time, but live music offered light.

JG: Some of the photographs here show performers posing with fans at clubs, including Dizzy Gillespie, Billie Holiday, and Oscar Peterson. Were the clubs places performers interacted with fans?

QJ: Yes, they always interacted.

JG: Thanks, Quincy, I'm so grateful for your perspective. ●

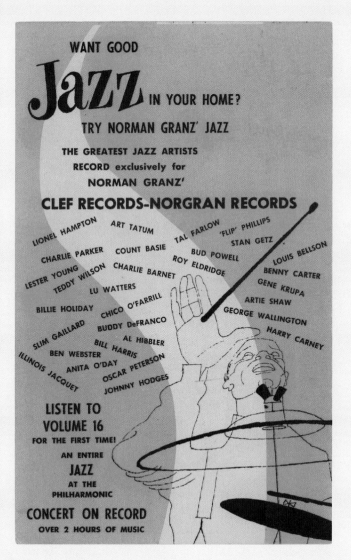

Greenwich Village

By the 1920s, Greenwich Village already had a small jazz scene, at clubs like the Cowboy and the Starlight Room. In the early 1930s, the Hot Feet Club speakeasy featured saxophonist Otto Hardwick's group, with Fats Waller. But it wasn't until 1937 that jazz in the Village began in earnest, with the opening of Nick's and, the next year, Café Society and the Village Vanguard.

In 1945, guitarist Eddie Condon opened his namesake club, which, like Nick's, presented primarily traditional and Dixieland groups. During the 1940s and 1950s, the same music could be heard in weekly jam sessions at the Stuyvesant Casino and Central Plaza. But in the 1950s, a new group of Village clubs began offering much more adventurous fare.

During the last few years of his life, Charlie Parker played regularly at the Open Door, a small, dark bar on West Third Street and Broadway. Café Bohemia featured modern jazz with groups led by Miles Davis, Charles Mingus, and the Horace Silver/Hank Mobley Quintet. The newly emergent hard bop, a bebop offshoot that incorporated influences from gospel, rhythm and blues, and blues, began to take hold at various Village clubs. And in 1957, the Five Spot Café, a small storefront bar that held only seventy-five people, opened on Cooper Square, with the Thelonious Monk Quartet featuring John Coltrane. Two years later, the Ornette Coleman Quartet, from Los Angeles, brought avant-garde jazz to the club; its original booking had been for two weeks, but the group generated so much interest—and controversy—that it was extended to ten weeks. Musicians including Lionel Hampton, Leonard Bernstein, and the Modern Jazz Quartet came and were vocal in their support, but Miles Davis and Dizzy Gillespie were not won over; the latter was quoted in *Time* magazine as saying, "I don't know what he's playing, but it's not jazz."[53]

In 1958, the Village Gate opened on Thompson and Bleecker Streets, and for the next thirty-eight years, the club hosted shows by established artists like Coleman Hawkins and Duke Ellington and younger innovators like Coltrane, pianist Bill Evans, and Dave Brubeck.

Though most of the Village's jazz clubs closed long ago, the Village Vanguard, after more than eight decades, continues to be a center for jazz in New York City.

← OPPOSITE **Jazz clubs in Greenwich Village.**

VILLAGE VANGUARD

178 SEVENTH AVENUE

In 1935, law school dropout Max Gordon opened the first Village Vanguard in a basement on Charles Street at Greenwich Avenue. Gordon initially planned for his club to be a hub for local poets, but after he decided to add live music, the police department denied him a cabaret license, deeming the premises insufficient. He soon relocated to the former home of a basement speakeasy, the Golden Triangle.

The new location offered a mixed bag of poetry readings, comedy, cabaret acts, folk and popular music, dancing, and some jazz. During the 1930s and 1940s, the Vanguard booked some small swing groups and musicians, including Mary Lou Williams and Sidney Bechet. In her memoir *Alive at the Village Vanguard*, Gordon's wife, Lorraine, recalled that before she knew Max, "the biggest reason my pals and I went to the Vanguard, though, was because there were jazz jam sessions in the afternoons on Sundays. You could go hear Lester Young, Ben Webster, all the greatest jazz musicians for fifty cents at the door, or something like that."[54]

Sensing jazz might be something to focus on, Max Gordon brought in more musicians, and as jazz began to shift from big bands to smaller combos, he hired a resident trio featuring clarinetist Jimmy Hamilton, pianist Eddie Heywood, and drummer Zutty Singleton.

In the late 1940s, Gordon ran into his future wife at a Fire Island bakery. Lorraine, then married to Blue Note Records cofounder Alfred Lion, recognized Gordon. She approached him, suggesting he book Blue Note's Thelonious Monk at the club, and he agreed. On September 14, 1948, Monk opened at the club. As Lorraine recalled: "Nobody came. None of the so-called jazz critics. None of the so-called cognoscenti. Zilch. Alfred and I sat there in a banquette at the Vanguard, and Thelonious got up at one point and did this little dance and announced, "Now, human beings, I'm going to play. . . ." Max came running over to me in acute distress. . . . There was almost no audience. And Max kept crying, "What did you talk me into? You trying to ruin my business? We're dying with this guy.""[55]

By the late 1950s, Gordon was focusing primarily on jazz, and the Vanguard was thriving, bringing in countless important artists including Miles Davis, Art Blakey, the Modern Jazz Quartet, Charles Mingus, and Horace Silver. Bill Evans was a regular. John Coltrane's groups played the club numerous times, resulting in his classic albums *Live at the Village Vanguard* (1962) and *Live at the Village Vanguard Again!* (1966).

More than fifty albums have been recorded at the club, including titles by Sonny Rollins, Dizzy Gillespie, guitarists Kenny Burrell and Charlie Byrd, drummer Elvin Jones, singer Betty Carter, pianist Junior Mance, and saxophonist Gerry Mulligan.

When Max Gordon died in 1989, Lorraine closed the Vanguard for a single night. She then reopened and continued to run it until her death in 2018 at the age of ninety-five. The Village Vanguard continues to present important jazz today.

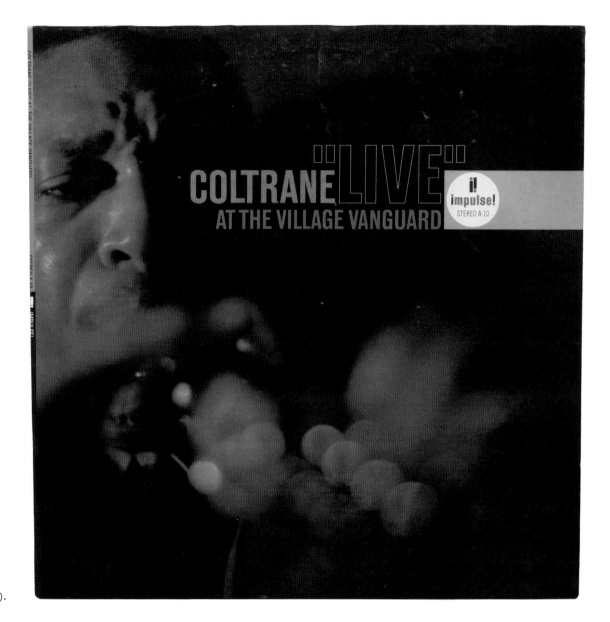

→ RIGHT **John Coltrane**
album *"Live" at the*
Village Vanguard (1962).

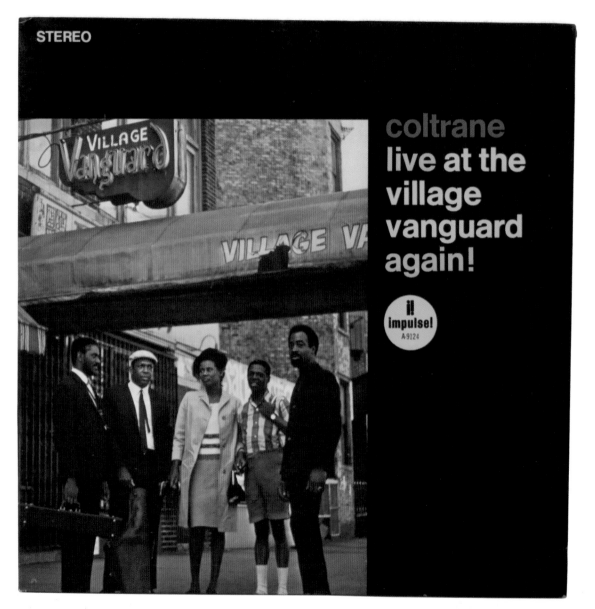

STEREO

coltrane
live at the
village
vanguard
again!

il
impulse!
A-9124

← LEFT John Coltrane's album *Coltrane at the Village Vanguard Again!* (1966).

→ OPPOSITE Miles Davis at the Village Vanguard, 1958.

→ RIGHT **Nick's postcard,
date unknown.**

→ OPPOSITE **An unidentified
singer at Café Society
downtown, date unknown.**

NICK'S
170 WEST TENTH STREET AT SEVENTH AVENUE

Opened in the mid-1930s, Nick's was the eponymous club and steak house of jazz pianist and former lawyer Nick Rongetti. Rongetti favored improvised traditional and Dixieland music and mandated that music stands and written scores be barred from the bandstand. Cornetist Muggsy Spanier, Bud Freeman, and Sidney Bechet were just a few of the musicians who played residencies at the club. Sax player Benny Carter was booked for a single night but stayed for more than a month. Boogie-woogie giant Meade "Lux" Lewis played intermission piano at Nick's, and Rongetti organized regular jam sessions featuring musicians like Fats Waller and Eddie Condon.

Pianist Johnny Varro, who played at Nick's with different bands for more than ten years, recalled of the club, "It had atmosphere. They had moose heads all over the walls. From the kitchen they'd bring out these sizzling steaks and poured brandy on the platter and the sweet smell would permeate the place."[56] Customers ordering dinner were served by tuxedoed waiters, but less affluent patrons could listen from the bar, where a beer cost only twenty cents.

The club drew an extraordinary variety of patrons, from students with meager funds to celebrities including baseball hero Joe DiMaggio, *Honeymooners* star Jackie Gleason, and writer John Steinbeck. Reportedly John Coltrane and Miles Davis hung out at Nick's after their own shows.

Eventually, Rongetti's predilection for improvised traditional music and Dixieland led to Nick's demise. In 1963, the club lost its lease, and the property was seized for nonpayment of internal revenue taxes. A 1963 article in the *Village Voice* commented: "As new [jazz] forms have developed, Nick's has become somewhat of a museum for a certain sound. . . . [F]or Dixie buffs a mecca of an old, slowly dying form, for others a place to recapture one's youth briefly, for out-of-town collegians the only familiar name on a first tour of Greenwich Village. But it has been perhaps merely a matter of time until Nick's would succumb. Commercially, it was an anachronism."[57]

CAFÉ SOCIETY
2 SHERIDAN SQUARE

Visits to cabarets in Prague and Berlin inspired New Jersey jazz fan and shoe salesman Barney Josephson to start his own club. After securing a $6,000 loan, he opened Café Society in December 1938. The fully integrated club—Manhattan's first south of Harlem—booked African American performers, and Josephson made sure both Black and white people were treated equally, often seating people of color at the most desirable tables.

Josephson mockingly named his two-hundred-seat basement club after journalist Clare Boothe Luce's term for high-society patrons of nightclubs. He advertised Café Society as "The Wrong Place for the Right People" and "the rendezvous of celebs, debs and plebs" and decorated the walls with satirical paintings lampooning the upper crust.

Jazz producer and writer John Hammond served as the club's unofficial music director, and it was his idea to hire Billie Holiday, who had just gone solo after stints in both Count Basie's and Artie Shaw's bands, to open the club. During her engagement, Josephson first heard "Strange Fruit," a poem set to music by Bronx high school teacher Abel Meeropol, who had written the piece in response to seeing a photograph of two Black men lynched in 1930 in Marion, Indiana. "Strange Fruit" had achieved some success as a protest song, and Josephson brought it to Holiday.

Reticent to perform it at first because of the song's subject matter, Holiday added it to her set in January 1939. In *The Guardian*, Dorian Lynskey wrote: "Josephson, a natural showman, knew there was no point slipping Strange Fruit into the body of the set and pretending it was just another song. He drew up some rules: first, Holiday would close all three of her nightly sets with it; second, the waiters would halt all service beforehand; third, the whole room would be in darkness but for a sharp, bright spotlight on Holiday's face; fourth, there would be no encore. 'People had to remember Strange Fruit, get their insides burned by it,' he explained."[58]

In her 1956 autobiography, *Lady Sings the Blues*, Holiday recalled, "There wasn't even a patter of applause when I finished. Then a lone

person began to clap nervously. Then suddenly everybody was clapping."[59] "Strange Fruit" became Holiday's best-known song.

Following Holiday's nine-month engagement, the club booked many of the greatest names in jazz, including pianist Teddy Wilson, Ella Fitzgerald, Count Basie, Lester Young, Coleman Hawkins, and Fletcher Henderson, who played his last shows there. Josephson also presented comedians, with Jack Gilford, Zero Mostel, and Imogene Coca all performing there. African American intellectuals like Ralph Bunche, Richard Wright, and Langston Hughes visited Café Society, as did white luminaries including Ingrid Bergman, Ernest Hemingway, and even Eleanor Roosevelt.

The downtown club was such a success that in 1940 Josephson opened a location on Fifty-Eighth Street between Park and Lexington Avenues. Acts would start out in the smaller Village room, and when they'd generated enough of a following, Josephson moved them to the larger uptown room. Plans were afoot for a third club, but the United States' entry into World War II and Josephson's avowed leftist politics led to Café Society's downfall.

During the early 1940s, J. Edgar Hoover, then head of the Federal Bureau of Investigation, looked into Hammond's and Josephson's doings, compiling a 2,100-page dossier on the latter. As a result, Josephson was placed on the FBI Security Index and the club put under surveillance. During World War II, Café Society hosted a number of Communist-affiliated events, and Josephson's brother Leon was a well-known member of the Communist Party and alleged to have ties to Soviet intelligence. In 1947, Leon was convicted of contempt of court after refusing to answer questions before the House Un-American Activities Committee. As Michael Riedel wrote in the *New York Post*, this provoked "the ire of powerful red-baiting columnists such as [Walter] Winchell, Dorothy Kilgallen and Westbrook Pegler. They savaged Josephson, implying that anybody who frequented his clubs was probably a Commie and a traitor. Winchell, who favored the Stork Club over Café Society, took to calling it 'Café Pink.'"[60] Business at both clubs dropped precipitously and Josephson sold them in 1949.

Footage of Café Society can be seen in the 1946 *March of Time* newsreel "Night Club Boom," with Josephson self-consciously coaching his protégée, Guadeloupean singer Moune de Rivel.

← LEFT **Charlie Parker poses with fans at Café Society's Fifty-Eighth Street location, date unknown.**

↑↑ ABOVE **Playbills from Café Society uptown and downtown.**

EDDIE CONDON'S

47 WEST THIRD STREET

Jazz guitarist, banjoist, and bandleader Eddie Condon opened his first nightclub in 1945. He'd come of age musically in 1920s Chicago, and the club featured music from that era, played by Condon's own band, which at various times included Muggsy Spanier, drummer Dave Tough, and Pee Wee Russell. Stride piano innovator James P. Johnson often performed between band sets.

In 1957, the club moved to 330 East Fifty-Sixth Street, but the music remained the same. The *Syncopated Times* critic Scott Yanow noted, "The revival of interest in Dixieland resulted in many amateur bands playing a repertoire that overlapped with Condon's, but Eddie Condon's recordings and nightly performances outshone the competition. It was said that at Condon's (particularly when [cornetist] Wild Bill Davison was in the band), 'every night was like New Year's Eve.' Condon saw no need to modernize his music, once saying that "the beboppers play flatted fifths: we drink them."[61]

The Fifty-Sixth Street club closed in 1967, and Condon died in 1973, but a third incarnation of his club opened in 1975 on West Fifty-Fourth Street and stayed in business for the next ten years. Condon and his band can be seen performing at his club in a 1946 *March of Time* film called "Night Club Boom" on YouTube.

↖ OPPOSITE, LEFT **Eddie Condon's souvenir photograph and photo folder** (*opposite, right*)**, date unknown.**

↑↑ ABOVE **Postcards advertising shows at Central Plaza, 1950.**

CENTRAL PLAZA
111 SECOND AVENUE AT SIXTH STREET

After World War II, many of the Jewish immigrants who had settled in the area around Central Plaza in the East Village moved, leaving the five-story kosher catering hall struggling for business. With a ballroom on each floor, Central Plaza was a perfect place for jazz shows and dancing. In 1949, Commodore Music Shop manager Jack Crystal began producing "Jazz at the Plaza" jam sessions in the largest room.

The shows, like similar ones held at the nearby Stuyvesant Casino, were publicized by postcards, which listed each week's lineup and were sent to a mailing list of regulars. Many of the performers were Dixieland musicians or traditional jazz performers who had been members of big bands, including stalwarts like cornetist Jimmy McPartland, Willie "the Lion" Smith, Sidney Bechet, Wild Bill Davison, Roy Eldridge, and Max Kaminsky. The occasional non-jazz musician would appear, like folk singer Pete Seeger or blues giant "Champion Jack" Dupree. Two documentary films, *Jazz at the Plaza* and *Jazz Dance* (1954), were shot during Central Plaza performances.

The venue also hosted weddings and bar mitzvahs and rented out rehearsal space for Broadway shows like *The Music Man* and television programs like *Playhouse 90*, sometimes in the same ballroom where a jazz show had been the night before. But Central Plaza was best known for its jazz shows, which continued until Jack Crystal's death in 1963. Five years later the building became the first home of New York University's School of the Arts. In 2015, the school renamed a theater built on the site the Jack Crystal Theater, in recognition of continued support from Crystal's son and NYU alum, entertainer Billy Crystal, and his family.

← OPPOSITE **Clockwise from top, right: Roy Haynes, Charlie Parker, Thelonious Monk, and Charles Mingus at the Open Door, September 13, 1953.**

→ RIGHT **Open Door photograph folder, mid-1950s.**

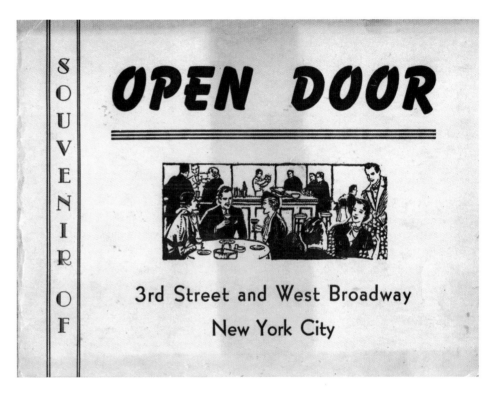

OPEN DOOR

55 WEST THIRD STREET AT WASHINGTON SQUARE SOUTH

In the spring of 1953, jazz critic and future Charlie Parker biographer Robert Reisner convinced the owner of the Open Door, a Greenwich Village bar, to let him organize jazz shows on Sundays in a large back room. Booking well-known artists and paying the musicians over scale, Reisner was able to draw top talent. Parker played many of the sessions alongside many of bop's leading lights, including Bud Powell, Charles Mingus, Max Roach, Sonny Rollins, and Thelonious Monk.

Jazz at the Open Door was a short-lived phenomenon, though. At some point Reisner left the club, which continued for a short time hosting jam sessions, anchored by a house band featuring saxophonist Brew Moore and trumpeter Tony Fruscella. But within two years of Reisner's initial shows, the bar had stopped presenting live music.

→ RIGHT Handbill advertising a January 1955 show by Charlie Parker at the Open Door. Parker died two months later, on March 12, 1955.

BOB REISNER

presents

THE GREATEST IN MODERN JAZZ

"BIRD"
CHARLIE PARKER
AND HIS ALL STARS
SUNDAY, JAN. 9th, *1955*

2 PERFORMANCES

Matinee: 5.30 to 7.30   Eve: 9.30 to 2 A. M.

OPEN DOOR
55 W. 3rd STREET

↑ ABOVE **Open Door souvenir photograph, mid-1950s.**

ATLANTIC C ★ I ★ T ★ Y

Atlantic City featured jazz in its nightclubs as early as the 1920s. From the 1930s through the 1960s, most of it was played in clubs in the Northside, the city's main African American district.

After World War I, most large American cities were segregated, the result of deed restrictions placed on properties known as "racial covenants." These were created on behalf of developers and homeowners who wanted to keep their neighborhoods as white as possible. Consequently, most city-dwelling Black people lived in large concentrations in a single neighborhood or two, with numerous businesses catering to African Americans and an entertainment district that usually included jazz clubs.

In 1948, the Supreme Court ruled these covenants unconstitutional, and slowly Black people began to move to areas outside their historically segregated neighborhoods. But by that time, many of the Northside's clubs were well established.

One of the first resort towns to cater to the working class, Atlantic City welcomed thousands of vacationers from nearby cities like Philadelphia, Washington, D.C., and New York. Murray Fredericks, solicitor of Atlantic City for more than twenty-five years, said, "If the people who came to town had wanted Bible readings, we'd have given 'em that. But nobody asked for Bible readings. They wanted booze, broads and gambling, so that's what we gave 'em."[1]

Many people wanted music too, and though the city was segregated, most of the Northside's clubs welcomed patrons of all races. One major concentration was around Kentucky and Arctic Avenues, known as KY and the Curb. Tourists, locals, politicians, and celebrities filled the clubs, most of which offered multiact revues.

New Jersey's place in the history of jazz was further secured by the 1942 founding of Savoy Records—the Newark label released seminal recordings by Miles Davis, Charlie Parker, Dexter Gordon, and Fats Navarro—and the Englewood Cliffs recording studio of Rudy Van Gelder. Van Gelder, a New Jersey–born former optometrist, became the most celebrated engineer in jazz history, recording such legendary albums as John Coltrane's *Blue Train* (1958) and *A Love Supreme* (1965), Art Blakey and the Jazz Messengers' *Moanin'* (1959), and Sonny Rollins's *Saxophone Colossus* (1957). Rutgers University's Institute of Jazz Studies houses the world's largest archive of jazz recordings and books on its Newark campus.

PARADISE CAFE

50 FOREMOST COLORED STARS

presents "BIRDS OF *Paradise*"

Atlantic City's Gayest Spot

A FAST SIZZLING SEPIA REVUE

SONG HITS by EDDIE LIEBERMAN

DANCE CREATIONS by CHARLIE MARANO

↑ ABOVE Paradise Café napkin exterior, 1941.

PARADISE CAFÉ
220 NORTH ILLINOIS AVENUE

Hyped by owner Harold Abrams as "the oldest nightclub in America," the Paradise Café, also known as the Paradise Club, opened in the 1920s and was allegedly the first club to offer early-morning breakfast shows. While both Black and white people were admitted, most of the audience members were white guests from a nearby resort, the Traymore Hotel; likewise, an equally high percentage of the performers were Black. Come daylight, the white attendees returned to segregated life.

In *Boardwalk of Dreams*, historian Bryant Simon wrote: "During the 1930s, Count Basie's Orchestra regularly performed at the Paradise. Basie said that playing there was 'a gas.' Before his hard-swinging, hard-living band took the stage, Black vocalists entertained the crowd with risqué vaudeville tunes, and Black comedians in overalls and straw hats told raunchy jokes. Then the half-dozen, dark-skinned, full-bodied Sextuplet Dancers, dressed in top hats, short black shorts, and tuxedo vests a size or two too small, took the stage. . . . Count Basie, Jimmie Lunceford, Lucky Millinder, and the other musicians who played the Paradise knew they were sometimes sideshows. White tourists came primarily to watch the Black women do their shake dances, not to listen to music."[2]

As trumpeter Johnny Coles described it, "This gig was about playing the show; it wasn't about playing jazz. . . . We'd get a chance to do maybe a jazz tune or two before the show started."[3] Nonetheless, following the evening's final show, the players often went over to Club Harlem to jam with its band into the early-morning hours, and musicians performing at the Steel Pier would make their way to the Paradise for the same reason. Top-name Black musicians dropped by to jam; a session could begin in one club and continue in another, such as when trumpeters Clifford Brown, Art Farmer, and Joe Gordon started at the Paradise and continued at Club Harlem in the early 1950s.

During his orchestra's 1947 summer residency at the latter, Count Basie, on a boating trip, fell overboard trying to reel in a fish; the owner of the former, Harold Abrams, leaped into the water and saved him. In 1954, the Paradise Café merged with Club Harlem.

← LEFT **Paradise Café napkin interior, 1941.**

CLUB HARLEM
32 NORTH KENTUCKY AVENUE

Few clubs prospered longer than Club Harlem. From 1935 to 1986, it was Atlantic City's premier club for Black jazz musicians. Black and white patrons mingled at the club, eager to enjoy a night of African American entertainment in an upscale environment similar to that of New York's Cotton Club. Atlantic City's version featured a nine-hundred-seat main showroom, two lounges (each with continuous entertainment and capable of holding up to four hundred people), and seven bars. In its original 1930s incarnation, the venue included a rooftop basketball court flanked by rows of slot machines.

Atlantic City's proximity to New York allowed the club to book a steady stream of top headlining artists, including Louis Armstrong, Billie Holiday, Duke Ellington, Ella Fitzgerald, Count Basie, Sarah Vaughan, and Dinah Washington. From 1946 to 1971, the club was home base for producer Larry Steele's *Smart Affairs* revue, a show with a weekly $35,000 budget that rivaled that of a Broadway production. The extravaganza offered a varied lineup of acts accompanied by a blistering house band: risqué comics dressed as clowns, dowdy old ladies, and Cuban ritual dancers, all in an atmosphere Lena Horne described as having "a naked quality that was supposed to make a civilized audience lose its inhibitions."[4] Some of that atmosphere was provided by a dozen shaking, shimmying chorus girls, clad in high heels, exotic headdresses, and little else.

The club's customers didn't applaud performers, instead showing their approval by banging "table knockers"—wooden balls attached to long sticks—on their tables. Club Harlem was often in and out of business between 1968 and 1986, when it finally closed. Scenes from Louis Malle's film *Atlantic City* (1980) were shot at Club Harlem.

↑ ABOVE **Club Harlem postcard, date unknown.**

→ RIGHT **Club Harlem table knocker, date unknown.**

CLUB HARLEM

↑ ABOVE **Club Harlem souvenir photograph, date unknown.**

↓→ RIGHT **Club Harlem photo folder
and souvenir photograph** (*below*),
date unknown.

Souvenir of

HARLEM CLUB

Your Genial Host
ATLANTIC CITY, N. J.

↑ ABOVE **Club Harlem** souvenir photograph, date unknown.

500 CLUB
6 MISSOURI AVENUE

Known to locals as "the Five," the 500 was a go-to spot for Black and white revelers and the site of Atlantic City's first illegal casino. During its 1940s and 1950s heyday, the club was owned by mobster Paul "Skinny" D'Amato, who presented performances by stars such as Nat King Cole, Eartha Kitt, and Louis Prima. D'Amato pals Frank Sinatra and Sammy Davis Jr. also appeared, and Dean Martin and Jerry Lewis debuted their slapstick comedy act there in 1946.

Outside the Five's street entrance, the names of various celebrities who'd appeared within were written in cement. Guests were welcomed by doorman Roy "Slim" Gaines, reputed to have stood seven feet, seven inches. Inside, the main bar was black and wound around a large room covered in black-and-white zebra-patterned wallpaper. At one end was a waterfall surrounded by fake exotic vegetation.

The club was open from five P.M. to ten A.M., with the last show starting at four A.M. Away from the main stage, a series of back rooms welcomed gamblers—many of them mobsters and politicians making deals with each other—to a world of blackjack, high-stakes poker, craps tables, and roulette wheels. A nod or a word from D'Amato to the doormen guarding the rooms authorized admittance for these special guests.

Responding to pressure from the Senate's Kefauver Committee, which was investigating organized crime, D'Amato closed the back rooms in the early 1950s. The 500 Club was destroyed by a fire in 1973.

← ↑ OPPOSITE **500 souvenir photograph and photo folder** (*above*), date unknown.

A Conversation with

SONNY ROLLINS

Saxophonist and composer Theodore Walter "Sonny" Rollins was born in 1930 in New York City. He grew up surrounded by music in Harlem's Sugar Hill neighborhood and soon came under the influence of bebop, recording and performing with Miles Davis, Charlie Parker, Thelonious Monk, and Bud Powell by the time he was in his early twenties.

In 1955, Rollins joined the Clifford Brown–Max Roach Quintet, and during the next two years he released the highly acclaimed albums *Saxophone Colossus* and *Way Out West* before taking a three-year leave of absence from the jazz world in 1959. "I was getting very famous at the time and I felt I needed to brush up on various aspects of my craft. I felt I was getting too much, too soon, so I said, wait a minute, I'm going to do it my way." Living in the Lower East Side of Manhattan with nowhere to practice, Rollins took his horn to the Williamsburg Bridge. "I would be up there 15 or 16 hours at a time spring, summer, fall and winter." When he finally returned to the recording studio, in 1962, he named his new album, appropriately, *The Bridge*.

That same year he resumed performing in public, playing with his idol Coleman Hawkins, as well as guitarist Jim Hall, pianist Paul Bley, and trumpeter Don Cherry before, in 1969, again taking time off to travel and study Eastern religions. In 1972, he returned to touring and recording, ultimately releasing more than sixty albums as a leader.

Recognized as one of jazz's greatest improvisers, Rollins has written a number of compositions that have become jazz standards, including "Oleo," "Doxy," and "Airegin."

In 2010, President Barack Obama presented Rollins with the National Medal of the Arts. Rollins is a Kennedy Center Honoree, a Grammy Lifetime Achievement Award winner, and the recipient of ten honorary doctor of music degrees from institutions including the New England Conservatory, Berklee College of Music, and the Juilliard School.

Jeff Gold (JG): I recently bought a big collection of jazz memorabilia, which included club photos from the 1940s and 1950s. We've seen so many photographs of the musicians playing in these clubs, but you never see pictures of the audiences. These pictures are a fascinating window into the scene, and I wanted to speak with you to get a feel for jazz clubs at the time.

Sonny Rollins (SR): I'm enjoying the photos you sent—going on a real nostalgic trip here with this stuff.

JG: You've said, "Harlem was my conservatory." It certainly was the epicenter of jazz when you were growing up. Your neighbors were Duke Ellington, [composer and pianist] Billy Strayhorn, Coleman Hawkins, Bud Powell, and many more important musicians. And it was a hotbed of live music too, with the Apollo, Savoy, Minton's Playhouse, Smalls' Paradise, and a number of other clubs.

SR: Right.

JG: I was wondering, when did you start going out to see live music? Where did you go?

SR: Well, these places were really jumping when I was a kid. And as I began to get older and get into the music, I eventually began playing in some of these places. I actually played in Smalls' Paradise in New York. I played at another club in New York called the Celebrity Club—you have pictures from there. And that's a big joke with me, because I played there with Randy Weston, the pianist, years ago. And every time I called Randy, I'd mention the Celebrity Club and we'd have a big laugh. Because I think the piano wasn't always in tune—and so he'd always say, "Oh yeah, the piano was never in tune." But it was great. I played there with Connie Kay, the drummer—

JG: But when you were really young, where would you go to hear music? Or did that start happening when you started playing live?

SR: Well, where I grew up, when I was a boy, I passed by the Savoy and Cotton Club every day going to school. They were right in the neighborhood. By the time I got into jazz and to the point of being a professional—or

↑ ABOVE **A 1941 Savoy handbill.**

wanting to be a professional—I was still too young to really get into a lot of these clubs. I couldn't get in at all. The earliest thing that I remember was going to clubs on Fifty-Second Street. And we used to go over there and I used to have eyebrow pencil to make me look like I had a mustache.

JG: [*Laughs.*]

SR: I used to go get into some of those clubs on Fifty-Second Street, the Three Deuces and those places. So I was, at that point I was in my teens, you know? But prior to that I wasn't really able to go to any clubs. Let's see, I'm trying to think. What we did, we had a lot of jazz music on the radio. And so that filled in the gaps for me. They'd broadcast from the Apollo every Wednesday, amateur night in Harlem. And like that, but before I got to my teens I wasn't really able to get into any clubs.

JG: I watched an interview where you talked about playing gigs when you were very young. I think you said your first gig was on Jerome Avenue, in the Bronx, when you were thirteen or fourteen. And then soon after that you had your band with [saxophonist] Jackie McLean and [drummer] Art Taylor and [pianist] Kenny Drew—was that called the Counts of Bebop?

SR: [*Laughs.*] That's right! The Counts of Bop, yeah.

JG: And what kind of places did you play with those guys?

SR: Okay, now with those guys, we played a lot of really local dance halls. You know? A lot of clubs where they had dances in, functions like that. None of which were very famous. I think they were just neighborhood ballrooms.

JG: Did they have liquor, or were they mostly—?

SR: Oh yeah. They had liquor, sure.

JG: What was it like to be so young in a scene full of older professional musicians and club owners and adult audiences? Were the club owners reticent to hire you?

SR: Well, you know, we were a good young group of very upcoming talented musicians, so . . . One thing that I remember very well is that often in these places we'd be playing and people would be dancing sometimes, and we'd be playing and before the night was over, there was a huge fight! The whole place you're playing at was fighting. And that happened several times in places we played at.

JG: It's such an amazing hotbed of talent you grew up in. There were so many musicians who were already established and so many people who became established, like those guys you were playing with.

SR: [Saxophonist] Andy Kirk Jr.—he's another one.

JG: He died young, right?

SR: Oh yeah, yeah. He got messed up with drugs. But he was a little more advanced than we were because he played with his father's band [Andy Kirk's Twelve Clouds of Joy]. And he went out on several tours with his father's band. Andy had more experience than we did. But he was a member of the crowd, you know?

JG: As you began to play on bills with more established musicians, were they approachable, receptive to younger players? Did they let you guys sit in? I know you played on a bill with [Thelonious] Monk, and he took you under his wing.

SR: Right. Right, that was at a club—you know, I'm not sure whether that was at Club Harlem. It could have been at Club Harlem, one of the clubs that you have [pictures of] there. But, in general, the older musicians that we were trying to get mentored by were all very nice to me and I think to everybody else. They were all very nice. And I mean, I was a real bug. I would go up to [saxophonist] Eddie ["Lockjaw"] Davis's house—he lived in the Bronx—and I would go up there after school and be ringing his bell, and I'm sure these guys didn't get home till five, six o'clock in the morning, and here's this young guy . . . But they were all good. I never got into Eddie Davis's house, but I did get into Denzil Best's, the great drummer. And I remember I knew of him because the family knew of him. And he was playing with Coleman Hawkins, you know? So I rang his bell incessantly one day. Over and over. Finally, he came to the door. This guy was probably out till five, six in the morning, and he had this young kid just asking him questions about, you know, jazz and all this stuff. But they were all good. They were all good to me. I had no problem. They all sort of realized how sincere we were, you know?

JG: You've said you started out playing for dancers, which was toward the tail end of the swing era. But as bebop starts developing in places like Minton's, it starts to gravitate toward smaller groups playing music meant for listening more than dancing. What was the transition like for the bands you were playing in, and in the clubs, and for the more established musicians? Was it a slow thing? Or did it happen kind of rapidly?

SR: Well, I can't say whether it was rapidly—I mean compared to what—but I observed it happening. When I was pretty much getting established, getting a name and everything, I played at the Audubon Ballroom [where Malcolm X was assassinated in 1965]. And what would happen at the Audubon was that the real jazz aficionados would be near the front of the stage, and then the rest of the people would be farther back. So we'd play, and people would be dancing, but then the guys that were listening to the music were up toward the front of the stage. And then the other people a little farther back would be dancing. And I was at another job where [saxophonist] Gene Ammons played—I forgot where it was, but it was the same phenomenon. The guys that are really listening to the music, beginning to appreciate the music, were up near the front, listening close. And then the rest of the people were dancing, you know, a little bit back. I observed this happening a few times.

JG: It's almost a physical manifestation of that transition. And during your early years, were these clubs integrated? I mean, I know the Cotton Club wasn't.

SR: Well, I would say these early clubs in Harlem that I know about—like I know the Savoy Ballroom, there was some integration out there.

→ RIGHT **Dancers in a Washington, D.C., jazz club, sometime between 1938–1948.**

JG: How about the dances you guys were playing?

SR: The dances we were playing at were basically not integrated. Because we were right in the thick of—the heart of the neighborhood, you know? And it was, more or less, less sophisticated.

JG: Were drugs and alcohol as big of a factor as they became ten or fifteen years later?

SR: Well, I think alcohol was always there for the people. Drugs began coming in after a while. By the time drugs were coming in, I was already establishing myself on the older circuit. It wasn't so much in the young kid stage. Drugs sort of really came into being . . . I would say that must have been in the late 1940s. And the places we were playing at first were just mainly dances. And the people . . . it wasn't a sophisticated audience of people that would be involved with drugs.

And we had to play a lot of calypso as well as other jazz music.

JG: Because there were a lot of Caribbean people in your neighborhood, like your parents?

SR: Right, right. It was a lot of Caribbean people. And calypso is dance music really, so any place we played, we played calypso and people would dance. We played a lot of calypso, as well as anything else that we could play.

JG: By the time you graduated from high school, you were basically a working professional musician and your career picked up momentum really quickly. You recorded with [trombonist] J. J. Johnson and Bud Powell when you were nineteen, with Miles Davis when you were twenty-one; you played with Monk and the Clifford Brown–Max Roach group and even Charlie Parker. So how did the Harlem scene you started out in differ from the Fifty-Second Street club scene?

SR: Well, you asked [about Harlem], was it integrated—now, Fifty-Second Street of course was integrated. [At that point] in the uptown scene, there wasn't a lot of integration, although at the end of the twenties and the thirties, there had been a lot of integration in Harlem. There were a lot of these clubs located around 134th Street, 133rd Street. And I think after that sort of disseminated [in the mid-1930s], then there were clubs, just places to play that didn't really have a lot of integration.

JG: I know Smalls' Paradise was integrated.

SR: Oh yeah. Smalls' may have been integrated. Smalls' was a very famous club—I had the privilege of playing at Smalls', actually, but this was of course later years. That was another club that you had [photos of] that I played, with my group.

JG: Quincy Jones told me when he got to New York in the early 1950s, he was going to Fifty-Second Street. From his perspective, race wasn't an issue at all in those clubs. It was all about whether you could play or not. Was that your experience?

SR: Well, I think that was what set the bebop apart from some of the earlier music, although there was some integration [in earlier bands]. I know Roy Eldridge used to play with Artie Shaw and Billie Holiday sang with his band.

JG: And Benny Goodman had Lionel Hampton and Teddy Wilson.

SR: Benny Goodman, of course, had an integrated group. But it wasn't the norm. Now, when Fifty-Second Street began blossoming and bebop became the music of the day, that was a much more integrated music. Much, much more, I mean, we accept anybody. Anybody that can play great bebop was accepted.

JG: And the audiences too. In the early, early 1950s, Quincy said you could go to a jazz club on Fifty-Second Street, and Black people, white people, everybody got along.

SR: That's one of the things that jazz musicians never get credit for—the way it was such an integrated scene. We never really get credit for that.

→ OPPOSITE **An integrated audience at the Downbeat Club, New York City, circa 1948.**

The Famous

COTTON CLUB

The Aristocrat of Harlem

142ⁿᵈ Street & Lenox Ave

PROGRAM

Reservations advisable   *Bradhurst 2·7767-1687*

↑ ABOVE **Cotton Club program, circa 1930.**

Everybody else gets credit—or blame, if you want to put it like that, depending on your point of view. But you know, for that, jazz was really where the racial barriers were broken down heavily. I've always thought that. It was a matter of if you were good enough to make it, then that was it. There were a lot of great white musicians playing around that time. Of course, Artie Shaw, but later we had [saxophonist and bandleader] Georgie Auld—remember him?

JG: I do, yeah.

SR: Sure. So yeah, people like that.

JG: [Saxophonist] Gil Mellé.

SR: Gil Mellé, right, right. [Clarinetist] Tony Scott.

JG: Red Rodney.

SR: And many others. Yeah, jazz was really the music that facilitated this integration among the races in this country and never got credit for it. There was lots of integration.

JG: And also a lot of the guys running record labels that were recording this music early on were white guys. You know, like Alfred Lion of Blue Note.

SR: That's right. Of course.

JG: And they really supported their artists, at least in the case of Blue Note. They seemed to treat their artists well.

SR: Well, I think especially in the case of Alfred Lion. He was really a very—he was a person who was just a very good human being. The way that Black people were treated just offended him as a human being. And he really demonstrated that in his relations with his artists. But everybody, they were all good. I mean, the company I was with early on, Prestige with Bob Weinstock. You know, because really, we had to be together, it was a matter of, you know, race didn't matter. Race and politics, that's something that had nothing to do with the music. So jazz really, especially the bebop era, but coming into that—Benny Goodman and all of that, melding into that—by the time bebop was there, it had nothing to do with race.

JG: That's fantastic.

SR: Yes, that's fantastic. I hope you put this in your book.

JG: I am absolutely going to put it in my book!

I have another question about jazz and race. I'm fascinated by the phenomenon of the Cotton Club, a racist place that Black people couldn't get into.... Yet they hired Black performers exclusively and, in some cases, paid them very well. And they created opportunities and exposure for these artists, especially through their national radio broadcasts. It was a really important place for Duke Ellington, Louis Armstrong, Cab Calloway. That Black people couldn't get in was terrible, yet something good came of it. What did musicians of your era think about all that?

SR: Well, as I told you, I'd pass the Cotton Club going to school every day. And you know, something else, which was somewhat offensive to me, was some of the names—they called Duke Ellington's band Duke Ellington's Jungle Orchestra.

JG: And the [club's] artwork is super racist!

SR: Right. Super racist! Now, you know, that might have just been what was necessary as things progressed. So I can't speak to that, because that was sort of the way things were. But that soon changed. You know, that was the Cotton Club, but there were many other places that would shy away from this kind of stereotypical Black representation. I remember a place called the Ubangi—

JG: The Ubangi Club. I've got some photos from there; they had a racist graphic too. There's a kind of dark dichotomy between the stereotypical racism of some of these clubs and the positivity and exposure they afforded Black artists.

SR: Well, I think it was positivity, but don't you think, Jeff, that that was because there was a money incentive there? Those racketeers that owned the Cotton Club didn't care anything about integration. They knew that the music had a great commercial potential, so they presented it. And they presented it in a way that made it as stereotypically offensive to Black people as much as they could. But they were in it to get the money. So I don't give them a lot of credit for what they were doing. They did it because it was money. That's how I feel about that!

JG: It's my perspective too, but I wasn't there. And I wasn't a musician.

SR: [*Laughs.*] And also places like the Savoy, a lot of great music happened at the Savoy. But they didn't have these offensive stereotypes of Black people and all of this stuff to sell it. Who was the guy from the Cotton Club? One of those racketeers?

JG: The owner was a gangster and bootlegger named Owney Madden.

SR: Right, so they had a strong racist element there. So I don't give them anything, except that they saw the potential and that's what they did. Although, you know what, somebody told me that in Chicago, Al Capone was really a very fair-minded, nonracial person.

JG: How wild! He was part owner of a jazz club in Chicago, the Green Mill.

SR: Yeah, he had a jazz club. And he treated the musicians like people. It wasn't a lot of this racist stuff. And Al Capone was very good to this guy—I don't know if it was [double bassist] Milt Hinton or somebody of the older jazz people. [In the 2003 documentary *Keeping Time: The Life, Music and Photographs of Milt Hinton*, Hinton talks about his happy teenage experience working for Al Capone in Chicago. Hinton was injured in a car accident while running Prohibition liquor, and his boss, Capone, knowing he was a bass player, wouldn't let a doctor amputate his injured finger.]

JG: Skipping ahead, in 1957, you recorded a live album at the Village Vanguard [*A Night at the Village Vanguard*] during the first shows you played leading your own group. As you began playing shows as a leader, what was it like dealing with club promoters and being the focus of attention in clubs? Did that change things? Were you being paid well? Were you having any problems getting paid?

SR: Right! Right. Well, at that point, by then I had established a name for myself. I'd played at Birdland and everything. And they did have some very notorious owners of some of these clubs. I remember there was a guy in Birdland, [manager] Oscar Goodstein. Well, Goodstein was a very imperious type of guy. Of course, I wasn't the top echelon at that time, but I was good enough to be playing, headlining in Birdland. But no, Goodstein, nobody liked him. And another guy that they didn't like was Sol Weinstock, Bob Weinstock's father—he was also a pretty rough character and didn't respect the musicians too much. Bob was different, but his father, who we had to deal with often to get checks and everything like that, he was a pretty rough guy to deal with.

JG: Was it difficult to get paid playing clubs?

SR: No, it wasn't for me. No, not at that point. When I was playing the Vanguard and all that stuff, no. I mean, the money, who knows? The money may have seemed like a trifle today, but it was no problem getting paid. Now sometimes in other clubs, before I got to that position, you know, you always had trouble, as I told you, at a lot of those places where [I played with] Jackie McLean and Arthur Taylor, we had better get paid up front.

JG: Yeah. [*Laughs.*]

SR: And often you'd get these big fights that would break out. And then forget about it! In fact, I had a beautiful—my mother had just bought me a great herringbone raglan coat from Barney's in New York. And I went out to this club, Tony's in Brooklyn, which was another club. So I was out there playing, man, and a great fight broke out, and that was it. That was the end of the night and the end of my coat. And so that happened to me, these are just some of the stories coming up. Tony's was a club a lot of guys played, Monk, Miles, everybody.

JG: Was there a Mob presence that you felt in these clubs?

SR: No, I didn't feel a Mob presence. I'm trying to think if I've ever felt a real Mob presence . . . I don't think I did. There was a place in Chicago on Fifty-Fifth Street. Do you know which I mean? [There were a number of jazz clubs on Fifty-Fifth Street in Chicago, including the Beehive Lounge, Cadillac Lounge, Lee Loving's Hi-Hat, and Rhumboogie Club.]

JG: I've got a list of Chicago clubs. Downbeat, Blackhawk, Club DeLisa, El Grotto, Rhumboogie, Hurricane—

SR: I played at the Rhumboogie, by the way. I worked the Rhumboogie. There was another club. It was on Fifty-Fifth Street, over on the east side. And the owner was a guy named Sol. Sol was a very good guy. Everybody that had these clubs were not mercenaries. [Sol Tananbaum owned the Beehive Lounge, where Rollins first played with the Clifford Brown–Max Roach group in 1955.]

JG: In New York, where did you like to play? Or where did you not like to play?

SR: Well, of course, when I was coming up, as a kid, I liked to play any place I could play. You know? And by the time I was playing places like the Club Harlem, and Smalls' Paradise, and the Celebrity Club, and of course Birdland, I mean, it didn't matter to me. I was happy to be playing my horn.

JG: Any places where you were treated particularly well or particularly badly?

SR: Well, I would say Birdland had—not only did they have Oscar Goodstein, but they had the emcee Pee Wee Marquette. And he was quite a problem for a lot of the musicians because you had to pay him to get your name pronounced right.

JG: He was the small-of-stature guy, right? [Marquette was three feet, nine inches.]

SR: Oh yeah! Pee Wee was a little guy. In fact, Lester Young used to call him a "half a motherfucker."

JG: That is genius!

SR: It's genius. But he was a rough guy. Unless you got him when you worked there, he's going to mess up your name! He's going to mess it up, until you realize hey, I got to pay this guy! I got to sweeten him! You know, put something in his palm. Then he was okay, but boy . . . so that was a drag, Birdland. And Oscar Goodstein was sort of an imperious type of guy. So that club had its problems, but it was such a great place and everybody was completely integrated . . . right on Broadway!

JG: To the extent you played around the country, there were pretty vibrant jazz club scenes in Chicago and D.C., and Detroit and L.A., San Francisco—

SR: Oh yeah!

JG: Did the scenes in those cities differ from New York? Were the clubs different? The audiences?

SR: I don't think so. I was looking at some of your pictures of the clubs in Chicago, where I spent a lot of time. And basically they're about the same. The Black people that came, the white people that came. I don't know how—well, no, the clubs that I played at were integrated in Chicago as well as New York. The people, you know, they were dressed up to come to the club. And they were similar. When I first went out to San Francisco, there was a bohemian feel to the whole town. So that was always there, that was great.

JG: You've said you prefer playing live to recording, because of the energy you get from audiences.

SR: Right.

JG: And I'd imagine that's even more the case in small clubs—

SR: Yes.

JG: Can you talk about that for a minute?

SR: Well, for instance, the Vanguard, where I played a lot, is a small club. The people are closer to the stage. And they sort of played with you. They're like part of the band. You know what I mean? That's the best way I can put it. The audience is part of the band, and that inspired me to play. It inspires everybody to play. Because it's a big community jazz fest, and you have to be good, you have to take your best product in there when you're playing so close to people.

JG: It seemed like it was survival of the fittest, when you're in that intense of a situation.

SR: Well, you better be fit or else you wouldn't get up there. Some of the earlier clubs that I played at, they would really, the musicians, they wouldn't allow you to play up there if you weren't of a certain caliber. There used to be a guy named—we used to call him the Demon. He was a saxophone player who didn't know any music, but he really wanted to play and somehow he always got onstage and he would be playing awful. So the guys, I think, sort of took a liking to him, and they knew he was awful and they allowed him to play anyway. [Dizzy Gillespie remembered that the Demon "played with everybody—Lester, Charlie Parker. He was the first freedom player—freedom from harmony, freedom from rhythm, freedom from everything."][5]

And then there was a great club on 110th Street called the Paradise, and Big Nick [Nick Nicholas] the saxophone player ran the sessions there. And guys would just come in—these were top musicians that played there. You know, you had to [be]. I played there a few times, sessions with some of them. Great, I mean great people. People like Hot Lips Page, [trumpeter] Blue Mitchell, and Charlie Parker. Everybody that was somebody wanted to jam; they'd come by the Paradise Club. I don't know how long it lasted . . .

JG: And if you weren't great, you didn't last long.

SR: Well, in that club—in clubs like that, Big Nick wouldn't let you on the stand. You couldn't get on the stand. You had to be of a caliber at a club like that. Now there's some other sessions around where guys would be able to get up, and then [if they didn't deliver] everybody would try to ignore them and they wouldn't get back on, you know. But the Paradise was a top-notch place run by a top-notch jazz musician, and that was it really—just the top people.

JG: Did the musicians have much interaction with the audiences when you weren't onstage? I know in some of the photos I've got there are musicians posing—seemingly happily—with fans. Would people come up and talk to you? Was there interaction?

SR: Oh yeah, there was interaction. It was quite gratifying in fact, when we played places like Birdland and some of these clubs that were well-regarded clubs, totally integrated. Yeah, it was quite rewarding and fulfilling for the jazz musicians who'd never get credit for their work otherwise, to be appreciated by these people that they never get a chance to come in contact with often. You know, back to the original days in the Cotton Club, jazz musicians I'm sure didn't get an opportunity to fraternize with the [audiences]—or think back to Las Vegas when Sammy Davis Jr. and those guys had to come in the back door. You know this kind of stuff would prevail. So yes, the jazz musicians, their fans got a chance to pose and the photos and yeah—that was great. It was all great.

JG: I know many of these clubs had photographers, so the patrons could get a souvenir photo. Was that anything you guys paid attention to? Or was it just another profit center for the clubs?

SR: It was a profit center for the clubs, but often the audience asked the musicians to take a photo with them. You know, so a lot of guys did that. There's one you had there with Dizzy. And there's one with Oscar Peterson.

JG: In 1959, you toured Europe for the first time. In 1963, you played in Japan. I know a lot of jazz musicians felt they got much better treatment outside the United States, and the audiences were extremely reverential. What was it like for you to play outside the U.S.?

SR: Well, I think that's absolutely right. It was great in Europe, you know. When I first went to Europe—what'd you have? '59, was it?

JG: Yeah, 1959.

SR: Yeah, okay. So it was great. I mean, the fans were fantastic, and I think in general, we Black jazz musicians felt a little more appreciated. Also the politics as a country were a little more progressive than the United States. And in Japan, of course, the people are very reverential. Good word. And in Europe too. That's why people like [saxophonist] Don Byas went to Europe early and stayed over there. Because they were treated better. And they were treated as the great artists that they were. I loved it in Europe; I was there quite a bit. I think I went to Japan every two years. I think I was in Japan maybe more than twenty times in my career.

JG: My last question: something that almost surprised me a little bit with the photographs in this book—you see how big a deal going to a jazz club was for people. They dressed up in their most stylish clothes. There are families. There are fathers and sons. There are people on dates, and everybody's obviously having a great time. What do you think going to see live music meant to audiences during that era, especially to African Americans?

SR: Well, I think you've got it exactly right and some of your pictures depict that. People were really dressed. They were happy. They were smiling. Everything was great. It was really a paradisiacal place to be, the jazz club. And of course the great, great music. It was a paradise. It was a paradise. Paradisiacal.

JG: Sonny, I can't thank you enough for your music and for your time.

SR: Well, I think it's wonderful, the work that you're doing here. A story that needs to be told! ●

Washington D.C.

From the early 1900s, Washington, D.C., was one of the nation's prominent centers in the development of jazz. As early as 1912, ragtime orchestras performed at the Howard Theatre on Seventh and T Streets. Soon after, the city's musicians began experimenting, mixing blues, ragtime, gospel, and brassy marching band music into a new style now recognized as jazz. Most of this activity took place in the city's African American entertainment district, the U Street corridor, which came to be known as "Black Broadway." Commercial and cultural activity was centered there from the 1920s through the 1950s, with jazz providing one of the area's major forms of entertainment, drawing white jazz fans as well as locals.

Many clubs thrived along the U Street corridor, most notably the Crystal (later the Bohemian) Caverns, one of the country's oldest jazz rooms, established in 1926 as a basement speakeasy. In 1935, with ragtime's popularity fading, the legendary Jelly Roll Morton moved from New York City to D.C. and worked at the Jungle Inn as the house pianist, manager, emcee, bartender, and bouncer.

Small clusters of clubs dotted the downtown area: the Offbeat, Flora's Cocktail Lounge, and Little Harlem were at Seventh and T Streets; less than a half mile away near Fourteenth and U Streets were Club Bali, Club Bengasi, and the Republic Gardens.

Tony Taylor, a Washington promoter who operated the Bohemian Caverns from 1959 to 1968, dubbed 1947 the best year for local jazz, citing the after-hours Villa Bier at Nineteenth and California Streets as a magnet for musicians: "[They'd] come over from the Howard Theater and play all night long. . . . When those clubs closed, they'd all go to the Villa and play till daylight."[1]

Live jazz in the city started to dim in popularity in the 1950s, with competition from rock and roll and television and the exodus to the suburbs of middle-class families. Times worsened for the U Street scene the following decade; in the mid-1960s, Bohemian Caverns was the only major club still open. The 1968 race riots furthered the neighborhood's decline. Jazz fans now found their music at such established Georgetown-area clubs as Blues Alley and One Step Down, nearer to the center of D.C.

CRYSTAL CAVERNS

2001 ELEVENTH STREET NW

Housed in a drugstore basement, D.C.'s most famous jazz club opened in 1926 as Club Caverns, changing its name during the 1950s to Crystal Caverns and then later to Bohemian Caverns. Designed by Italian craftsmen to look like a cave adorned with stalagmites and stalactites, the room attracted Black and white jazz-loving members of D.C.'s smart set.

In Prohibition days, when other nightspots closed at midnight, the Caverns stayed open until daybreak, serving chicken, pork chops, and bootleg liquor in teacups to artists and audiences. As with other Washington clubs, musicians from other venues regularly dropped into the Caverns to enjoy late-night jam sessions—with a caveat: they were denied admittance unless they agreed to play. Throughout the Caverns' historic run, performers such as Billie Holiday, Miles Davis, John Coltrane, Duke Ellington, Pearl Bailey, and singer and pianist Shirley Horn played there. In 1964, the Ramsey Lewis Trio recorded its live album *Ramsey Lewis Trio at the Bohemian Caverns*.

The club went out of business in 1968, was reopened in the 1990s, but closed for good in 2016.

→ OPPOSITE **Party at the Crystal Caverns, circa 1945.**

↑ ABOVE **Club Kavakos souvenir photograph, mid-1940s.**

CLUB KAVAKOS

727 H STREET NE

Opened in 1935, the family-owned Club Kavakos was a bar and grill located well outside D.C.'s downtown club quarter. It offered live music as well as ballroom dance teams and nude women dancers. It was especially popular with servicemen and -women during World War II as well as a popular spot for Redskins fans to stop by for a drink after a football game.

During the 1950s, Sundays at the Kavakos featured the Orchestra, a group led by drummer Joe Timer comprising D.C.-area jazz stars and journeymen players from lesser-known out-of-town bands. Presumably the need to boost attendance at the Orchestra's weekly performances was what prompted club management to book a major jazz star to sit in on Sunday, February 22, 1953. According to pianist Bill Potts, Charlie Parker showed up that day minus his saxophone and had to perform with a borrowed clear plastic practice model. Nonetheless, Parker's successful appearance led to the group backing other famous jazzmen, including the Bud Powell Trio with Charles Mingus as well as Dizzy Gillespie (recordings of both sessions have been released).

Not long after Gillespie's gig, Club Kavakos closed, in 1955, due to unpaid taxes.

↗ TOP **Club Kavakos** photo folder, mid-1940s.

→ BOTTOM **Club Kavakos** postcard, date unknown.

⇉ RIGHT **Club Bali photo folder and souvenir photograph (*opposite*), 1946.**

Souvenir of a Pleasant Evening at
CLUB BALI

Capital of the United Nations

1901-14th STREET, N. W.   -   WASHINGTON, D. C.

CLUB BALI
1901 FOURTEENTH STREET NW

In 1943, Benjamin Caldwell, an African American, opened Club Bali, a Pacific-themed venue serving Korean food and featuring performances by a fourteen-piece orchestra behind the bar. Jazz and pop acts attracted a multiracial clientele, but, like other clubs, the Bali's bill of fare also included chorus girls and tap dancers. A then-steep cover charge of five dollars assured Caldwell of drawing an elite crowd.

Sarah Vaughan and Dinah Washington played Club Bali, as did Cab Calloway, Erroll Garner, Charlie Ventura, and singer Johnny Hartman. Following her 1947 arrest on narcotics charges, Billie Holiday was required to surrender her New York City cabaret card and was no longer able to perform at clubs in Manhattan that served liquor; consequently, she hit the road, and in the difficult years of touring that followed, she performed at Club Bali in 1948 and 1949.

In 1950, Caldwell was found guilty of jury tampering in a gambling case. Throughout the 1950s and 1960s, the Bali was the site of several clubs and restaurants; Holiday returned to play one of them, Café Trinidad, in 1954.

Jan. 19, 1940

1. "Jackie"   3. "Dump"   5. "Red"
2. "Joey"   4. "Zeke"   6. "Babes"

TURKISH EMBASSY

1606 TWENTY-THIRD STREET NW

One of Washington's most historically significant jazz venues was not a club or ballroom but the Turkish embassy. Inside the diplomatic residence, the music, which had previously been a segregated art form, began to integrate. The catalysts for this change were Ahmet and Nesuhi Ertegun, who moved into the embassy with their father, Ambassador Mehmet Munir Ertegun, in 1935.

The teenage brothers were jazz fanatics and immersed themselves in the city's rich music scene, attending shows at the Howard Theatre and seeing artists like Duke Ellington, Jelly Roll Morton, and Joe Marsala.

Surprised to find D.C.'s bandstands and audiences segregated, they took to inviting their favorite artists to the embassy—regardless of their ethnicity—to jam and share lunch. "Nesuhi and I made the most out of the extra-territorial situation offered by the embassy by inviting musicians who'd played in town the night before over for Sunday lunch," Ahmet recalled in his book *"What'd I Say": The Atlantic Story.* "They all loved the idea of having lunch at an embassy, particularly one as well-appointed and in such grand surroundings as the Turkish embassy in Washington. After lunch, jam sessions would inevitably develop."[2] Musical legends, both Black and white, played together in the embassy living room. Among them were Louis Armstrong, Duke Ellington, Lester Young, Benny Goodman, Tommy Dorsey, Benny Carter, and Teddy Wilson.

When some of the Erteguns' neighbors, including one southern congressman, complained about Black guests entering through the embassy's front door, Ahmet and Nesuhi's father defended his sons and the musicians. "You can't imagine how segregated Washington was at that time," Nesuhi said. "[Black and white people] couldn't sit together in most places. . . . Jazz was our weapon for social action."[3] In 1942, the brothers staged D.C.'s first integrated concert, at the Jewish Community Center on Sixteenth Street. The mixed audience enjoyed Black and white performers including Sidney Bechet, pianists Pete Johnson and Joe Turner, and Pee Wee Russell—although the center's management didn't know the event would be integrated. By the time the center found out, the concert had been publicized and it was too late to cancel it.

The Erteguns next organized the National Press Club's first integrated event, a concert by the folk-blues artist Lead Belly. In 1947, with $10,000 lent to him by his dentist, Ahmet cofounded Atlantic Records; Nesuhi joined him there a few years later. Atlantic went on to become one of the most successful independent labels ever, releasing legendary recordings by jazz artists including John Coltrane and Thelonious Monk, rhythm and blues stars like Ray Charles and Aretha Franklin, and rock groups including Led Zeppelin and Cream.

← OPPOSITE **Musicians at the Turkish Embassy, February 8, 1943. Seated at center: J.C. Higginbotham** (*left*) **and Art Hodes** (*right*)**. Standing, clockwise from top right: Sidney de Paris, Lou McGarrity, Red Allen, Lester Young, Sadi Coylin, Nesuhi Ertegun, Mert Oliver** (*with cigarette*)**, Ralph Hawkins, Ahmet Ertegun, and Mezz Mezzrow.**

↖ ABOVE, LEFT **Musicians playing at the Turkish Embassy, Washington, D.C., 1930s: Front row, from left to right: Rex Stewart (cornet), Harry Carney (alto saxophone), Barney Bigard (clarinet), and Joe Marsala (clarinet). Back row: Adele Girard (harp).**

BOSTON

While jazz had been played in Boston since the early 1920s, the United States' entry into World War II was the catalyst that turned the city into a major destination for the music. Soldiers, sailors, and defense workers streamed into the Massachusetts port, and as in other cities, musicians followed. New clubs opened and old ones thrived. When the war ended, the GI Bill offered subsidized education to veterans, and the area's many colleges and universities drew former enlisted men and women to the area.

The city was a hotbed for musicians: the New England Conservatory and the Boston Conservatory, though oriented toward classical music, educated many who played jazz—and both admitted students of color. In 1945, musician Lawrence Berk founded a school that became the Berklee College of Music, now the largest independent music college in the world, which from its earliest days offered a jazz curriculum.

During the 1940s and 1950s, many of the city's jazz clubs were concentrated in the South End, particularly around the area near the intersection of Massachusetts and Columbus Avenues, which had a growing African American population. The Hi-Hat, the Big M, the Pioneer Club, Estelle's, the Savoy Cafe, and Wally's Paradise (later Cafe) were part of an area characterized as the city's version of Fifty-Second Street.

But even during this time of booming creativity, Boston was overall a conservative city. Founded by Puritans, Massachusetts had blue laws in place to protect its citizens from films, literature, theater, and music that might offend. As George Wein, owner of the upscale club Storyville, recalled in his memoir, *Myself Among Others*: "[A] stipulation of the Blue Laws was that all entertainment, music, and serving of alcohol had to halt at the stroke of midnight on Saturday night. One Saturday night, three or four burly cops in uniform appeared in the club at ten minutes before midnight. . . . It so happened that we were packed that night [Sarah Vaughan was appearing]. . . . I went to the side of the stage during a piano solo, motioned Sarah over, and whispered a request: 'When I point to you, ring in Sunday morning by singing "The Lord's Prayer," *a capella*.' . . . Midnight struck, and the police began a predatory walk toward the stage. I signaled to Sarah, and she started singing: 'Our Father, which art in Heaven, hallowed be Thy Name . . .' It stopped the officers in their tracks. . . . The Boston Irish Catholic policemen were flummoxed. Perhaps they said a few Hail Mary's after leaving the club."[1]

In 1955, Harvard graduate and future Bob Dylan producer Tom Wilson founded the independent record label Transition in Cambridge, recording and releasing the debut albums of trumpeter Donald Byrd, pianists Sun Ra and Cecil Taylor, and bassist Doug Watkins.

As music and Boston changed during the 1960s, the South End became the city's place for jazz. Today, with musicians from all over the world coming to study at the New England Conservatory and Berklee, the city's jazz scene remains active.

SYMPHONY HALL

301 MASSACHUSETTS AVENUE

Built in 1900 as a home for the Boston Symphony Orchestra, Symphony Hall was acoustically designed for classical music. But jazz was played there, and on April 18, 1947, it played host to a "Birth of the Blues" concert featuring Louis Armstrong and Billie Holiday. A film starring the two, *New Orleans*, was released earlier that year (Armstrong played a bandleader, Holiday a singing maid), and their manager, Joe Glaser, added Holiday to Armstrong's tour to create some buzz for the film. Both artists were extremely popular at the time, but each was about to experience major challenges. With the decline of swing, Armstrong broke up his big band later that year, downsizing to the six-piece "All Stars." Holiday was arrested for possession of narcotics just one month after this show, resulting in ten months in a prison camp and the loss of her New York City cabaret card.

→ RIGHT *Birth of the Blues* concert program, 1947.

HI-HAT
566 COLUMBUS AVENUE AT MASSACHUSETTS AVENUE

The home of "America's Smartest Barbecue" opened its doors in 1937; though located in a Black neighborhood, the dinner and dance club catered to a white crowd. But in the summer of 1948, the management noticed jazz was drawing larger crowds to nearby clubs like Wally's Paradise and the Savoy Cafe. As a result, African American bandleader Sabby Lewis was hired to perform at the Hi-Hat, and the club opened up its admission policy to include Black customers.

Boston jazz historian Richard Vacca noted: "In the first half of the 1950s, the Hi-Hat was one of Boston's busiest clubs, and the best jazz and rhythm & blues artists performed there regularly. Charlie Parker appeared five times, Oscar Peterson six, Dizzy Gillespie seven, Illinois Jacquet eight.

But the most popular star was [singer and multi-instrumentalist] Bulee 'Slim' Gaillard, who played the Hi-Hat eleven times in 1951–54."[2]

After a marijuana bust, Symphony Sid Torin had relocated from New York City to Boston, and in 1952, he began hosting live broadcasts from the club. Inspired by Birdland's motto "the Jazz Corner of the World," he christened the Hi-Hat "the Jazz Corner of Boston."

Charlie Parker, Miles Davis, Lester Young, Stan Getz, and saxophonists Serge Chaloff and Sonny Stitt released live recordings of their performances at the Hi-Hat.

The Hi-Hat closed in 1959 after a fire.

→ RIGHT **Hi-Hat menu,**
date unknown.

STATE ARMORY - North Adams
THURSDAY, MAY 22nd

18 - ARTISTS - 18

COUNT BASIE

Columbia Records Artists

AND HIS ORCHESTRA
JAMES RUSHING
VOCALIST

JAMES RUSHING, *Vocalist*

They'll thrill you with their superb Musical Invocations and perfect Dance Tempos!!!

Basie's distinct rhythm style set the pattern for most of the name bands on Tin Pan Alley today!

Don't Miss this Attraction!!

DANCING 8.30 till 1
ADMISSION $1.00
Auspices Co. K., M. S. G.

← LEFT **Handbill for a May 1953 show at the North Adams Armory by Count Basie and His Orchestra.**

NORTH ADAMS ARMORY
206 ASHLAND STREET, NORTH ADAMS

The North Adams Armory, located 150 miles west of Boston, served as a National Guard headquarters until 1914, when it was decommissioned and repurposed into commercial space. Part of the space was used to present live entertainment, including concerts and professional wrestling.

Hurricane Club

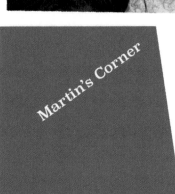

Martin's Corner

PART TWO

Hotel Garfield

Mirror Show Bar

THE MIDWEST

Flame Show Bar

Club DeLisa

Club 77

CLEVELAND

Jazz took hold in Cleveland in the 1920s, when speakeasies and clubs like the Golden Slipper were segregated by hours of operation: white musicians and patrons before midnight, their Black counterparts afterward. In the 1930s and 1940s, as Cleveland became the country's sixth-most-populous city, the jazz scene integrated.

The first Cleveland club to gain a national profile was Val's on the Alley, Art Tatum's home away from home until World War II. Touring musicians including Duke Ellington and Benny Goodman often stopped by the club to listen and jam with Tatum.

At the same time, a "second downtown," known as Doan's Corners, was taking shape, centered on East 105th Street and Euclid Avenue. Filled with movie theaters, restaurants, clubs, and a huge indoor skating rink, the scene was affordable for most, with live music all night.

Venues in the neighborhood included Cafe Tia Juana, the Loop Lounge, Club Rendezvous, and the renowned Lindsay's Sky Bar, which brought in many top performers including Coleman Hawkins, Charlie Parker, and Billie Holiday. Between the end of World War II and the mid-1960s, Cleveland had more than two dozen clubs booking nationally known performers.

In 1953, the Dave Brubeck Quartet recorded a concert at nearby Oberlin College; the resulting live album, *Jazz at Oberlin*, was "the watershed event that signaled the change of performance space for jazz from the nightclub to the concert hall," according to Wendell Logan, former chairman of the school's jazz studies program.[1]

But come the next decade, the scene began to change. Cleveland jazz historian Joe Mosbrook noted, "It used to be that even the top jazz people would play for low fees, but during the 1960s, those fees climbed enormously as they became more popular." Eventually "local clubs couldn't afford it—instead of a couple of hundred dollars a week, it was a few thousand."[2]

Jazz in Cleveland faced other challenges too; as journalist Evelyn Theiss observed: "The '60s brought civil unrest. Bomb threats began to be called into clubs where audiences were racially mixed. Eventually, a bomb [destroyed] a popular club known as the Jazz Temple. Students from nearby colleges began to seek out something different, too—folk music at La Cave, which was also in the neighborhood and featured such performers as Judy Collins and Peter, Paul and Mary."[3]

"For a long time in this neighborhood, you had the students, the traffic, girls, prostitutes—there was never any friction," saxophonist Ernie Krivda told Theiss. "You had exploding Black consciousness, white students, mavericks like me, and no police issues. Then, the police started seeing trouble. They stepped in, and it wasn't so much fun anymore."[4]

CHATTERBOX
5121-23-29 WOODLAND AVENUE

John "Chin" Ballard opened the Chatterbox in 1949, aided by Cleveland Browns player Marion Motley. The well-appointed club featured a then-gigantic twenty-one-inch television, reportedly "the largest television set in any Cleveland café," so patrons could watch baseball.

In 1956, the club welcomed Billie Holiday and the doo-wop group the Future Tones, which included future Motown solo artist Edwin Starr (who had a hit in 1970 with "War"). Two years later, the club had a huge success with the *Idlewild Revue*, featuring blues giant T-Bone Walker, singer Della Reese, future Motown legends the Four Tops, and exotic dancer Black Velvet.

In 1959, a massive fire destroyed the club as well as a number of adjacent businesses.

CLUB 77
7541 KINSMAN ROAD

Little is known about the short-lived Club 77. Brothers Dick and Woody Haddad opened the club in 1954, with entertainment mostly by local jazz groups, including the Bill Brooks–Jimmy Slaughter duo, the Rip Bivins Orchestra, Bamba Jones and His Cosmic Sounds, Willie "Guitar" Lewis, and the Three Sounds with Jerry Lovano. "King of the Jukebox" Louis Jordan appeared at the club at some point before it closed in 1957.

↖ OPPOSITE, LEFT **Chatterbox photo folder, date unknown.**

↖ OPPOSITE, RIGHT **Club 77 photo folder, mid-1950s.**

← LEFT **Multi-instrumentalist, singer, and bandleader Louis Jordan, the "King of the Jukebox," at Club 77, date unknown.**

← LEFT **Mirror Show Bar souvenir photograph, 1956.**

MIRROR SHOW BAR

12376 SUPERIOR AVENUE

The Mirror Show Bar operated in Cleveland's University Circle neighborhood from 1956 to 1962. Pianist Bobby Few told Joe Mosbrook that he'd played at the club with saxophonist "Big Joe" Alexander, trumpeter Bill Hardman, drummer Lawrence "Jacktown" Jackson, and singer Gene Jordan. Other local musicians who played the Mirror include drummer James "Chink" McKinney, saxophonist William "Weasel" Parker, and pianist Bill Gidney.

DETROIT

Society and big bands played Detroit's famed Graystone Ballroom during the 1920s and 1930s. Co-owned by bandleader Jean Goldkette, the Graystone was the Motor City's only large venue presenting African American groups, and only on Monday nights. The best-known group was McKinney's Cotton Pickers, who had been known as McKinney's Synco Septet before Goldkette forced the band to adopt the new, racist name.

Billie Holiday played the Fox Theatre with the Count Basie Orchestra in 1937; in *Lady Sings the Blues,* she recalled: "Detroit was between race riots then, and after three performances the first day, the theater management went crazy. They claimed they had so many complaints about all those Negro men up there on the stage with those bare-legged white girls, all hell cut loose backstage. The next thing we knew, they revamped the whole show. And when the chorus line opened the show, they'd fitted them out with special black masks and mammy dresses. They did both their numbers in blackface and those damn mammy getups."[1]

During the first half of the twentieth century, the promise of auto industry jobs drew huge numbers to the city; from 1910 to 1950, the city's African American population grew from 5,700 to 300,000. As with other cities, discriminatory housing covenants meant most Black people lived in only a few neighborhoods, and many in one dubbed Black Bottom. Adjacent was Paradise Valley, a Black entertainment district with restaurants, gambling dens, theaters, and many of the city's numerous jazz clubs. The area drew a mixed crowd; Black Bottom historian Ken Coleman noted, "It wasn't very uncommon to see wealthy or upper middle class [white patrons] from Grosse Pointe partying in Paradise Valley on a Saturday night."[2]

In 1942, Earl Hines brought his big band to Detroit's Paradise Theatre. His saxophonist, Charlie Parker, had been missing shows but promised to get his act together. As Hines's then-vocalist Billy Eckstine recalled in Nat Shapiro and Nat Hentoff's *Hear Me Talkin' to Ya*: "One time . . . Bird [Parker] says, 'I ain't gonna miss no more. I'm going to stay in the theater all night to make sure I'm here.' We answered, 'Okay. That's your business. Just make the show, huh?' Sure enough, we come to work the next morning, we get on the stand—no Bird. As usual. . . . This is the gospel truth. We played the whole show, the curtains close, and we're coming off the band cart, when all of a sudden we hear a noise. We look under the stand, and here comes Bird out from underneath. He had been under there asleep through the entire show!"[3]

During the 1950s, Detroit became a major hub for bebop. The economy, boosted by the auto industry, supplied a steady stream of workers looking for diversions, and a seemingly endless number of clubs, bars, dance halls, and the like provided venues for the city's extraordinary homegrown talent.

In the late 1950s and early 1960s, however, urban renewal projects spelled the end for Paradise Valley and its clubs, and changing musical tastes—and the ascent of the city's Motown Records—supplanted local interest in jazz in Detroit.

CLUB THREE 666

666 EAST ADAMS

The "Three Sixes" opened in Paradise Valley in 1941. The luxurious nightclub featured local acts like the Ted Buckner Orchestra (with future bop vibes legend Milt Jackson), out-of-town artists, and its own chorus line. Club manager Richard King remembered, "During this time, Black [people] couldn't eat just anyplace.... Our club was first class all the way, and our clientele was well dressed at all times.... During the week we'd average two hundred people per night, on Saturday we'd have a complete turnover.... When we lost the white business that we were getting, it was time to get out of the business. We sold the business in 1949." [4]

← OPPOSITE **Club Three 666 souvenir photograph dated January, 1947. Both Black and white people were welcome audience members at the "Three Sixes."**

↗ ABOVE, RIGHT **Club Three 666 photo folder.**

→ RIGHT, TOP AND BOTTOM
Garfield Hotel's Wal-Ha Room photo folder, 1956.

GARFIELD HOTEL

445 JOHN R. AT GARFIELD

The Garfield Hotel opened its Wal-Ha Room in 1950, when owner Randolph Wallace was granted "the first Negro-operated hotel-lounge license in Michigan."[5] A 1952 article in the African American newspaper the *Michigan Chronicle* described the club: "The circular bar is flanked by 35 chairs . . . plush booths line the walls. . . . The Wal-Ha Room is entered through accordion-like doors from the main lounge . . . recitals by local singers and dramatic readers are staged often in the Wal-Ha on Sunday evenings. . . . [T]he name is a contraction of Wallace and Harris (after Charles Harris, the former manager)."[6]

The Wal-Ha played host to small combos led by locals like jazz harpist Dorothy Ashby and guitarist Kenny Burrell.

Here's Hoping you and the Song Success to the Tops

fred =
2/17/56

↑ ABOVE **Wal-Ha Room souvenir photograph of jazz harpist and composer Dorothy Ashby with unknown musicians in 1956.**
Critic Tom Moon hailed Ashby as "one of the most unjustly under-loved jazz greats of the 1950s."[7]

→ RIGHT **Flame Show Bar photo folder, date unknown.**

FLAME SHOW BAR

4264 JOHN R. AT CANFIELD

According to the *Detroit Metro Times*, from its 1949 opening until it closed in 1963, "the Flame was *the* outlet for upscale Black entertainment in Detroit, hosting giants like Billie Holiday, Della Reese, Etta James, Dinah Washington, B.B. King, and Joe Turner."[8] The Flame was a Black and tan club with a difference; it also booked white entertainers, including pioneering pre-rock singer Johnny Ray (he recorded the hit "Cry"), who was discovered there. The venue featured a revue format, with a headliner preceded by singers, dancers, and perhaps a comedy act.

House band member Beans Bowles recalled: "The Flame was Black and tan and more white than Black. On the weekends the traffic would line up; you could not drive down Canfield or John R. That was hustle night, girls were on the street, pimps were out, everybody was makin' money. It was like Las Vegas. . . . Everything there was just poppin'. Lights and glitter, valet parking. . . . Nobody bother you or nothing. White people would come from all over to come to the Flame, because we had the top shows."

The club may have been jammed, but tipping the doorman often got a patron through the door. Bowles noted, "That was one, and only one, of the little hustles going on. You could get anything at the Flame if you had enough money."[9]

A Conversation with

JASON MORAN

Jason Moran is a pianist, composer, educator, and visual artist who was born in Houston, Texas, in 1975. A graduate of the Manhattan School of Music, Moran has released fifteen albums as a leader and performed and recorded with musicians including singer Cassandra Wilson, bassist Christian McBride, and saxophonists Charles Lloyd, Lee Konitz, and Greg Osby, as well as with his own trio, the Bandwagon.

The 2010 *DownBeat* critics poll named Moran's album *Ten* the Jazz Album of the Year, and Moran himself won Pianist of the Year and Jazz Artist of the Year. The same year, Moran was named a MacArthur Foundation Fellow.

Moran has composed music for his own multimedia shows as well as for theater, ballet, art installations, and feature films, including the sound track to the acclaimed *Selma* (2014). He has had works commissioned by institutions including the Walker Art Center, the Philadelphia Museum of Art, the Dia Art Foundation, the Whitney Museum of American Art, Harlem Stage, and Jazz at Lincoln Center.

Moran teaches at the New England Conservatory and is the artistic director for jazz at the Kennedy Center in Washington, D.C. His sculptural installation series *STAGED*, which re-creates the performance stages of the Savoy Ballroom, Three Deuces, and Slugs' Saloon, was part of his first solo museum exhibition and opened at the Walker Art Center in Minneapolis in 2018.

Jeff Gold (JG): Quincy and Sonny had a lot to say about playing these clubs. But I'm curious what you, a younger musician whose work is so informed by the musicians and music that came before you, make of these images.

Jason Moran (JM): The thing is that jazz is usually focused on lore of the musician. And so the images musicians get accustomed to are all about making icons out of the people on the stage. But every person on the stage understands that the only reason they even do it is because of the people sitting in front of them, who've shown them enough respect to come, sit down, and listen. Or talk and drink. But they do it within the relationship to the music. And seeing these images is powerful because we never document the jazz audience. Even to this day, even at the Kennedy Center, I tell my photographer, "Take pictures of the people on the stage, but you got to take pictures of the people in the audience!"

We have to know what it looks like to listen to this music too. We have to know what people are feeling, how it shows up on their face. This is a thing I've seen blues musicians continue to do where they take photographs with their fans. "Oh, you can get a five-dollar Polaroid! Come take a picture with Buddy Guy," or whatever. Now we do it with our phones so frequently that it doesn't feel like it's so formalized. But seeing these images in rapid order is the first time I feel like I understand what people are—how the music functions for the people that are coming to listen to it. That it is as much serious music as it is social. This is how we look when we go listen. This is how we look when we hang out. And this is how we document our moment together. I mean, this is the 1940s—it's still a terrible time!

JG: I know. It's during World War II and the audiences looked great!

JM: And then in these photographs with all these servicemen getting into the city, going to hear music, documenting who they're with—their buddies and their girlfriends or whatever—it's powerful to see. Because it tells that other part in history about where the music sits. We listen to Charlie Parker and all those musicians in the 1940s so frequently without ever asking ourselves who's in that room. Phil Schaap does that show *Bird Flight* every morning in New York—he goes through detail by detail, song by song, take by take of Charlie Parker. And to finally see some of these places, kind of like what it felt like.

I've been interested in the architecture of these rooms. The way the ceiling feels. The way the tables feel, close to each other. What is the stage made of? How much fabric is there in the room to soak up the sound? And how many bodies can fit in there to soak up the sound? How they do this. What it looks like. So to see now, okay, this is the table, this is what we drank, this is what we ordered, who I'm with—it's a revelation.

JG: I think there's so much information to be teased out of these things. I was staring at these photographs and I realized: these photographs turn the camera around. We've countless pictures of performers performing in these places—but you never see pictures of the people.

JM: And that separation has been a dangerous one over the years, as there's a way of erasing the relationship to the audience in performance. You know? So it doesn't ever leave a trail of how the music is experienced by generations.

JG: Sonny Rollins told me that, especially in small clubs, but in any clubs, that his whole performance was based on who was in the audience and how they were reacting. And they were really a part of the band.

JM: And it gets said so frequently you might just think it's a cliché. But any serious performer knows that we depend so much on that energy. Even the guy who's heard you play thirteen times, right? And he lets you know he's in the club that night—"Oh, okay, well, I can't just play the same thing over and over again." You know what I mean?

JG: I love the artwork on these folders too . . .

JM: Yeah, and also just seeing the number of clubs that you never hear about. And you know in New York, clubs turn over.

JG: So here's one from the Cotton Club, which I'll talk to you about in a bit. That's a hard-core racist club.

JM: Whoa.

JG: And it's such an interesting, complex issue, because they gave Ellington, Louis Armstrong, Cab Calloway—all these people—very important exposure through their national radio broadcasts but wouldn't let Black people in [as customers] and were completely segregated. Sonny Rollins said, "You don't think they were doing that for any reason other than that they thought they could make a buck doing it."

JM: Hmm . . . there's something I'm sure that someone has written a history about (or is waiting to write), but over the summer we were living at the American Academy in Rome. I gave my talk about the Three Deuces, Savoy, and I'm about to make one on Slugs' Saloon, the 1970s club. And in that talk, I talk about the Lenox Lounge, which has now just been destroyed and demolished. It's vacant now. It's an hour-long presentation about these spaces and the music that comes out of them and the need to preserve them. Then a historian said—started asking a question: "Well, you know, it's also just really closely related to money."

Whose money is this? So we know this is a lot of Mafia money. But there hasn't really been that deep dive into the economics around these spaces, because either there's an underground economy that's funneling through or maybe a laundering that's happening here. There's constantly, even to this day—I won't say the festival that operates now that is closely tied to the Mafia—that every musician understands.

JG: Want me to turn this off so you can tell me?

JM: Nope! But it always points to a place that we don't know, like Sonny might point out, which is that we aren't really sure where that trail goes. Or that famous story about Fats Waller being kidnapped by Al Capone and being made to play. [In 1926, Waller was kidnapped by four men, who forced him to play at gunpoint at one of Capone's clubs, the Hawthorne Inn. Eventually he realized he was at a birthday party for the gangster and was expected to provide the entertainment. Supposedly Waller stayed at the club for three days and left with his pockets stuffed with thousands of dollars in tips from Capone and his friends.]

But we're also considering the history of African Americans up to this point too. So here comes the style of music that allows the platform for each musician in the band to have a say—

JG: Right. Solos . . .

JM: Right. So as a musician I don't give a fuck what space you give me, you know? I don't care where it is, if I can get to say my piece. You know what I mean?

JG: So you see good in the Cotton Club and those places? Just in terms of giving exposure and . . .

JM: Well, look, there's always a—for us, we have to take anything. Because every generation of African Americans is reaching for something that has not been there the generation before. Look, what do we think of the ring shouts that happened on the slave plantation fields? What that becomes is a tradition for African Americans to generate sound and generate repetition and generate exhaustion through singing and dancing as a ritual. Not as a performance, but as a ritual. That kind of an excavation can only happen through movement—and what that makes the constant breathing through your body. You feel in your body and in your head. So we're looking for any space. Any space. And that's even before technical freedom that comes with the civil rights movement. These places are always tied up in—look, each musician is still getting robbed of their publishing at the same time. [Laughs.] In hindsight, we're still trying to learn our way, especially as a part of creating culture.

[*Leafs through some of the club photographs.*] It's unbelievable. I didn't even know that these things existed.

JG: They're an obscure thing. This was Earl "Fatha" Hines's place for a while, El Grotto. And this one was owned by a Black [Detroit] man, but it's called the Plantation Club. The Last Word on Central Avenue [in Los Angeles], "East Side['s] Smartest Sepia Nightclub." Murrain's up in Harlem.

JM: You know, an artist friend of ours has this term "adjacency." I'm thinking about that in relationship to, say, Fatha Hines having a club or noticing

↑ ABOVE **Photo folder from the Cotton Club's midtown location, late 1930s.**

how many clubs are uptown, which very few of these clubs I've ever heard of. Adjacency—like being near other people and other venues kind of like you will help you. Theaster Gates is his name; he has all these projects in Chicago, so we talk all the time. Because there's a point that I see coming, as I watch these clubs diminish—fortunately we still have the Village Vanguard and the Apollo—but as places get knocked down and developers come in, finding space, it's going to take artists to really go buy themselves a space to make sure at least that we own our places.

JG: Yeah, you got into that with [owning your own] record label.

JM: Yeah, it's a step. Because it's—how else?

JG: Makes all the sense in the world. The jazz scene of the 1940s and 1950s is very well documented and still fascinates fans and musicians and historians. Why do you think that is?

JM: I was saying this last night in thinking about Thelonious Monk. It's because they were predicting the change that would happen fifteen years later. And they predicted it in basements. They saw the future. But they were showing it to us in musical form. And they were showing us that there were many languages that may be spoken at once, and you'd have to follow really closely to understand it. And you'd have to give it time. And you'd have to understand that everyone was allowed that platform. That's the ideal. I think that's part of what it is. I think that it's part of one of the first generations—I may be making, I am making this up, because we all are, we're all making this up. You can hear Thelonious Monk in this Town Hall concert. You hear him in rehearsal, and he's talking with his arranger Hall Overton about how he didn't want his band to sound like a big band, because the big band idea is too stiff. Now "stiff" has many connotations. Stiff is restrictive, oppressive. You know, it has all those connotations built into it. Now we know he's talking about a generation of big bands that—not only the great big bands, but just the idea of the big bands is that you work in this way—

JG: And it's very formatted.

JM: Yes, this [music] happens here. It happens every time. And he didn't want his large ensemble to feel this way. And he also says under his breath, "It's not that I don't like it, I don't want to say that." He says this. But it's critical of the generation before him, right? There's a critique in there that bebop addresses, with not forty people, all dressed up the same, kind of behind a platform with all these formatted music stands—

JG: One guy calling all the shots.

JM: Yeah. [Bebop is a] small group in a basement. Pared down, showing you what recklessness looks like. And they do it in such a way because they rehearse it. It's kind of like modern dance, like, *What the fuck? They're not dancing! That's not choreography!* But you know, as you learn the language, you understand: *Ah, oh my goodness!* Whereas the big band shows it to you in visual form, we show it to you en masse. [Big bands have] twenty bodies on the stage, right? We have all these uniforms. We have these moves that everybody does. [*Hums and stomps a tune.*]

JG: A very controlled environment.

JM: [*Humming.*] HEY! HEY! HEY! You know, right? We have all that, which is a part of the party. Bebop is suggesting that we're not just party. We're not just the party, we're also complex individuals. And us picking that up and finding that as a music form, that's why that era becomes like . . . I hope it continues to be, I hope we still have a relationship to it because it's still kind of close by. I think it's going to change in a couple of years—maybe twenty years—[bop] won't be regarded the same way because people won't be here. Roy Haynes won't be here anymore.

So something else will happen: we'll have to start thinking of the 1970s or something. But I think for we who are living now, we know that [bop] was kind of like a thermometer saying, *The country has a flu, it's going through a war. You think it's across the water, but it's right here. We're showing you that it's about to change. And this won't happen with all of us in uniforms, it'll happen on a small scale with us shouting.* [*Laughs.*]

JG: The cabaret tax during World War II really supercharged bebop too.

Any club with dancing or bands with vocalists had to pay an additional 30 percent tax. Club owners are going, *Screw this! We're not going to pay 30 percent extra. We'll just hire these smaller bands that don't have singers and that people don't dance to and make more money.*

JM: Yeah, yeah. It's combined. You know, people often ask: If you could go back and live in another era or witness things ... ? You know. These are the things I'd like to walk downstairs and just see for three hours.

JG: That's why I think [these photographs are] as close as it gets. That's why I was looking at these pictures realizing they have to get out!

JM: Yeah, they do. They do! Because also it helps humanize, as people die. You know I think Thelonious Monk is great. But also, I only think of him as part of his family's history, you know? I mean, he changed my life, but it's his parents and it's his grandparents and his great-grandparents. They changed a lot of people's lives too. So we have to think about him in the continuum, not as like the point.

JG: And jazz is such a continuum, being passed down. Older musicians mentoring younger musicians.

JM: It's also the only way that I've been able to learn where the music's at in different cities and how it's presented. Say in Chicago, [composer and multi-instrumentalist] Henry Threadgill would talk about going to a movie house and staying all day. Because they'd show a movie, and then Art Blakey would play, and then a comedian would come out. Then they'd show another movie and then Miles Davis would play. Like, what are you talking about, where this is a night? Where this is a format and people would just skip school—

JG: Sinatra was playing at the Paramount Theatre in New York. They'd have a movie and then Frank Sinatra, and these kids would mob this place and go nuts and see a movie they might or might not want to see, [just] to see Frank Sinatra. I mean, it's crazy for people of our generation to contemplate.

So let's talk about what these evoke for you.

JM: Well, they mostly tell me that I need to document my audience and that I have not even documented myself in an audience. I mean, when I think about all the shows I've been to, the times I've been in the Village Vanguard to see whomever, whether it was [pianist] Geri Allen or [saxophonist] David Murray or [pianist] Mal Waldron. That many times, if I had a camera with me, I took a picture of the people on the stage, and I probably could have also turned that camera around and tried to take a photo of myself in the space, because it's a necessary part of the narrative. To really understand what the music is doing and who it's doing it for and who's helping support it. It's not only the venue, it's the audience and it's the musicians. And that's the ecosystem that keeps it healthy, is acknowledging everyone in it.

JG: And it is an ecosystem. Looking at these pictures of musicians, you can fall into this false perspective that it's the crowd watching, that it's a spectator sport, rather than a participatory experience on the level that Sonny talked about.

JM: I remember asking [saxophonist] Wayne Shorter once about playing in clubs back when he was with Art Blakey. And there was one point where, I guess, Art had played Carnegie Hall, and he had felt what it was like to be on a concert hall stage where the audience was quiet. And then he went back to a club and he was like, "Wait a minute!" [*Laughs.*] And Wayne said [Blakey] said something to the audience like, "You wouldn't do this at Carnegie Hall!" There was a shift in the relationship with how we experience music.

'Cause there's all those great records where you hear John Coltrane or Monk or anybody playing like the most amazing stuff and the audience is just like whatever. I mean, they're not whatever, they're there. But they're also just talking to each other.

So there's music now that we made like, wait a minute, let's actually listen to the music—oh, this is profound what's happening back here. But it was also just background. So [these pictures] kind of keep it—'cause seeing is believing. And that's a really important part to see.

Jacob Samuel, a friend of Moran and Gold, (JS): One of the things that really struck me when I first looked at the photographs was the dignity of the audience. People were happy to be out and they were dressed for it. The clubs gave people an opportunity to move into a different spirit than they might have had in their day job. And how important, having a venue for that expression.

JM: And these places were that. A club that has recently closed, but the space is still there in D.C. . . . It's called the Bohemian Caverns. It closed, but the basement is still there. A recent article about it was saying this was also a place where people were proud to be able to go to. There was a sense of status for them: *Okay, I'm going to go hang out for the night. That's where I'm going.* And so people arrived there looking their very, very best.

JG: I'm interested in what your thoughts are about what music meant to the Black community from what you know and from what you see looking at these pictures.

JM: I think it's aspirational music. And also I think as the music continued to change, it didn't pose necessarily what the answer was for the future, as much as it would propose that you reconsider where you stand.

And that's what I mean by kind of like a self-reflective kind of space, which I think W. E. B. DuBois sort of unlocked and would take generations for us to understand. Same for, say, James Baldwin or Toni Morrison. That they continued to unlock aspects of some of the psychology and psychosis that centuries of oppression leaves in people.

And we can't work through them in one generation. And I think the music— I mean, look, I play the music so I think it's great—it's totally tied up in some totally awful aspects of how it works too and who it marginalizes. So within that, I also understand, because of my distance away from a hundred years ago or ninety years ago or fifty years ago, there's a way that we can think about what it means to people.

↗ ABOVE, RIGHT **Bohemian Caverns photo folder from the John Coltrane Quartet's engagement, mid-1960s.**

JG: To shift gears a bit: I'm really interested in the issue of race. I was really surprised when Quincy Jones told me by the time he was playing clubs, race wasn't an issue, and that "racism would've been over in the 1950s if they listened to the jazz guys."

JM: That's what I mean. You could tell they were predicting that.

JG: That really surprised me, so I asked Sonny about it, and he said, "Yeah, that's one of the things jazz musicians never get credit for." Does it surprise you to hear that?

JM: No, it doesn't. Look, I've looked at enough art—and I mean looked at, visually, with my eyes—to know that. And it wasn't just them; it was also how forms started to change then too. Whether it's in wood construction, with how [designer Charles] Eames sees things. There's just enough things changing at once, that is the marker that okay, we should—if we could go back, we could start this work earlier. But it's impossible to know, because these are abstract forms that they've chosen to work—not chosen, this is how it evolves, right? I actually asked the audience last night. Someone out here is predicting what the next twenty years is looking like right now. And it probably sounds like something we don't quite understand yet. But someone's doing it right now, you know? Some sculptor is making it. I saw [artist] Mike Kelley's show. This show is—I mean, it's the last body of work he made. It's not a soulful show, but it's all soul.

So now I kind of look at things within a relationship to each other. There's some choreographer making the work, there's some filmmaker making it. There's some musician making it. And we're trying to work out something that hasn't quite formulated itself into language yet. There are enough tensions inside people that are like, *I'm working through it, but I haven't quite found a way to say it yet.* Monk says it. Hall Overton asks him about how he learned [something] and he says, "Well, rather than say it, can't I just play it?"

JG: But back to the issue of race. You read about these shows in the 1950s and the 1960s in the South, shows are racially segregated. Rock shows were segregated. The Beatles had it put in their contracts that when they went to the South, "we won't play in front of segregated audiences." I had no idea that in the late 1940s—as early as the late 1940s and maybe earlier—on Fifty-Second Street, everybody got along.

JM: Yeah, here's a block where this is working, right? I'm not a real historian, so I couldn't say anything factual associated with it, but when you see those images of what Fifty-Second Street looked like, or Chinatown, Little Italy, or Harlem—it's just it's that one block, that one block that becomes a neighborhood within a neighborhood. It's where the rules change and

it satisfies everyone. And so Fifty-Second Street became a place where enough voices said this is how it can work. And it's not like a commune either. This is New York City. It's not out west in some remote plains. This is in the middle of a metropolitan city. And that always strikes me too.

JG: Kind of an oasis.

JM: Yeah, yeah.

JG: Some of these photos have the artists posing with the fans. I asked Sonny whether there was much interaction between the fans and the performers, and he said yes, it was kind of a shock for someone from Harlem, who hadn't had much interaction with white people, to be so embraced by them. Not just playing in front of them but meeting these people and getting this positive reinforcement, and people wanting to take pictures with them.

JM: Oh my god! That's kind of heavy. But it mostly just deals with humanity, like the feeling that everybody, that people, are on the same level. You know [in the club] Three Deuces, the stage was the floor. It wasn't vaulted in the air. Yeah, that's kind of stunning. I hadn't considered that there would be a line between the performer and the audience, an audience member, in the generation before Sonny. I would've figured that people in Duke's band or Chick Webb's band, or whoever, just would be hanging out.

JG: Remember, at the Cotton Club, you could play in front of these people, but you couldn't go out into the audience. You probably came in through the back way. And Sonny was living up in Harlem, probably not meeting a lot of people like those [white audience members] except at work. And Quincy and Sonny both said as a musician—you know, in terms of band integration—it was about whether you could play. Nobody gave a damn whether you were Black, white, whatever. And I think the people are reacting to that, you know? They're just looking at you for what you can do, not who you are.

JM: There's a lot that my generation might take for granted in that regard, and then the generation behind us. We also knew that there was a change with how an audience interacted with an artist. Because my generation didn't have Twitter or Instagram, where you can not only have that one snapshot, but trade messages [with an artist] and keep up with what they had for breakfast. And totally be a part of your life online.

JG: You know that ten thousand people are interested in what you're doing.

JM: Right! At any given moment. If I consider what that felt like, it's probably the same. Whoa, there's this extra layer sitting behind this device's door? That now an audience can feel with an artist. That feels so bizarre, because we remember the time when that wasn't there.

And that felt like enough! I never felt like I could just go up to anyone [and say], "Hey, can I have a lesson with you?" Now kids come up to me all the time—I mean, I teach a lot too, so maybe that's different—and say, "Oh, can I have a lesson? I got your email here." I'm like whoa, whoa! I couldn't just send [saxophonist] Joe Henderson an email, you know?

JG: In these photos everybody looks so happy. These people posing with Oscar Peterson (see page 247), here's my fantasy. He's got a small business and his wife, her mink coat is her proudest possession. And there they are at this club watching Oscar Peterson. It's like, "WOW! We get to meet him and take a picture with him!" Race mixing wasn't so fluid at that time, so it's really kind of amazing to look at them from that aspect too.

JM: Yeah. And also—what do you call that kind of photography? Social documentary.

JG: But it wasn't meant to be that.

JM: But it's a moment that people know that you smile for. You know you're—look, we look nice, we'll take this picture, y'all! Okay!

JG: It's personal. Very personal.

JM: Right, we do that because we're acknowledging how great of an evening this is. And we also are acknowledging how great the artist was. And look, the artist is now completing our picture.

JG: Look who we met.

JM: Yeah. And that's like—we all have photos with people like, "Hey! Look who I took a photo with."

JG: I mean, it's strange. It's kind of unintended documentary photography. It ends up being that, but that wasn't the intention. It was a souvenir.

JM: Souvenir. There it is.

JG: So you studied and played with a number of older, legendary musicians like [multi-instrumentalist] Jaki Byard, Charles Lloyd, Lee Konitz, and [drummer] Paul Motian, and I'm guessing that as well as picking up musical tips, you probably talked history with these guys too. And I was thinking that this music has been passed down from generation to generation by players. But the history has also been passed down to some extent, generation to generation, by players. And you've done these longer pieces based on the music of Monk, Fats Waller, and others. How does your close attention to the jazz of the past inform what you do today?

JM: There's no way for me to play anything without it. There's just no way. It informs every note that I make, every decision that I make. There's no way around it. A lot of us learn by following musicians that, we think, think how we think, that show us ourselves, show us who we can become. Thelonious Monk does it maybe the most profoundly for me.

At fourteen, when I hear him, I think I can be him. Just as you think you can be Superman or whomever. You know, you think, *I can do that. I can fly*, without having any idea of how difficult it actually is to be an artist. So I can't move without like bringing all of my baggage with me.

JG: It's in the algorithm?

JM: It is. And I'm thankful for it too. And I think I try to let younger musicians that I work with acknowledge that fact. And that it's also not just the musicians. You know, your parents teach you how to learn or how to be stubborn. You learn these things very early in your life, about how you process information and sounds. Do you listen to your mother when she tells you to take out the garbage the first time? Or does it take three times? You know what I mean? Does it then take her yelling—and whipping you? [*Laughs.*]

↑ ABOVE **Fans at Birdland with Count Basie, who added to his autograph the "Round Man," date unknown.**

JG: I didn't get my dollar allowance unless I took out the trash!

JM: [*Laughs.*] How does that manifest when you hit the stage? How much detail are you going to align yourself with? And I know from knowing my family, and having such respect for how I was raised, that then when I started to work, that history would always be a part of how I make musical decisions. And there will always be a place for you to say something. Or you could interrupt someone, right? My place as a pianist is also to kind of move like that. Thelonious Monk tells me ways to do that. Mary Lou Williams tells me ways to do that. Earl Hines tells me. And I think of them as radical people. Radical—I don't think of them as stars, I think of them as radicals. Because they have decided to change the language, and what that takes is a kind of flexibility that is rarely found in people. I mean, in a population, right? People who decide, *I'm going to narrow it down to just like figuring this thing out.* That Earl Hines figures out virtuosity in that way. That then informs what Thelonious Monk can say: okay, well, virtuosity can work this way too. You know?

JG: There were so few channels to manifest genius.

JM: Yeah. And they weren't promoted. You may have generations of people that were doing magnificent things, but they have to do them underground. Because you can't be shouting how smart you are. That's just not a thing you can do. You can't even show nobody that you can read. Let alone, *Okay, now I'm going to show you something that probably is more fascinating than any bop you've ever heard. And that I can invent it on the spot. You know, I'm not going to show you the science behind this stuff.* And that's what I thought—talking last night, I was talking about Ellington, what he makes. Then that Charlie Parker and Dizzy and Monk can decide that okay, the melody can sound this way now, right? With all these starts and stops, and you have no idea where it's going to go next. And they're moving into this crazy, rapid pace. You know, like birds chasing each other, fighting over a worm. And then later, when [composer and pianist] Muhal Richard Abrams and all of them come along, that they say, *Well, okay, that could even go further. Now it could even be more gestural, to show you how great*

this is. At the same time that [composer] Elliott Carter is writing whatever he's writing too. And there's this stage that you can say, well, you know, you might just think this feels good, they sound great. Meanwhile . . . [*Laughs.*] Meanwhile, do you know what this is? Do you know what you're listening to right now? And these people are brave to do it.

JG: Yes. Look at what Coltrane did in the last few years of his life—going from being the superstar acknowledged by everybody as a god and just getting more and more out there and people not necessarily reacting well to it, but—

JM: Right. I'm keeping it moving.

JG: Just absolutely zero doubt in his mind that he was doing the right thing. And he just kept going.

JM: Yeah, yeah. These people are fascinating. And that, for me, then becomes the frame so that I can pull along. And also know that the teachers who taught me, the reason they shared all that they shared with me was because they felt that I could take care of it. You don't tell everybody your secrets—you tell some people. And every once in a while, I meet people who whisper in my ear. And they know!

We had the seventy-fifth anniversary of Blue Note Records and [pianist] McCoy Tyner came—it was probably one of the last times that [vibraphonist] Bobby Hutcherson was playing with him. And McCoy took me aside, because I had met McCoy when I was sixteen, and he said, "Man, I'm glad you have this job at the Kennedy Center, because I know you're going to take care of it." And he says, "Keep going." And they say "Keep going"; they don't say, *All right now, you're cool, just chill,* you know. They say, "Keep pushing at it." And I've had enough people give me that pep talk, of varying sorts. And the way that I know that we have to move forward, it's just being really respectful of all these trails that are left for us to be like, "Okay, we can consider all this, right?"

JG: I think that's a good place to end. Thank you so much.

JM: My pleasure. ●

C ★ H ★ I ★ C ★ A ★ G ★ O

Among the first musicians to bring the new sounds of New Orleans to Chicago were Jelly Roll Morton, cornetist Freddie Keppard, and drummer Warren "Baby" Dodds; but the one who made the biggest impact was cornetist and bandleader Joe "King" Oliver.

After the Storyville district in New Orleans closed, Oliver moved north, part of the great African American migration. Chicago had been a hub for foreign migrants, but when the United States entered World War I, European immigration was cut off. Resulting labor shortages meant jobs were plentiful in Chicago's stockyards and manufacturing, railroad, and retail sectors. And as in other cities, that meant more workers seeking diversion and more clubs.

King Oliver's Creole Jazz Band was already Chicago's top jazz group when Oliver wired his protégé, Louis Armstrong, to come north and join the ensemble at the Lincoln Gardens. The revolutionary music they created was a sensation, and among the many who flocked to see the band were local white musicians—and future stars—Benny Goodman, Eddie Condon, Hoagy Carmichael, and cornetist Bix Beiderbecke.

In the mid-1920s, Armstrong went solo and made a series of highly influential records with his Hot 5 and Hot 7 recording groups that altered jazz's focus, from ensemble playing to a sound that highlighted longer improvisations from a soloist.

Inspired by Oliver and Armstrong, a group of five students from Chicago's Austin High School—including cornetist Jimmy McPartland and saxophonists Bud Freeman and Frank Teschemacher—formed the Austin High School Gang, who came to exemplify the Chicago jazz sound, which featured quicker tempos, more solos, and an emphasis on the 4/4 beat. Guitar and string bass replaced the traditional New Orleans rhythm section of banjo and tuba.

The city's main African American entertainment district was centered on East Thirty-Fifth Street, in the South Side's Bronzeville neighborhood. In 1921, the Sunset Cafe opened; integrated from the beginning, the club welcomed people of all races and presented many legendary performers, including Earl Hines, who played a twelve-year residency there. Later renamed the Grand Terrace Cafe, the club was one of a number of Chicago venues controlled by gangster and bootlegger Al Capone. Capone was a jazz fan and made sure his clubs booked only Black musicians, considering them both talented and as oppressed as his Italian immigrant relatives. During the 1920s, Prohibition may have been the law of the land, but Capone and his associates made sure that liquor flowed freely in Chicago's many clubs.

On February 27, 1926, Okeh Records staged the world's first jazz concert, at the Coliseum, on Fourteenth Place and South Wabash Avenue. The "OKeh Race Records Artists Night" featured Armstrong, pianists Bennie Moten and Clarence Williams, and singer Sippie Wallace, and drew a crowd of thousands.

In 1927, the city's "Black Broadway" moved south to Forty-Seventh Street, with the opening of the deluxe Savoy Ballroom and, soon after, venues like the Palm Tavern, the Dreamland Cafe, and the Regal Theater.

As Chicago's jazz scene grew, new clubs opened in other parts of the city. But the thriving scene wouldn't last. Mob wars and the bloody 1929 Saint Valentine's Day Massacre brought increasing scrutiny on Capone and the city's speakeasies, while the Great Depression put economic pressure on the clubs. The growing jazz scene in New York City exerted an irresistible pull on many Chicago-based musicians, including Armstrong, Oliver, Jelly Roll Morton, Benny Goodman, and the Austin High players. By the 1930s, the center of jazz had shifted to New York City.

Though the innovators may have moved east, the fans remained, and for the next few decades Chicago still had plenty of jazz on offer. During the 1930s and 1940s, clubs like the DeLisa thrived. Downtown's Hotel Sherman had two clubs: the College Inn, which played host to the orchestras of Duke Ellington and Benny Goodman, and a basement club, the Panther Room, where Count Basie, Louis Armstrong, and Frank Sinatra appeared.

Racial barriers were breaking down too. On April 12, 1936, Goodman played an Easter Sunday show at the city's Congress Hotel, with African American pianist Teddy Wilson as part of his trio. This was the first public concert featuring an integrated group in a major venue. Soon Goodman added Wilson and African American vibraphonist Lionel Hampton as full-time members of his touring groups, a full ten years before Jackie Robinson broke baseball's color barrier. By that time, Goodman was such a huge star that he could draw crowds anywhere—even the South—no matter what the racial makeup of his band was. Not long afterward, white bandleader Artie Shaw hired Billie Holiday to sing with his group, and the first few mixed bands began playing Fifty-Second Street clubs.

The late 1940s and 1950s saw bebop take hold in Chicago, at clubs like the Sutherland Show Lounge and the Beehive, where Charlie Parker played one of his last shows. During the latter decade, the city experienced what the *Chicago Reader* called a "second jazz age," with "a host of jazz joints ranging from gin mills to fancy supper clubs," including the College Inn, the Hilton's Boulevard Room, Mr. Kelly's, and the Blue Note.[1]

In the 1960s, clubs like the Plugged Nickel hosted many modern-day stars, including the Miles Davis Quintet, who played a two-week residency in 1965. That same year, a group of Chicago avant-garde jazz musicians formed the Association for the Advancement of Creative Musicians, a collective organized to promote and present "serious, original music," which is still active today.

Chicago also became a major center for the blues and rhythm and blues music, but that's another story.

all colored revue

new *Club DeLisa*

4 SHOWS NIGHTLY

NO COVER OR MINIMUM CHARGE • Be sure to attend our Monday morning breakfast dance • 5521-23 SOUTH STATE ST.

← LEFT **Club DeLisa**
menu, date unknown.

↑ ABOVE **Club DeLisa** souvenir photograph with "Victory" logo on folder, World War II era.

CLUB DE LISA
NEW
4 SHOWS NIGHTLY

NO COVER
—OR—
MINIMUM CHARGE

AIR CONDITIONED

BREAKFAST DANCE
EVERY
MONDAY MORNING

← LEFT **Club DeLisa souvenir photograph with the American flag and Victory motif on its folder, World War II era. Both Black and white patrons were welcome at the DeLisa.**

CLUB DELISA

5521 SOUTH STATE STREET

In 1934, after the repeal of Prohibition, the four DeLisa brothers turned their South Side speakeasy into a legal nightclub. Seven years later the club burned down, but they soon reopened in a larger space. The integrated DeLisa offered revue-style entertainment, with singers, dancers, comedians, and chorus girls, all backed by a seven- to nine-piece house band. An additional, less public source of income was illegal gambling in a basement room.

During the 1930s and 1940s, the DeLisa was open around the clock, offering a breakfast dance on Monday mornings. Many name performers played the club, including Billy Eckstine, pianist Albert Ammons, and singer LaVern Baker. Drummer Red Saunders led the house band for nineteen years; Count Basie discovered his longtime vocalist, Joe Williams, singing in Saunders's band.

In 1946, pianist Herman Blount, later to become famous as experimental musician Sun Ra, was hired by the DeLisa's then-bandleader Fletcher Henderson to play piano and arrange music for the club's floor shows.

The DeLisa closed in February 1958, after the death of two of the DeLisa brothers. *Jet* magazine quoted Saunders saying, "I haven't had a vacation since 1952. I guess I'll take one now."[2]

→ RIGHT **Martin's Corner souvenir photograph, date unknown.**

MARTIN'S CORNER
1900 WEST LAKE STREET

This Black and tan club was opened in the 1930s by Big Jim Martin, "the biggest policy [numbers] king on Chicago's Westside," according to *Crime Magazine*"; with friend Ed Jones, Martin "controlled gambling in Black Chicago."[3] Along with the small club's musicians, dancers, singers, and comics, Martin offered his customers illegal gambling, including craps, roulette, slot machines, and card games. Upstairs, patrons could see if the policy wheels had spun the numbers they'd chosen.

Sometime around 1940, female impersonator Valda Gray produced a revue in the club's back garden, featuring a male Joan Crawford impersonator. In 1944, legendary blues singer Memphis Minnie played at the club for six weeks.

At some point during the early 1950s, Martin sold the club.

→ OPPOSITE **Louis Armstrong** (*second from left*) posing with fans. Armstrong's longtime band vocalist, Velma Middleton, is seated fifth from the left, and his adopted son, Clarence Armstrong, is seated second from the right.

JOE'S DELUXE CLUB

6323 SOUTH PARKWAY

Former Golden Gloves boxer and honorary Bronzeville mayor Joe Hughes and his wife, Velma, opened the Deluxe in 1939. The club booked top jazz performers for its weekly swing session and was popular for its Monday "celebrity nights," with names like Cab Calloway, Sarah Vaughan, and Bill Robinson.

But what really distinguished the club was its nightly floor shows, featuring female impersonators including Sandra (Chester P. Frederick), Petite Swanson (Alphonso Horsley), and Dixie Lee (Robert Johnson). An article in the African American newspaper the *Chicago Defender* characterized the club as an "impersonator's mecca."[4]

The OutHistory.org website noted, "In Bronzeville, female impersonators were very respected as entertainers. . . . [T]he *Chicago Defender* often cited them in articles, as legitimate entertainers beside musicians or dancers,"[5] adding, "As a proof of Hughes' respectability, *Ebony* magazine stated that [he was] friends with the Eddie 'Rochester' Andersons and Joe Louis, along with other celebrities, proving that Black Queer entertainment was recognized as financially rewarding but also a way to access the upper class."[6]

Joe's Deluxe closed in the mid-1950s.

JOE'S DeLUXE CLUB
THREE FLOOR SHOWS NIGHTLY

6323 SOUTH PARKWAY   **CHICAGO, ILLINOIS**

Every Monday Celebrity Night

ENGlewood 3050—NORmal 2261

JOE HUGHES, Prop. ——— **G. HUGHES, Mgr.**

PHOTOGRAPHS BY—WILLA CORUM AND RICHARD JOHNSON

← ↑ OPPOSITE **Hurricane Show Club souvenir photograph and photo folder** (*above*), **1940s.**

HURRICANE SHOW CLUB

347 EAST GARFIELD BOULEVARD

Not much is known about this 1940s South Side club. Saxophonist and blues shouter Joseph "Buster" Bennett played here in 1943, as did singer and pianist Rudy Richardson, sometimes advertised as "America's only male torch singer."

→ RIGHT Rhumboogie menu with
Joe Louis on cover, 1940s.

RHUMBOOGIE CAFE

343 EAST GARFIELD BOULEVARD

Boxing champion Joe Louis and car salesman Charlie Glenn opened the Rhumboogie in April 1942. The club kicked off with an eight-week residency by Tiny Bradshaw and His Orchestra, but the best-known performer associated with the club was T-Bone Walker. His nine-month residency drew large crowds, and during the next three years, he played a number of extended runs at the Rhumboogie. Other acts that played the club include Fletcher Henderson, Sarah Vaughan, and the International Sweethearts of Rhythm, the first integrated all-women band in the United States.

In 1944, the club founded a record label, the Rhumboogie Recording Company, to record Walker. A fire on December 31, 1945, shuttered the Rhumboogie; it reopened in mid-1946 but never truly recovered, closing for good the next year.

↑ ABOVE **Rhumboogie postcard, 1940s.**

The Luxurious NEW

RHUMBOOGIE

Famous for the Finest Entertainment in America

GARFIELD BLVD. AT SOUTH PARKWAY IN CHICAGO

← ↑ OPPOSITE **Rhumboogie photo folder and souvenir photograph** (*above*), 1940s.

BLUE NOTE
56 WEST MADISON STREET

On November 25, 1947, Frank Holzfeind opened his newly remodeled jazz club, rechristening it the Blue Note, inspired by the name of a café in a radio drama. Writing in the *Chicago Reader*, Dan Caine noted, "The Blue Note was the first truly integrated club [in Chicago's] downtown." "Number one rule, don't discriminate. If you do, you're dead," observed Holzfeind in the same article. "Among jazz fans there is no color line." Caine wrote, "Until the Blue Note came along, however, facts seemed to say otherwise. North-side and south-side jazz in Chicago were almost totally separate scenes. While it was not uncommon for Black singers and musicians to perform for white audiences all over town, Black customers were themselves restricted, de facto, to the expanse of the city south of Roosevelt Road."[9]

In 1953, the club moved to a much larger space on the second floor of a building on North Clark. Count Basie considered the Blue Note to be his "Chicago headquarters," playing there frequently, and at various points the club had resident Dixieland bands led by cornetist Doc Evans and trombonist Miff Mole. Holzfeind booked a cross-section of music, including big bands (Duke Ellington, Chico O'Farrill), singers (Billie Holiday, Maxine Sullivan), boppers (Dizzy Gillespie, Lennie Tristano), and cool jazz players (Dave Brubeck, trumpeter Chet Baker).

But by mid-1956, Holzfeind found many of the artists he'd previously booked were no longer affordable, being paid more by and finding bigger crowds at more upscale clubs like the London House and Mr. Kelly's. The end came suddenly. On June 14, 1960, after New Orleans trumpeter Al Hirt played his second set to a sparse crowd, Holzfeind told the musician that he'd decided to close, effective immediately. "I knew I had to make the grim decision or get trapped in serious financial problems," Holzfeind told reporters. "I have closed the Blue Note. I've had my first good night's sleep in years."[10]

↑ ABOVE **Blue Note souvenir photograph, late 1940s.**

↑ ABOVE **Blue Note photo folder, late 1940s.**

EL GROTTO
6412 SOUTH COTTAGE GROVE AVENUE
AT SIXTY-FOURTH STREET

El Grotto opened in the basement of the Pershing Hotel in 1944. At the time, *Billboard* reported: "The Grotto's talent, unusual in its quality for a Chicago Negro night spot, will consist of Johnny Bradshaw's orchestra; the Charioteers, singers; Jessy E. K. Scott, tap dancer; Olive Brown, blues singer; Johnny Taylor, comedian; Rosita Lockhart, shake dancer; Dorris Woods, singer, and the 10 Zigglettes [chorus] line. Ziggie Johnson, well-known night club impresario, will produce the El Grotto's show and act as its emcee."[7]

A few years later, Chicago-based pianist and bandleader Earl "Fatha" Hines bought the club; he'd played there previously, and the club became his home base. When his band was touring, he booked local and nationally known musicians including saxophonist Eddie "Lockjaw" Davis and trumpeter Roy Eldridge.

In 1946, singer Johnny Hartman, the "Bronze Sinatra," played a six-month stand at the Grotto. "That's where I started," he later recalled. "I won an amateur hour in Chicago and the prize was a week's work in a club and fortunately for me Earl Hines' band was like the house band. This was a top club in Chicago, right? And Earl liked my singing and he kept me on."[8]

The club closed in 1947.

↑ ABOVE **El Grotto photo folder, January 1946.**

El Grotto Supper Club
Chicago, -:- Illinois

1-17-46

↑ ABOVE **El Grotto souvenir photograph, January 1946.**

Harry Fields

EL GROTTO SUPPER CLUB

PRESENTS THE 10th EDITION OF

STAR-TIME

1st SECTION

1. Opening Tipping in Entire Cast
2. Dolores Parker Songs That Soothe
3. Patterson and Jackson, Sons of Fun
4. Rhumba with Jive Grottoettes
5. Mable Scott, Bomb Shell of Song
6. Holmes and Jean, Ballet-Hoo
7. Finale Destiny's Tots

2nd SECTION

INTERUPTION

1. Lord Essex, Prisoner of Love
2. Grottoettes, Just You
3. Patterson and Jackson, Sons of Fun
4. Rhumba with Jive Grottoettes
5. Mabel Scott, Sweet and Hot
6. Holmes and Jean, Cigarettes Period
7. Finale Drums Grottoettes Featuring Chick Booth

EARL FATHA HINES

PRESENTS THE BAND IN CONCERT

A DEDICATION TO THE LATE GEORGE GERSHWIN

1. Opening A Medley of Fascinating Rhythm, Lady Be Good and Liza
2. Biding My Time, Vocal Arthur Walker
3. Embracable You, Vocal Dolores Parker
4. s'Wonderful Vocal, Lord Essex, Supported By Kermit Scott and Mr. Hines
5. I Got Rhythm, Featuring Scoops Carey, Chick Booth and the Rhythm Quartet
6. Love Walked In and The Man I Love, Vocal by Essex Scott and Dolores Parker
7. A Medley of Somebody Loves Me and Swanee Vocal, Fats Palmer
8. RAPSODY IN BLUE, Featuring Clifton Small at the Piano

Music Written by George Gershwin

Entire Score Arranged By Buggs Roberts

In-colaboration with Mr. Hines

SHOW PRODUCED BY JOE SLIP STEVENSON

↑ ABOVE **Program from 10th Edition of El Grotto's Star-Time show, mid-1940s.**

KANSAS *City*

From the mid- to late 1920s, pianist Bennie Moten's Kansas City Orchestra played a vital role in the early development of the city's unique jazz sound. But equally important to the city's emergence as a thriving center of jazz was the fourteen-year rule of the city's corrupt Democratic political boss, Tom Pendergast.

Kansas City's central location made it a commercial center for a huge part of the United States. All that business begat a thriving entertainment district, and under Pendergast, it was a "wide-open" town. Prohibition and vice laws were ignored in the city's numerous brothels, bars, cabarets, and gambling dens, many of which featured live music as part of their entertainment.

In *Bird Lives!*, Ross Russell wrote: "There was more music in Kansas City than had been heard in America since the gilt palaces and funky butt dance halls of the Storyville section of New Orleans closed. . . . There were more jobs for musicians than anywhere else in America, and more bands. . . . A remarkable feature of music in Kansas City was that nobody told the musicians what to play or how to play it. Jazzmen were free to create as the spirit moved them. So long as the music was danceable and lively

and the visiting firemen were satisfied, the gangsters who ran the clubs did not interfere. As the result of favoring conditions—steady work, isolation, a concentration of talent, and almost total lack of commercial pressures—Kansas City had developed a jazz style of its own."[1]

At its peak, the "Paris of the Plains" boasted more than fifty jazz venues along Twelfth Street, with more clubs in the city's main African American neighborhood, at Eighteenth and Vine Streets. Some clubs had loudspeakers over their front doors, blasting the music being played inside to the people on the streets. The city had some Black and tan clubs. The Reno was fully integrated, while other clubs offered white customers prime space on the dance floor and Black customers balcony seating only.

The music began to take on a distinct character when Moten hired Count Basie, Hot Lips Page, and bassist Walter Page. The new sound was more spontaneous and riff oriented, with a blues influence and extended solos. Bands played "head arrangements" instead of relying on written music.

In *Bop Apocalypse*, Martin Torgoff wrote, "The musical life of the city revolved around marathon jam sessions, and the traveling bands passing through included those of Duke Ellington, Fletcher Henderson, Jimmie Lunceford, and Cab Calloway, featuring a host of great musicians—Chu Berry, Coleman Hawkins, Johnny Hodges—always looking for cutting sessions like visiting gunslingers."[2]

The competitive atmosphere was unrelenting. "Jam sessions in Kansas City?" pianist Sam Price recalled in Shapiro and Hentoff's *Hear Me Talkin' to Ya*. "I remember once at the Subway Club, on Eighteenth Street, I came by a session at about ten o'clock and then went home to clean up and change clothes. I came back a little after one o'clock and they were still playing the same song."[3]

Bandleader Jay McShann told the Associated Press, "You'd hear some cat play, and somebody would say, 'This cat, he sounds like he's from Kansas City.' It was Kansas City style. They knew it on the East Coast. They knew it on the West Coast. They knew it up north, and they knew it down south."[4]

The Kansas City sound went national after John Hammond heard a live broadcast on his car radio from the Reno Club, featuring Count Basie's group. "I couldn't believe my ears," Hammond recalled.[5] As soon as possible, he drove to Kansas City and, after hearing the music in person, made it his mission to bring the new sounds to New York City and the rest of the country.

Other prominent Kansas City bands at the time included Andy Kirk and His Twelve Clouds of Joy, featuring pianist Mary Lou Williams, one of the first women to come to prominence in the male-dominated jazz world, and the Jay McShann Orchestra, with Kansas City native Charlie Parker. "Bird would pull out his horn . . . and just run it up and down," McShann remembered. "I mean, he knew his instrument backward."[6]

In 1939, Tom Pendergast was jailed for income tax evasion and his political machine collapsed. Reform elements took over the city's government, and many nightclubs, bars, and cabarets were closed. Without jobs, many of the city's musicians moved elsewhere or were drafted when the United States entered World War II. Kansas City's golden era as a jazz city may have ended, but its musicians carried the new sounds far and wide.

↓ BELOW **Gilmore's Chez Paree souvenir photograph, 1940s.**

GILMORE'S
CHEZ PAREE

**The Gayest Nite Spot
In Greater Kansas City**

**1822 Vine Street
Kansas City, Mo.**

hard keys, like E-flat and B-natural. That took care of quite a few of the local characters right away. Not many piano players were eager to mess with that stuff. I knew I wasn't."[8]

Mary Lou Williams picked up the story: "Around 4 A.M. I awoke to hear someone pecking at my screen. I opened the window on Ben Webster. He was saying, 'Get up, pussycat, we're jammin' and all the pianists are tired out now. Hawkins got his shirt off and is still blowing. You got to come down.' Sure enough, when I got there Hawkins was in his singlet taking turns with the KC men. It seems he had run into something he didn't expect. Lester's style was light and . . . it took him maybe five choruses to warm up. But then he would really blow, then you couldn't handle him on a cutting session. That was how Hawkins got hung up. The Henderson band was playing in St. Louis that evening, and Bean [Hawkins] knew he ought to be on the way. But he kept trying to blow something to beat Ben and Herschel and Lester. When at last he gave up, he got straight in his car and drove to St. Louis. I heard he'd just bought a new Cadillac and that he burnt it out trying to make the job on time. Yes, Hawkins was king until he met those crazy KC tenormen."[9]

In 1944, the Cherry Blossom became Gilmore's Chez Paree, home to Jay McShann and singer Walter Brown. The club had its own record label too, releasing Gatemouth Moore's "I Ain't Mad at You Pretty Baby."

GILMORE'S CHEZ PAREE
1822 VINE STREET AT EIGHTEENTH STREET

Chez Paree was opened in 1944 by Quincy and Alberta Gilmore. Quincy was also the owner of the National Negro Detective Agency and a public relations man for the Negro Baseball League's Kansas City Monarchs.

In the early 1920s, the venue had been a silent movie theater, the Eblon, where a young Bill (not yet Count) Basie played organ, accompanying the films. Ten years later, it became the Cherry Blossom nightclub. In his autobiography *Good Morning Blues*, Basie recalled playing there as part of Bennie Moten's band: "It was designed to look like an Oriental spot. All of the decorations were Japanese, including a Buddha on the stage, and the waitresses wore costumes that made them look like they were Japanese. That was about as far as it went. You couldn't get any Japanese meals in there or anything like that."[7] Eventually Basie took over the Moten band, and the group became Count Basie and His Cherry Blossom Orchestra. The club was the site of a famous "Battle of the Saxes." Basie wrote about this too: "[Saxophonists] Herschel [Evans] and Ben Webster and Lester [Young] and a few others were up there jamming, and [Coleman] Hawkins came by and decided to get his horn. Somebody kept asking him to play, so he finally went across the street to the hotel, and . . . he came back in with his horn. . . . All those other saxophone players were up there calling for their favorite tunes, and then Hawk went up there, and he knew all of the tunes, and he started calling for all of those

TOOTIE'S
NEW MAYFAIR
40 HIGHWAY AND CITY LIMITS

After the arrest of corrupt Kansas City boss Tom Pendergast, club owner Tootie Clarkin moved his Mayfair Club beyond the county line, hoping to avoid trouble from police. Author Chuck Haddix described it in *Bird* as "a roomy, stucco building with large, painted-over front windows [that] served steaks, fried chicken, hamburgers, and other home-style favorites."[10] The club had live music from nine o'clock at night until four o'clock in the morning, booking name acts including Earl Hines, Sonny Stitt, and Kansas City's own Charlie Parker.

← LEFT A newspaper advertisement for Tootie's New Mayfair, 1951.

At the turn of the twentieth century, St. Louis was a nexus for ragtime pianists, most notably Scott Joplin, the "King of Ragtime," who moved to the city in 1901. In 1914, "Father of the Blues" W. C. Handy published his song "St. Louis Blues," a jazz and blues standard, reportedly written as Handy sat on the city's riverfront.

While the city had a long history of racial segregation, after-hours clubs like the Barrel and the Chauffer's Club had integrated jam sessions as early as the 1920s. During World War II, the fully integrated Club Riviera opened, and after the war ended, the city's jazz scene matured, centered on DeBaliviere Avenue and, during the 1950s, the Gaslight Square entertainment district.

Trumpeters Clark Terry and Miles Davis came of age in St. Louis. Jazz historian Dennis C. Owsley noted, "The sound of a St. Louis trumpet player is unmistakable," adding that "a trumpet player in St. Louis has the vocal inflections of the Mississippi Delta blues laid over the German brass [band's] singing tone."[1]

Memories of . . .

CLUB PLANTATION

3617 Delmar Boulevard, Saint Louis

⇆ OPPOSITE **Club Plantation souvenir photograph and photo folder (*left*), date unknown.**

CLUB PLANTATION

3617 DELMAR BOULEVARD

Gangster Tony Scarpelli opened the Plantation in 1931, later moving it to a former roller-skating rink down the street. Like the Cotton Club, the Plantation offered African American entertainment to, as its bigoted advertising proclaimed, "Strictly White Patronage Only." As liquor laws required taverns to close at one o'clock in the morning, the club devised a work-around, offering "setups" of soft drinks and glasses, with customers bringing their own libations.

The house band, the Jeter-Pillars Orchestra, featured at various times trumpeter Harry "Sweets" Edison and Clark Terry, who recalled that "all the acts from Nat King Cole to Ella Fitzgerald, Sarah Vaughan, the Nicholas Brothers—all acts came to the Club Plantation because it was a very, very popular place. They brought their music and we would play their music better than anybody ever played it."[2]

In his memoir *To Be, or Not . . . to Bop*, Dizzy Gillespie recalled, "The Plantation Club in St. Louis was a white club. They fired Billy Eckstine's band because we came in through the front door, and they wanted us to come through the back. We just walked right in with our horns, in front. And the gangsters—St. Louis was a stronghold of gangsterism—said, 'Them guys got to go.' . . . We went over to work at another place."[3]

The Plantation closed sometime during the 1950s.

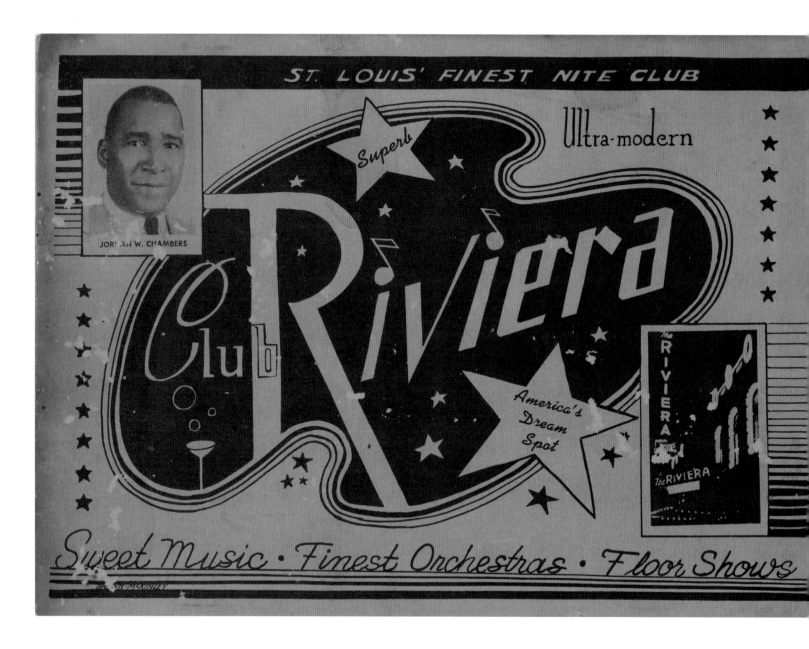

↰ OPPOSITE **Club Riviera** photo folder and souvenir photograph (*right*), date unknown.

CLUB RIVIERA

4460 DELMAR BOULEVARD

In 1944, mortician and civic leader Jordan Chambers opened the Riviera as an integrated alternative to the Club Plantation. The Gaslight Square venue, which advertised "everyone welcome," first presented a mixed band during an October 1945 jam session, with members of the Lionel Hampton, Cootie Williams, and Jack Teagarden bands playing together.

In 1947, a near riot occurred when the Riviera presented a free concert featuring Cab Calloway, Dinah Washington, Cootie Williams, and Frankie Laine. Other acts who headlined the club included Illinois Jacquet, Miles Davis, the Billy Eckstine Orchestra (with Charlie Parker and Dizzy Gillespie), Lucky Millinder and His Orchestra, and white bands led by Woody Herman and Georgie Auld.

A Conversation with

DAN MORGENSTERN

Jazz author, archivist, historian, and educator Dan Morgenstern was born in 1929 in Munich, Germany. Raised in Vienna and Copenhagen, Morgenstern moved to the United States in 1947 and almost immediately became immersed in jazz.

Beginning in 1958, Morgenstern began writing about jazz for publications including *Metronome*, *Jazz Journal*, *Jazz*, the *New York Post*, the *Chicago Sun-Times*, and *DownBeat*, where he was chief editor from 1967 to 1973.

From 1976 until 2012, Morgenstern was director of Rutgers University's Institute of Jazz Studies, teaching and overseeing the world's largest collection of jazz recordings, documents, and memorabilia. Morgenstern has also taught at New York University, Johns Hopkins University, Brooklyn College, and the Schweitzer Institute of Music in Idaho.

Both of Morgenstern's books, *Jazz People* (1976) and *Living with Jazz* (2004), won the American Society of Composers, Authors, and Publishers' Deems Taylor Award, and Morgenstern has won a record-setting eight Best Album Notes Grammy Awards.

In 2007, *DownBeat* honored Morgenstern with its Lifetime Achievement Award, the Recording Academy honored him with a Legacy Award, and the National Endowment for the Arts awarded him the A. B. Spellman NEA Jazz Masters Fellowship for Jazz Advocacy.

Dan Morgenstern (DM): I'm amazed at the things you sent—that you were able to find these. I remember the days when you went to a nightclub and there was a cameraperson, usually a girl, and they would take photos of you with your party. And then you'd get them in a folder. I don't know where you found these things.

Jeff Gold (JG): I bought them, most of them from one collection.

DM: Well, that makes sense, because when I was still active at the Institute of Jazz Studies, there was a guy who came to us who had a lot of stuff; he went around Harlem and other Black neighborhoods and rang doorbells and asked people if they had anything. [*Laughs.*]

JG: That's a smart way to do it! I'm interested in looking at the phenomenon of jazz fans and clubs through the lens of these photographs. I'm trying to gather different perspectives. I wanted to speak to you as a jazz historian who was actually there at the time. You grew up in Europe and immigrated to New York in 1947, when you were seventeen?

DM: Right.

JG: When you were around nine, in 1938, your mom took you to see Fats Waller. I was wondering if you saw other jazz performances before you came to the United States.

DM: Well, this was just before World War II broke out in Europe. I did see Fats, and then there was the Hot Club of France with Django [Reinhardt], which was fun. And not to sound as if I was very precocious, but I remember Django best because he was the heart of it. And he moved a lot. He moved, so he was adventurous. And then the Mills Brothers. And then the war broke out and that was the end of, you know, American groups. But there was a lot of jazz in Denmark—like in other European countries that were occupied by the Nazis, jazz became very popular. And Django is a case in point—he rose to be a star in France after the Germans came in. Because it represented everything that was the opposite of what they were about.

JG: When you got to the United States, you've said your first night in New York, you found Symphony Sid playing on the radio, I think from the Royal Roost.

MONTE KAY
— Presents —
SYMPHONY SID'S
'BOP' CONCERT

Sunday Afternoon, October 10, 1948 4-8 p.m.

CHANO POZO
(MONTECA)

Tadd Dameron   **Fats Navarro**
(*The* SQUIRREL)

Dexter Gordon   **Allen Eagers**
TENOR SAX

Max Roach   **Art Blakey**
The ,Gonest' on DRUMS

Al Haig   **Milt Jackson**
PIANO   VIBES

James Moody   **Cecil Payne**
Dizzy's TENOR & BARITONE SAX STARS

Nelson Boyd   **Tommy Potter**
Two Great BASSISTS

ADMISSION $1.50   No minimum or cabaret tax

THE HOUSE THAT BOP BUILT

Royal Roost
1580 Broadway, Cor. 47th St., Opp. Strand Theatre

↑ ABOVE **Handbill for Royal Roost *Bop Concert*, 1948.**

DM: Well, actually no, it wasn't live. He was in the studio. But I was looking for—I thought there would be jazz all over the radio. [*Laughs.*] And this was before FM, we're still talking AM only, but you know, I went through the dial and I couldn't find anything. Finally, I caught onto Symphony Sid, and it was hard for me to understand him. [*Laughs.*] You're probably too young to have experienced him, but he was very slangy.

JG: Can you tell me what those shows were like? Jazz on the radio and Symphony Sid and what role they played in promoting jazz in the clubs?

DM: We're talking about spring, early summer of '47 when I came to the U.S. Bebop was still something that wasn't widely accepted, commercially speaking. Sid was kind of unique because he was about the only guy who played it on the air. He cast himself in the role of a missionary, so to speak. Sid's real name was Sid Torin. He was important and doing what he could to promote what he called "the modern sound." People called in and made requests, but if somebody requested Louis Armstrong or Benny Goodman, he'd say, "We only play the modern sound!" [*Laughs.*]

But in retrospect, you learn things. Actually, he was getting some of what they later called payola [a payment to play a particular record], and it wasn't very big, you know. But there were record labels that were recording modern jazz, and they'd give him a little taste. But it was sincere on his part. He had started out in radio [with] something called *After School Swing Session* at a small station, I forget which one, it was before my time. Anyway, he had a late-afternoon show. Aimed at teenagers, I guess. And that was still in the swing era. John Hammond told me that when he first met Symphony Sid, Sid was working in a record store that handled used records. That was pretty much in the era of 78s; you would go to junk shops and comb things to see what you could find. But he said that Sid, whenever he found anything rare like Paramount label, he would call John. Sid didn't start out with bebop.

And there was other jazz on the radio, but it was not like Symphony Sid. Ted Husing was a guy who really was a professional announcer on a fairly regular station, and he had a music show. He was a jazz fan, so he squeezed in as much jazz as he could. And, of course, there had been Martin Block—he was a famous disc jockey; he had the *Make-Believe Ballroom*. He was also a big jazz fan and he would have live music in the studio, I guess it was once a week, a [show] called "Saturday Night in Harlem." He would play Black bands for an hour or so.

Anyway, when I caught Symphony Sid, it was like—finally. I found some jazz there. And Sid was also on the scene as live emcee at Birdland and originally at the Royal Roost, which was kind of a predecessor of Birdland, owned by the same people.

JG: Were those radio shows—as well as playing and promoting the records—promoting the live appearances in clubs?

DM: Sure. When Sid was just on the verge there in '47, he moved to WJZ, which was part of ABC. WJZ was their main New York station. He would be on late at night, and he would broadcast from Birdland. He was in a cubicle there. And he would also emcee there; he played records, but live music was going on too.

JG: What was it like for you as a recent immigrant listening to these shows? Did it stoke your imagination? Get you wanting to go to these clubs?

DM: Sure. That's the first thing I wanted to do when I came to New York. And I said that in Ken Burns's [documentary film] *Jazz*—most people want to see the Empire State Building when they come to New York. I said I wanted to see Fifty-Second Street. That was true. I was enough of a jazz fan to have heard about Fifty-Second Street, and that's what I wanted. I wasn't quite of legal age to go to a bar, a place where they sold liquor. But I was very close to eighteen so I could get away with it. So that's what I started to do. But I would say my parents were not too happy about my hanging out at night. The first place I went to was Jimmy Ryan's on Fifty-Second Street.

JG: And that was more of a traditional scene?

DM: Well, to an extent. But it wasn't like what we called Dixieland. Sidney Bechet worked there a lot, and I would call it mainstream. The Dixieland tradition—although he hated the word "Dixieland"—[was] at

Eddie Condon's in the Village. And Nick's. Eddie did not want labels on his music. That's why when he wrote his autobiography, the title was *We Called It Music*. He didn't want labels.

JG: How long did it take you to actually get to Fifty-Second Street? And what was it like when you got there in terms of your expectations?

DM: It didn't take very long. I lived in Denmark and Sweden before I came here, and over there, you start English in sixth grade. English is almost like a second language in a small country like that. My English was pretty good and I wasn't worried about going out by myself. It was also a question of money, which I didn't have. You could sneak into a club and there wasn't usually a door charge, but there was a minimum at tables. But you could stay at the bar and there was generally no minimum there; you could buy a beer and nurse it.

What surprised me was how easy it was in the clubs to access the musicians. Of course, they were sitting ducks, or when they went outside for a break when the weather was nice. They would be there and people wanted to talk to them. I became somebody who got up the nerve to talk to musicians. Some were really proselytizers. One was Art Hodes, a piano player originally from Chicago who was very active in New York. And another was Wilbur de Paris, who was trying to establish a jazz society.

They were kind of proselytizing for jazz, so if they saw a young person who was interested, they were perfectly willing to chat with you and all that. So I became acclimated pretty quickly. I was also surprised at how close you could get to the musicians. In the clubs, it's an intimate situation. None of the clubs were huge, not until the Metropole. I mean, Birdland was a little bigger than most, and then the Metropole had that huge long bar. So that was hardly an intimate place. But most of the clubs were small, especially on Fifty-Second Street. They were in brownstones or other buildings that had been residential buildings. People still lived above the clubs. It was hard to shoehorn a big band into some of these places.

JG: Would you go, as I've read people did, from club to club during a night?

DM: No, I didn't really do that because I couldn't afford it. [*Laughs.*] You'd try to stay in one club and, like I said, nurse a beer. That was something that I was taught by musicians. They told me not to order a drink because I'd get a transparent . . . translucent glass. Get beer. The bottle is opaque, so the bartender can't tell how much you've had.

Then another trick was that when you order your first drink, leave a tip. And then the bartenders would leave you alone. So those are little things that you learn. But I couldn't move from club to club, no. That would cost me more than a week's salary. But when you hear about prices then—it's hard for people to realize how much a dollar was. Compared to at least fifteen dollars today. [*Laughs.*]

Fifty-Second was very interesting and there was still a lot of music going on. It was all on one block, except for the Hickory House, which was by itself on another block. That was the only Fifty-Second Street club to have food, by the way, and it was very good. But otherwise, all the jazz joints were in one block there.

JG: Were the audiences pretty much integrated by that time?

DM: That's an interesting question. I was very much aware of what the problem was with race relations. Because as someone Jewish who went through the Nazi thing in Europe, and as somebody who was interested in jazz and in America, this was something I became aware of early on. And I had read a lot of stuff. There was a Swedish sociologist named Gunnar Myrdal who wrote a big fat book called *An American Dilemma*, which was about race relations, about the Black situation. I read that even before I came here. And I thought that New York would be a place where you wouldn't encounter prejudice, but that was far from right.

A little later on when I made Black friends, sometimes when we felt like it, if we were a little bit loaded or something, we would go to a place where we knew that we would not be welcome. [These places] had to be careful about that because [discrimination] was against the law, of course, too. But they would say, "We don't have room," "We're all full," or whatever. So we would say something like, "Well, there are a lot of tables . . ."—just to try to put them through the wringer a little bit. But it was amazing. I mean even in the Times Square area, there was a chain of restaurants called Toffenetti's. They were, you know, lily-white.

So in the clubs, yes [they were integrated], since the musicians were predominantly Black. And the bands were mixed, so it wasn't anything. But once in a while you got the feeling that some of the service personnel—that there might be a waiter who clearly was giving you somewhat of a cold shoulder, if you were in a mixed bunch.

I met a girl . . . she was the first one to take me to Harlem and to the Apollo. And I was really lucky that my first time at the Apollo was Dizzy's big band, with Chano Pozo, so it was tremendous. This girl had a girlfriend, who was married to a Black guy who was not a jazz musician, but he was a musician. And he had ambitions to become a classical—a serious composer. He was a pianist and once in a while he would take a jazz gig, but he wasn't very good at it. But he had a circle of friends, and that's how I got into becoming friends with Black people. That was even before I befriended musicians, but that was a very important part of my early life in this country.

JG: When I talked to Quincy Jones and Sonny Rollins, who were both starting to play clubs at about that same time, they said Fifty-Second Street was really an oasis from racism for them. From your perspective, out in the audience, was the race mixing pretty fluid in Fifty-Second Street?

DM: Yes . . . pretty much so, yes. Yes. It was exceptional. It was kind of an oasis. Because as I said before, even in midtown Manhattan there were places who wouldn't serve a mixed couple. Actually, if I walked down the streets, say, with an interracial couple—a white girl, a Black man, and a white man—people would turn around and look. They would fall over their own feet. Later on when I was in the army, I was stationed in Georgia, at Fort Benning, and there I really got to experience and to see what that was

→ RIGHT **Unidentified jazz group in Harlem, circa 1930s.**

like. Even the bit of prejudice that you encountered in New York was miles apart from that. It did exist. But on Fifty-Second Street, no. I mean everything was cool there.

JG: I know you were going up to Harlem to see music and down to the Village too—how did the clubs, the venues, and the audiences differ from Fifty-Second Street?

DM: Well, the difference with Harlem was that in Harlem, the clubs and the music were part of the social fabric. In other words, the club would be in a neighborhood and the people who came—not exclusively, but much of the clientele—would be local. Fifty-Second Street was not a residential street then. There were a few people who still lived there, but most of it was business. And that whole neighborhood right there in midtown Manhattan was not much of a residential area. The people who came to Fifty-Second Street came from all over the place. They would come not only from all the corners of New York City but also from out of town, even from Europe—there were a lot of Europeans that came to Fifty-Second. And in Harlem, the clubs were populated by people who lived in the community. There was a different feel to it.

JG: In the 1920s and 1930s, there had been a lot of people from downtown coming uptown to see African American performers. Was that still happening when you got there?

DM: The people who came to Harlem were musicians and music fans. There wasn't a tourist element, which would have existed at the time with the Cotton Club, which, incidentally, had moved downtown. And the downtown Cotton Club wasn't even around anymore when I started going out.

But that was a whole different thing. You know, we're talking 1920s, so of course neither of us were around then. No, but going to Harlem . . . Remember "The Lady Is a Tramp" . . . "Won't go to Harlem, in ermines and pearls"?

My father was friends with Al Hirschfeld, the great cartoonist. Al was a big jazz fan. He had done a Harlem book, actually, in the mid-1930s. He told me a few things about what it was like in the 1920s. One thing was that the people

who went to Harlem in those days were people who wanted to dance. Jazz is great dance music. A place like the Savoy Ballroom was pretty well integrated. A lot of dancers would come there from other boroughs. Later on, I met a guy from the Bronx who told me that he used to go to the Savoy, for dancing.

And there were places, I guess, when you came to Harlem, where you would encounter reverse prejudice [*laughs*], where white people were not particularly welcome. But by and large, I had very little experience of that nature.

JG: What were the clubs like in the Village?

DM: In the Village there were two major clubs: Condon's and Nick's. Condon's had a very nice atmosphere, because Eddie was a great guy. And it was frequented by John Steinbeck, who was a big jazz fan. He was there a lot. And other literary people and theater people and so on. And it had Eddie's name and he had started out in New York, on Fifty-Second Street, so he had a following. And then there was Nick's, which was owned by Nick Rongetti, a lawyer who was an amateur pianist and jazz fan. Nick's was different—I didn't like Nick's much. It was more expensive and it specialized in steaks. It was the home of sizzling steaks. They would bring the steak for the table, it would be on a platter with a lid on top. And then they would unveil the steak and it would bring out all the smell. I remember you could stand outside Nick's on the side, not at the main entrance, but on Seventh Avenue outside. And you could hear the music out in the street. The same was true on Fifty-Second. If you were poor you could listen to music out on the street. But with Nick's you could also smell that steak, which was way above anything I could afford!

Eddie, before he opened his place, worked a lot at Nick's. But the music at Nick's by then . . . well, Nick's still had some good music, but they also had what you would call Dixieland with a capital *D*. During my early years, Nick passed away and his wife took over. She was really musically prejudiced. And she only liked really bad Dixieland.

And there were other places in the Village. There was the famous Village Vanguard, which is still there. There was a place that I didn't experience, called the Pied Piper, which was notable for having great stride pianist James P. Johnson who worked there, Willie "the Lion" Smith. . . . But eventually it became the Café Bohemia in the bebop era—the same location, a little later. They had Miles Davis before he became a really big star.

One other place, and it's still there physically, was the Riviera, an Italian restaurant that had a room downstairs. For quite a while in the late 1940s and early 1950s, they had a solo pianist, and musicians used to come to sit in. The place encouraged that. Willie the Lion worked there for quite a while. Art Hodes was there for a minute. Hot Lips Page came and sang the blues for about half an hour. Roy Eldridge, the ubiquitous [clarinetist] Sol Yaged, [trumpeter] Jonah Jones—they all came. It was an intimate place and musicians liked to sit in there, because it was comfortable and small and the people who came to listen were pretty hip.

And there was Café Society, which was very important, especially in the 1930s. That's where Billie Holiday introduced "Strange Fruit." Barney Josephson, who owned the place, was someone who you would call an activist in today's language.

JG: I know Charlie Parker played there.

DM: Not much. I actually saw Bird at the second Café Society after the first one closed, I think due to the fact that they lost their lease or the place was going to be torn down, so they moved to a much less appealing physical location in the Village. Not that it was run-down or anything, it just wasn't as intimate and as nice as [the original] Café Society, which was downstairs and had a very nice feel to it. But Barney was really a pioneer. He opened in the 1930s, a time when Black people were not welcome in the Village. And he made sure that they knew that they would be welcome at Café Society. That was important to him. And most of the attractions there were indeed Black.

JG: As you had more experience and began seeing more acts, presumably your confidence built up. Could you go up to people like Bird and Lester Young and Basie? And were they receptive?

DM: Yeah, that's what I said before. I was amazed at how approachable musicians were. Because in a way they were trapped in the clubs. Some of the clubs were not very big. So yes. I was young and I was just a fan and I got to know some musicians. The young musicians, who were not established. But it was easy to exchange a few words with the famous musicians in a club setting. They'd go out for a smoke outside and you could encounter them on the sidewalk. By and by, I got to know some people who got me inside, so to speak. I got friendly with people and I got to meet a lot of—you mentioned a few names, yes. It was not hard if you were clearly interested. And in my favor too was the fact that I had come from Europe and I was somebody who would be . . .

JG: Exotic?

DM: No, no. Not that. But African Americans would be slightly . . . To place white people was sometimes difficult. I mean [white people] might be very nice and very friendly, but they could really harbor some prejudice. It would come out in certain situations, particularly if it was a Black guy with a white woman—that would be something that would trigger that kind of thing. But if you were European, you wouldn't be suspected of being that way. It created some openings. And I was very lucky. I very rapidly got to know, became friendly with, a little guy who played trumpet, who never made any records or anything. He never got famous, but he knew everybody and all the musicians liked him. He played a lot of jam sessions and things. And I got friendly with him—actually, we met on Fifty-Second Street, but not in a club. But on a corner, there was a chain called Nedick's. They had hot dogs. The famous thing was you could get an orange drink and a hot dog for fifteen cents. [*Laughs.*]

JG: Those were the days.

DM: Yeah. His name was Nat Lorber. I met Nat at Nedick's on Fifty-Second Street. And we got friendly. He was a big Louis Armstrong fan and he knew this girl who was taking care of Louis's fan mail, of which there was a lot. And eventually, before too long, there I was . . . in Louis's dressing room at the Roxy Theatre, which was just—it was enormous. It was the biggest movie theater in New York before they tore it down. And like all first-run movie theaters, they had stage shows. That was a great deal in those days. If you came early, for the first show—it was around 12:30 or so in the afternoon—you got in for thirty-five cents. You could stay as long as you wanted. [*Laughs.*] If you—if you wanted to see the movie over again, you could catch two shows. That's where I met Louis, at the Roxy. This would have been 1948, '49? Quite a bit later on, in 1965, I did a big interview with him for *DownBeat*, so you know I did have the good fortune of getting to know Louis . . .

That was one example. . . . Nat was very much at home uptown, because he was a big jam session guy, and that's where these things were happening.

JG: And everybody up there was friendly to you? You didn't have any problems?

DM: Well, I wasn't a musician. But I was with musicians, and I was obviously there for the music. The funny thing is there was a magazine called *Vanity Fair* . . .

At the Institute of Jazz Studies, where I was for almost four decades, Marshall Stearns, who founded it, had a great book collection. There were a couple of great volumes that [*Vanity Fair*] put out, the *Guide to New York*, in the late 1920s, early 1930s. There was a section on Harlem and it said there in the introduction, it's a good idea, if you go to Harlem, to go as a couple, because then you won't be . . . I mean, not in these exact words, but you won't be suspected of being a white person who comes to Harlem in order to find somebody to have sex with. You know? So that was pretty hip for a publication like that. [*Laughs.*]

But it was true—it was true even in my time. But if you were with musicians and you went. . . . I never encountered any cold shoulder or anything like that. It was very warm in Harlem. Like I said, jazz was more part of the social fabric than it was downtown. People would come in, people would know each other. There were regulars—I mean, you had regulars too, on Fifty-Second Street. But it's different.

I remember there was a place called the L Bar, which actually was on the outskirts of Harlem, up on Broadway around 136th Street or something. Pretty far west. This was a joint that you wouldn't read about in jazz magazines, although I did a little Caught in the Act piece on it later on when I was at *Metronome*. But it was a neighborhood joint. They had a very good organ player named Skip Hall who made some records. Organs were popular in Harlem. A good thing in a small club, you know, where you couldn't book a lot of larger bands. The organ had a sound that really filled up the place. And my friend Nat had a gig there for a while. And I got to know some of the people. One really big guy used to come in on a weekend, he was a longshoreman, and he would get happy after a while, buy everybody a drink. There was a Cootie Williams record called "House of Joy"—that was his favorite and he used to refer to himself as House of Joy. This was the kind of thing that wouldn't happen down on Fifty-Second Street. [*Laughs.*]

JG: You came to the U.S. as bebop was starting to take hold a bit. There's been a lot written about the back and forth between the "moldy figs," who only wanted to hear traditional jazz and swing, and bebop fans. I was wondering, did this exist in the clubs and among fans, or was it more a construct of people writing about jazz?

DM: This was more something that the critics indulged in than the musicians or even the fans. There were some people who only liked a certain kind of music, so somebody who was a patron of Nick's would not come up to Fifty-Second Street to find Charlie Parker and Dizzy Gillespie. But among the musicians, there wasn't any hostility like that. Musicians were musicians. They got along with each other. You played different styles, but you played music for a living. You didn't play it to make a statement in terms of politics or whatever. And you moved around. There were guys who might be considered beboppers, but if they got a job—you know everybody needs to work!—if they got a job playing with a swing group, or even some so-called Dixieland, that's just how it was.

Let me give you an example. This place, the Metropole, was an amazing place because it had this mile-long bar that went all through the length of the room. And it was a big room, where the band was above the bar on a so-called bandstand, which [was only deep enough to] accommodate one musician. They were lined up in a row like . . . at a police inquiry. [*Laughs.*] There was a piano, and you could put a set of drums there. But the fortunate thing was that there were mirrors on the wall opposite the bandstand, which was on an elevation above the bar, so the musicians could see each other. They had eye contact. Otherwise, they would've been lined up next to each other—and a musician would've only been able to see the guy who's right next to him to exchange glances or something.

The Metropole had music almost around the clock. They would have a trio in the afternoon. And then at night they would have two bands alternating. They were great bands. You know, you'd get Coleman Hawkins and Roy Eldridge. You'd get—Red Allen had the regular house band. J. C. Higginbotham, [clarinetist] Buster Bailey, Cozy Cole—all in one band! And it was wonderful if you liked what I would call mainstream jazz.

For instance, there was also a New Orleans clarinetist named Tony Parenti. Tony was somebody whose main thing was ragtime and New Orleans jazz. And when things changed and the big bands went downhill for economic reasons, and musicians who were really swing players were suddenly on the market and looking for work, some of the work would be in clubs that featured traditional jazz. And Tony would teach them. Buck Clayton told me that Tony taught him all these traditional standards like "Muskrat Ramble" and "Original Dixieland One-Step" and "Jazz Me Blues." Some of the standards were part of the general swing tradition, but you had to learn them.

I bring this up because Charlie Shavers—who for years was featured with Tommy Dorsey, one of the Black musicians who was featured in a white band—was a fixture at the Metropole. The band personnel kept changing, but on this particular occasion, the rest of the band was Tony Parenti on clarinet and I forget who the trombone player was. But who did Charlie send as a sub? He sent a guy he had first met in a band that had played together in Philadelphia around 1935, and that was none other than Dizzy Gillespie!

JG: There you go! [*Laughs.*]

DM: I lucked out, I was there that night. Diz came in and played with—you know they're musicians. Musicians were musicians. They didn't care about all this nonsense. There was a thing where bebop, when it first established itself, where it did run into some musical prejudice on the part of established musicians. That did happen. There were guys who said, "Oh, what is that? You can't dance to it! It's too fast. It's too this . . . ," but most guys with really good ears, they knew better. Coleman Hawkins was the first guy to hire Thelonious Monk for a regular job outside of Minton's—a small place in Harlem—and brought him to Fifty-Second Street and recorded him for the first time.

JG: And it seems like the musicians all hung out together and drank together, and when they were offstage, nobody had a problem.

DM: Sure, nobody had a problem. You know, people would come to listen to each other. Guys would come and sit in. There was a lot of sitting in. Which was great because you would go to hear somebody and then, oh, who would walk in? Maybe Roy Eldridge, who was off that night. Hot Lips Page was a great sitter-in—sometimes because he was out of work. [*Laughs.*] But you never knew what was going to happen. To get back to the thing about moldy figs and beboppers: this was much more a critical warfare, and there were critics who instigated this kind of thing, but it became almost like a form of political warfare.

JG: I was thinking it was almost like the newspaper wars, where people were all trying to gin up circulation.

DM: Yeah, but sometimes it would be fun because there were staged battles of bands. There was a guy named Rudi Blesh who actually was the veteran. I checked it out, and he was the oldest jazz critic who was still born in the nineteenth century. And he was a stone traditionalist. He wrote this book, *Shining Trumpets*. He was even prejudiced against swing, you know. And bebop, which wasn't around. . . . Rudi was actually a very nice man, but he was very deeply entrenched in traditional stuff.

They had this little battle of the bands. He put together a traditional band, and the other band, that bebop band, was Dizzy, Charlie Parker, Lennie Tristano, Max Roach. And this was done on the radio, so it exists on record, although it's hard to find. The beboppers won hands down, because that was an all-star band—my god, you couldn't do much better than that. Both bands played "Tiger Rag," and the "Tiger Rag" played by the beboppers was fantastic.

But there were times when clubs wouldn't hire one kind of musician because their customers expected a certain kind of music.

JG: I wanted to ask about the in-house photographers at clubs and whether that was something that you or your friends paid attention to, or whether it was more for people on dates.

DM: Yeah, it was very much for people on dates. And for foreigners—people from Europe or somewhere else. And also there were some family gatherings and sometimes there would be people on their honeymoon. Stuff like that. I have, if I could find them, some photos from Jimmy Ryan's with friends. This was a common thing. I made good use once or twice of the camera girl at the Metropole, because people would come in there. One time Benny Goodman, who never played there, came in, mainly to see his old friend Buster Bailey because, in Chicago, the two of them had the same teacher, a guy from the Chicago Symphony.

So Benny came in to see Buster, and they sat together in a little booth. And there was a camera girl there, so I enlisted her to take a picture of the two of them, which was cute. I was writing for a British magazine. The photo was published, and I got an extra copy of the magazine for her, and she was thrilled! She had a photo published! And I made sure that the editor put her name in there. I'm sure I'm not the only one who did something like that. It was a good thing. That was a little bit of a social thing that added to the atmosphere.

Oh, I want to tell you about this place in Harlem, the Celebrity Club. You've probably heard of—

JG: Yes, I've got some pictures from it, and Sonny Rollins told me a funny story about it.

DM: Well, this was a little different, because they were a place mostly renting out for parties, like after a wedding, for birthdays, and so on. That was their real stock and trade. There was always some kind of group there. But you could walk in off the street too, if they had room for you. Buddy Tate had a band there for years. It was eight or nine pieces, a really good band, and they had a long gig there. And it was nice, you would have all these parties coming in, it was like . . .

JG: I've got a picture of the Harriet Tubman Social Club there.

DM: That's perfect, right in keeping with it. You could bring your own booze there, then you've got setups. I guess they didn't have a liquor license or they didn't want to have one. So you brought a bottle and cups.

There was the same thing downtown, in what originally was a very Jewish neighborhood, the Lower East Side. You had these two places: the Stuyvesant Casino and the Central Plaza. They were wonderful for somebody like me because they had these weekend sessions. Bob Maltz ran the Stuyvesant, and Jack Crystal, who was [record producer] Milt Gabler's [brother-]in-law, ran things at the Central Plaza. And you would have a hard time deciding which one to go to because there were great bands in both places. You would bring your own bottle. The only thing they sold in the way of alcohol was beer—they had big pitchers of beer. And you could dance at the Central Plaza. I don't think there was dancing at the Stuyvesant. Maybe, maybe there was. They were catering halls, and they were available during Shabbos. [*Laughs.*] And they were empty in a Jewish neighborhood, so people could rent them out and have shows on Saturday nights.

JG: I've got a lot of postcards for those shows, and it seems like every week they had a different lineup and lots of really interesting people.

DM: I still have some of those cards too. You got a card every week with the lineup. Oh, it was fabulous, because—this was like I said before—when the big bands folded, there were a lot of musicians who were at liberty, more or less, who were available. And Bob Maltz especially had a tremendous

↑ ABOVE **Celebrity Club souvenir photograph of the Harriet Tubman Social Club, late 1940s.**

knowledge of older musicians who were still active. He would bring in really legendary figures.

JG: As you began to write about music professionally, I'm assuming you traveled to other places. There were very vital jazz scenes in Chicago, Los Angeles, and Detroit. What were the clubs like and the scenes like there, compared to New York?

DM: I would go to L.A. maybe once a year for some meeting with the Recording Academy, so I got to know some of the clubs there. But in Los Angeles, you know, to me, it's not a city. It's so damned spread out—it doesn't really have a core. There's one section where there are a bunch of skyscrapers and stuff, but . . . if you want to go hear some jazz, you have to drive fifty miles to get there. Well, there was Shelly's Manne-Hole—I was there a couple of times. There was the Lighthouse, which was out at the beach. And there was one place that I—was it Keystone Korner?

JG: That's in San Francisco.

DM: Yeah, that's right. Well, San Francisco's entirely different. That's a wonderful city, and it's a real city. [*Laughs.*] It's not like L.A. But I wasn't there very often.

JG: How about Chicago?

DM: I lived in Chicago when I was editor of *DownBeat* for close to four years. I got there in '67 and stayed until about 1971. Chicago is entirely different from New York, insofar as it had this blues component. It was a big blues city. When there was this big migration of African Americans from the South to the North, especially during World War I, when there was work, Chicago got a big influx of southern Black people.

JG: In World War II too.

DM: And they brought with them the blues. And Harlem you couldn't find—I mean forget it, there were no blues places in Harlem. But you could get a jazz band playing blues changes, you know, playing the "St. Louis Blues" or something like that. But even traditionally, Ma Rainey bombed in

Harlem, big as she was in the 1920s, because there never was an audience for the blues. In Chicago, there was this wonderful blues thing. . . . Muddy Waters was there, Howlin' Wolf. It was a whole different experience. On the South Side there's also jazz, of course, and there were some very nice clubs. Again, this was more, I think—compared to Harlem—a bit more down-home. There was of course University of Chicago—UC is very near there, so you also got an influx of jazz fan college kids. And then there was the Association for the Advancement of Creative Musicians, which happened during my stay in Chicago. That was really the avant-garde—

JG: The Art Ensemble of Chicago and those musicians.

DM: Yeah, I experienced that, that was interesting, you know—

JG: Was the Club DeLisa gone by the time you got there?

DM: I think the DeLisa was gone. That's a legendary name. The Plugged Nickel was the main club outside—that wasn't on the South Side, but that was near Rush Street, in the center of the city. Rush Street was just like a couple of long blocks, but there were a lot of clubs there and restaurants, bars, and so on. The Plugged Nickel was a pretty fancy club, you could compare it to Birdland or something like that. When Miles played in Chicago, that's where he played. The other places, they were usually small holes-in-the-wall.

JG: I'd like to go back to New York and talk about one more famous, even infamous, club—the Cotton Club. It was open in Harlem from 1923 to 1935 and then again briefly in midtown from 1936 to 1940. Though it had closed by the time you came to the United States, and predates the era covered in this book, I think it's a fascinating case. I'm interested in your thoughts on it, as a club that hired exclusively African American performers but was segregated and only allowed white patrons in the audience. Evidently, they treated the top performers pretty well, and they had a regular live radio broadcast from the club that gave performers important national exposure.

DM: The only Black people who got into that Cotton Club, as far as I know, were performers. If colleagues of the people who were performing there or [if they] had some name, like if Bojangles [Bill Robinson, a tap dancer and actor, who was reported to be the highest-paid African American performer during the first half of the twentieth century] wanted to come in, you know, that would be fine. But not off the street, that's right.

JG: I was talking to Sonny Rollins about it and asking about the exposure they gave to many artists, particularly from their national radio broadcasts. And he said, "I don't give them a lot of credit for what they were doing. They did it because it was money." Whereas Jason Moran felt it was much more nuanced and that any outlet for people to play, to express themselves and reach an audience, no matter how screwed up, had some value. I wonder what your thoughts are.

DM: Well, for instance, take Duke Ellington. The Cotton Club was extremely important in Ellington's career. And as you say, it had the radio wire; that was very important too. Because that would spread [the music] out beyond your physical realm, and radio was still pretty new then. It was exciting for people to be able to listen to something from far away, whatever. And for recording, if you played the Cotton Club, you were likely to get a recording contract. There weren't too many major labels; Duke Ellington and His Cotton Club Orchestra were recording for Victor, so that's very important regardless of that policy of white audiences. It really, career-wise, did not impede any of the Black artists who appeared there. I mean it was something that may have been somewhat of a bitter pill, but it was swallowed, entirely for practical and professional reasons. The shows were great; they were outlets for people other than musicians. There were choreographers, there were dancers—you could make yourself into a star there.

This was well before my time, and forget about the movie *Cotton Club*; it was mangled. There is this beautiful short of Ellington early in the days of sound. It's from 1929. It's called *Black and Tan Fantasy*, and it shows a pretty good replica of the Cotton Club and gives you a feel for the place. The same director also made the Bessie Smith short, which is also set in a club, most of it—not of the Cotton Club variety, but another way of seeing what that was like in the 1920s.

JG: And did they generally feel like it was something worth doing for their careers?

DM: Yes. I mean, it had to be. Also, not unimportantly, it paid well. If you played the Cotton Club, you got paid very nicely. More than if you worked in some little club in a side street. The feeling that I have from talking to people who actually were there—which are mostly Ellingtonians, also some people that were in Cab Calloway's band and so on—is that it wasn't an issue, really. I mean, it was there, but it wasn't something that was the elephant in the room. It was more like the skeleton in the closet. People took pride in working there. They could sneak their friends in, I think. That was something that could be done, I'm pretty sure.

JG: That's interesting. I hadn't heard that before. Well, Dan, thanks for being so generous with your time and sharing your stories. ●

← LEFT "Stormy Weather"
sheet music, from the
22nd edition of *Cotton
Club Parade*, 1933.

PART THREE

Last Word

Town Club

Joe Morris' Plantation Club

Downbeat

Oasis Club

Club Alabam

THE WEST COAST

L O S *Angeles*

Jazz came relatively early to Los Angeles. By 1919, New Orleans innovators Kid Ory and Jelly Roll Morton—the self-proclaimed inventor of jazz (an exaggeration, but not by much)—had relocated to the city, as did Louis Armstrong in 1930. From the 1920s through the late 1940s, most of Los Angeles's jazz activity was concentrated around a short stretch of Central Avenue, referred to as the "Jazz Corridor," a straight thoroughfare that cut through the heart of South Central, the city's main African American neighborhood. The Dunbar Hotel was the Jazz Corridor's epicenter, offering luxury accommodations to Black people at a time when most L.A. hotels were segregated. Many musicians, including Billie Holiday, Cab Calloway, and Duke Ellington, made the Dunbar their home away from home when they were on the road.

Numerous clubs, dance halls, and ballrooms surrounding the Dunbar presented a mix of nationally known entertainers and local talent, including the not-yet-famous Dexter Gordon, Art Farmer, Charles Mingus, drummer Chico Hamilton, and saxophonist Art Pepper.

In the lean Depression years, swing had become increasingly popular on radio. Black audiences had already embraced the music, but the swing era broke through to the white mainstream on August 21, 1935, when Benny Goodman and his band played a three-week engagement at the Palomar Ballroom on Vermont Avenue, not far from Central Avenue. On the first night, the band began playing its regular set to an indifferent audience. The group's discouraged drummer, Gene Krupa, said to Goodman, "If we're gonna die, Benny, let's die playing our own thing,"[1] and the band cut loose with its more swinging arrangements, many by Fletcher Henderson. Goodman recalled, "To our complete amazement, half of the crowd stopped dancing and came surging around the [band] stand. . . . That was the moment that decided things for me. . . . That first big roar from the crowd was one of the sweetest sounds I ever heard in my life."[2] News of the band's triumph spread like wildfire.

Writer Donald Clarke noted, "The Swing Era had been waiting to happen, but it was Goodman and his band that touched it off. . . . [H]e credited his success to the fact that there were a large number of dancers who were not being well served."[3] Cultural critic Gerald Early observed in Ken Burns's *Jazz*, "As an antidote to the Depression, I think swing music did as much as MGM musicals to help Americans through."[4]

The Central Avenue scene reached its zenith during World War II, when West Coast defense contractors—perhaps most notably Lockheed Aircraft Corporation, one of the war's major aircraft manufacturers—hired thousands of new workers to keep their plants running twenty-four hours a day. The population of the Los Angeles area exploded, with more growth than any other metropolitan area in the United States. With the influx of new residents and an increase in workers with more spending money, the clubs became a thriving scene and stayed open longer, even

into the morning. Factory shifts ended at all hours, so for those who worked at night, some venues began offering "breakfast club" shows. Middle-class white [guests] and Hollywood stars like Humphrey Bogart and Orson Welles came to the Jazz Corridor to take in the sounds.

When the war ended the defense plants wound down—in many cases, African Americans were the first to lose their jobs—and the economic boom was soon over. In 1948, when the Supreme Court struck down the restrictive racial covenants that kept African Americans from living where they wanted to, some began moving away from the Central Avenue area.

But as the Central Avenue–area jazz scene began to wane, new clubs opened on and around Western Avenue, in Hollywood, and about twenty miles south, in Hermosa Beach, where the Lighthouse became an important venue for the emerging West Coast "cool jazz" scene. Miles Davis and Gil Evans's *Birth of the Cool* recordings had kicked off the cool jazz movement, with a softer, mellower sound. While bop was impenetrable to some, Davis's new sound was ambitious but accessible.

The end of the war saw hundreds of thousands moving west in search of new opportunity, and that included a number of musicians, significantly *Birth of the Cool* saxophonist Gerry Mulligan. Film and television studios needed musicians, and as jazz writer Ted Gioia noted, "For the first time in West?—and many opted for the Pacific Coast. As I heard one musician opine 'I figured I could starve or freeze in New York, but in L.A., I'd only starve.'"[5]

West Coast jazz, sometimes described as a subgenre of the cool movement, thrived in 1950s Los Angeles, propelled by Mulligan and a group of musicians that included Chet Baker, Stan Getz, saxophonist and flautist Bud Shank, and drummer Shelly Manne. The Lighthouse Cafe was the hub of the West Coast scene, welcoming visiting headliners and providing a home base for bassist and bandleader Howard Rumsey and his Lighthouse All-Stars until 1971.

← ↑ OPPOSITE **Club Alabam souvenir photograph and photo folder** (*above*), date unknown.

CLUB ALABAM

4215 SOUTH CENTRAL AVENUE AT FORTY-SECOND STREET

Located next door to the Dunbar Hotel, the Club Alabam was the most prominent club in the Los Angeles jazz scene of the 1930s and 1940s. Drummer and bandleader Curtis Mosby's extravagant dance hall offered steak dinners and elaborate stage shows featuring comedians, showgirls, and top-flight performers, including Fats Waller, Lena Horne, and singer Johnny Otis. During World War II, drummer and singer Lee Young's band, featuring Dexter Gordon, Art Pepper, and Charles Mingus, played there. Frank Sinatra reportedly came as an audience member, but after the performance he spontaneously got onstage to sing.

⇆ LEFT Downbeat photo folder and souvenir photograph (*opposite*), August 1945.

DOWNBEAT

4201 SOUTH CENTRAL AVENUE AT FORTY-SECOND STREET

Two doors away from the more opulent Club Alabam, the Downbeat was "the hot spot on the Avenue,"[6] recalled flautist and clarinetist Buddy Collette. In 1946, Collette played the club with his short-lived septet, the Stars of Swing, featuring Charles Mingus and saxophonist Lucky Thompson. There are conflicting versions of who owned the Downbeat, but Collette recalled that gangster Mickey Cohen frequented the club and that his name was on the paychecks bandleaders received.

LAST WORD
4206 SOUTH CENTRAL AVENUE AT FORTY-SECOND STREET

The Last Word was a more modest venue owned by Curtis Mosby's brother Esvan, the honorary mayor of Central Avenue. Billing itself as the "East Side['s] Smartest Sepia Nightclub," it featured jazz and rhythm and blues artists such as Big Jay McNeely (whose band included then teenage pianist Hampton Hawes). After campaigning in the Central Avenue area, Richard Nixon spent the night of his 1950 election to the U.S. Senate drinking beer at the Last Word.

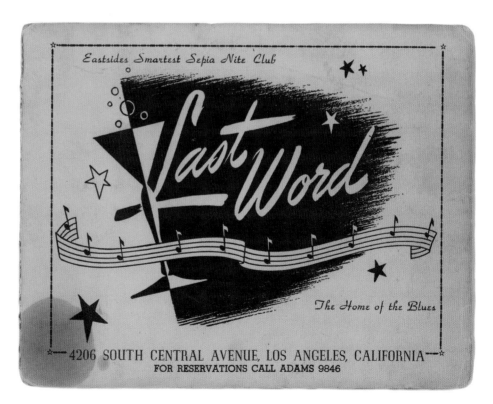

↹ OPPOSITE **Last Word** souvenir photograph and photo folder (*right*), date unknown.

JOE MORRIS'
PLANTATION CLUB

108TH STREET AND CENTRAL AVENUE

Self-billed as "California's Largest Harlem Night Club," Joe Morris' Plantation Club was in Watts, five miles south of Central Avenue's main concentration of clubs. Nationally known headliners included the bands of Count Basie, Jimmie Lunceford, Andy Kirk, and Billy Eckstine. In 1945, *Billboard* reported: "Morris is attempting to established [sic] his spot as a showcase for a Negro band playing for colored patronage. . . . Gimmick Morris uses to show his satisfaction with job band does at his spot is to present to leaders a Western-style belt with a diamond insert."[7]

↑ → ABOVE **Joe Morris' Plantation Club photo folder and souvenir photograph** (*opposite*), date unknown.

↓ → RIGHT **Billy Berg's** souvenir folder and photograph (*below*) with saxophonist Lucky Thompson (*right*) posing with soldiers, possibly during the Dizzy Gillespie Quintet's residency, mid-1950s.

1356 NORTH VINE STREET
HOLLYWOOD

BILLY BERG'S

1356 NORTH VINE STREET

Bebop came to the West Coast in December 1945, when the Dizzy Gillespie Quintet, featuring Charlie Parker, traveled to Los Angeles to play a controversial seven-week stint at Billy Berg's. As critic Leonard Feather wrote only a few years later, "Nobody who witnessed Dizzy's stint at Billy Berg's in Hollywood will forget it in a hurry."[8]

The first night Parker didn't play until late in the second set, emerging from the audience playing "Cherokee," having spent the first part of the show in the back of the club eating Mexican food. Parker's drug problem intensified when he met Moose the Mooch, whose Central Avenue shoeshine parlor was a front for his dealing. Feather recalled Parker's drug problems meant that "he showed up late or not at all on most evenings; as a result, Berg had Dizzy add a tenor, Lucky Thompson, to the group."[9]

While both club and band were integrated, Feather noted there were "prejudicial comments made about the presence of two white musicians, Al Haig and Stan Levy, in the group. Ray Brown's bass and Milt Jackson's vibes completed what was musically a very fine combination, but commercially a total flop." Feather recalled: "Business was bad at Berg's. Hardly anybody in California, except a small clique of young musicians, understood or cared about bebop, and the small clique in question earned so little money that it couldn't help Berg's much. Dizzy was not helped by the highly reactionary attitude of local critics and disc jockeys, who were not merely passively disinterested in his work, but actively desirous of seeing him fail. It was a happy day for the Gillespie men when they got back to the Apple."[10]

But the music was extraordinary. Milt Jackson told writer Ralph J. Gleason his "biggest kick was playing with Dizzy and Bird in 1945," saying: "[At Berg's] we had eight weeks and Bird was just so fascinating I would turn around on the bandstand, I'd be completely oblivious to the people. I was just listening to Bird play and one night we played 'Round Midnight' and, oh man, it was so moving I was just standing there and the tears...and everybody looked at me funny, what the heck is wrong with him, but then they'd know I was just so deeply moved listening to this man play there was just no other reaction I could get. That's actually definitely among the most memorable occasions that I've ever had. . . . [T]he audience didn't understand at all. . . . Nobody ever understood what Bird or Dizzy were doing, but I didn't care so long as I heard. It was something else."[11]

While the Berg's engagement wasn't a commercial success, it led to many important developments for both Parker and bebop. In Los Angeles, Gillespie and Parker recorded with Slim Gaillard and, in January 1946, played jazz impresario Norman Granz's first two Jazz at the Philharmonic concerts—these were Parker's first major concert appearances. At the second concert, Parker famously played with his idol Lester Young on "Lady Be Good," later released as a record. When the Berg's engagement ended, the rest of the band headed back to New York City, but Parker cashed in his plane ticket and spent the money, presumably on drugs. Soon afterward, local L.A. record store owner Ross Russell signed Parker to his nascent record label, Dial Records, recording Parker's bebop classics "Ornithology," "Yardbird Suite," "A Night in Tunisia," and "Moose the Mooche" with a handpicked group including Miles Davis and Lucky Thompson. Parker's addiction and alcoholism worsened; at the end of July, after setting fire to his hotel room, he was sentenced to a six-month stint at the Camarillo State Mental Hospital—where he wrote "Relaxin' at Camarillo"—before returning east in 1947.

OASIS CLUB
3801 SOUTH WESTERN AVENUE

The Oasis Club was a Middle Eastern–themed club on Western Avenue, four miles west of Central Avenue. Music historian Ted Gioia writes in *West Coast Jazz*, "Slim Gaillard's debut at the Oasis was the one owner Eddie de Sure remembered the longest." According to Gioia, Gaillard was late for opening night, and de Sure waited nervously for him outside. Gaillard finally arrived, stepped out of his cab, and said to de Sure, "'Pay the man, dad' and hurried into the club. The cabbie asked for two-fifty, and when given three dollars, replied, 'No, that's two hundred and fifty *dollars*. That guy won't fly. He caught my cab in San Francisco.'"[12]

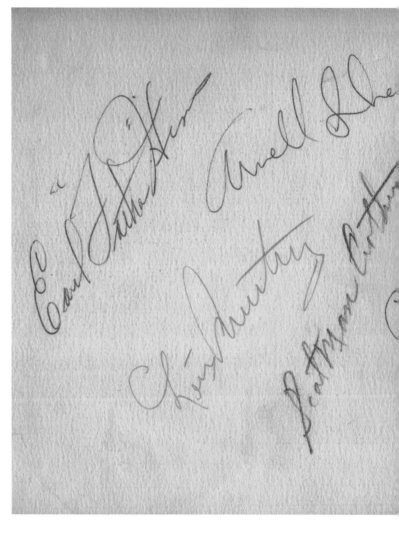

↑ ABOVE **Oasis Club photo folder, circa 1950.**

↑ ABOVE **Oasis Club souvenir photograph, signed by Louis Armstrong and band members Earl "Fatha" Hines, Arvell Shaw, Cozy Cole, and Jack Teagarden, and actor/musician Scatman Crothers, circa 1950.**

San FRANCISCO

Jazz was first played in San Francisco in the early 1920s, at clubs in the city's Barbary Coast district. Most were integrated, and some were owned by African Americans; pianist Jelly Roll Morton, in 1919, opened the short-lived Jupiter Club, on Columbus Avenue between Jackson Street and Pacific Avenue. Morton's club and some of the others closed as the result of a police clampdown on vice.

In the ensuing decade, a few jazz venues popped up in various areas of the city, but there wasn't another concentration until the end of Prohibition and the emergence of the Fillmore scene. Prohibition's repeal and the desire for a respite from racism—Black men who danced with white women in the city's integrated nightclubs had been subject to arrest—led to the opening of a number of Black-owned jazz and blues clubs. Jack's Tavern was the first, in 1933, soon followed by Club Alabam and the Town Club—the "big three" of the Fillmore district.

At the end of the 1930s, the city was home to a musical revival, when trumpeter Lu Watters and trombonist Turk Murphy, rejecting the era's popular swing music, found success looking back to the traditional music of New Orleans. Their Yerba Buena Jazz Band became a sensation, playing music in the style of Jelly Roll Morton and King Oliver.

With the United States' entry into World War II, the city's Japanese and Japanese American residents were forcibly relocated to internment camps. Many had lived in the Fillmore district, and the evacuation of their homes and businesses led to an abundance of inexpensive housing and commercial property. Soon, many African Americans—and their businesses—moved into the neighborhood.

Wartime jobs in the city's shipyards had drawn many Black people to the city; from 1941 to 1950, San Francisco's African American population grew from 4,864 to more than 43,000. Fillmore historian Elizabeth Pepin wrote, "The shipyard work was difficult and the hours long, and thousands of people crammed into small Victorian flats, but the money was good and racial barriers were slowly being broken down. People wanted to forget the war by being entertained. Within a few months, a network of musicians, bands, clubs, and bars began popping up to fill the void."[1]

The Fillmore scene was freewheeling, with musicians playing clubs during the evening and then jamming the night away at other after-hours venues. During the Fillmore's musical peak, major stars like Ella Fitzgerald, Miles Davis, Dizzy Gillespie, and Billie Holiday drew large crowds, and the area became known as the "Harlem of the West."

But the relaxed, racially mixed scene in the Fillmore didn't mean all of San Francisco was open to Black people.

Pepin observed: "African Americans weren't allowed to play in the major downtown clubs or in any of the clubs east of Van Ness Avenue until the late fifties. Now, if you were Duke Ellington or another prominent African American musician, you could play at the big hotel downtown, but even Duke Ellington couldn't stay there—he'd have to get in a cab and go back to the Fillmore District to spend the night. Additionally, none of his African American friends from the Fillmore could go and see him play in the downtown hotel, so after his downtown gigs, Ellington and other musicians of his caliber would play at the smaller clubs in the Fillmore for their own community. As a result, the Fillmore became a hotbed for African American music. The white musicians who were into hearing jazz would come to the Fillmore clubs, which led to them eventually jamming with the African American musicians. The police were not particularly happy about this form of integration, however, and there were many raids on the Fillmore clubs during the forties and fifties."[2]

After the war, bebop took hold among the city's jazz fans, and new clubs opened in other areas. In the Tenderloin district there was the Black Hawk, where Charlie Parker jammed and Billie Holiday and Lester Young played their last West Coast club dates. The club became home base for cool jazz pioneers like the Dave Brubeck Quartet (featuring saxophonist Paul Desmond), who recorded its 1956 album *Jazz at the Black Hawk* at the club; in 1961, the Miles Davis Quintet released two legendary albums also recorded there: *In Person, Friday Night at the Blackhawk, San Francisco, Volume 1* and *Volume 2*.

In North Beach there was the Jazz Workshop, where Cannonball Adderley, Charles Mingus, pianist Barry Harris, and organist "Brother Jack" McDuff all recorded live albums. And in the Western Addition neighborhood, there was Bop City, one of the city's most important clubs. As with other cities, though, changing musical tastes and municipal redevelopment projects presented insurmountable obstacles to many of the clubs, and by the 1970s, the Black Hawk, Club Alabam, and Bop City had all closed.

TOWN CLUB
1963 SUTTER STREET

Local businessman Jim Roberts opened the Town Club in 1936. In *Harlem of the West*, drummer Earl Watkins recalled the Fillmore's early "big three" clubs: "Jack's was a very nice club, considered more of an elite establishment, and the Club Alabam was smaller and a little more down-to-earth,"[3] while the Town Club, just a few doors down from Jack's, "was a small place, smaller than most of the other clubs, with a few tables and a piano. Ed Hammond on bass and Pat Patterson on piano made up the house band. They would have jam sessions in there on Sundays."[4] The club closed in the mid-1950s.

←↑ OPPOSITE **Town Club** souvenir photograph and photo folder (*above*), date unknown.

Cousin Jimbo

Welcomes You

The Survey showed that everyone in the world over 18 years of age, who likes American Jazz, has either been to Bop City, or heard of someone who has been to the Houses of Houses, Bop City . . .

Now Has Stereophonic Sounds and Scenery . . .

Cousin Jimbo's

BOP CITY

1690 post st.   san francisco, calif.

"Known the World Over"

BOP CITY
1690 POST STREET

In 1949, car salesman John "Jimbo" Edwards opened Bop City in a Victorian house previously home to Slim Gaillard's short-lived Vout City club. Edwards originally planned to open a café, Jimbo's Waffle Shop, but at the suggestion of some visiting musicians, he added a function room with a stage in the large back room.

Open from two A.M. until six A.M., the club was famous for its jam sessions featuring musicians who had finished their earlier gigs elsewhere; Count Basie, Miles Davis, Duke Ellington, Dizzy Gillespie, Ben Webster, Dinah Washington, and John Coltrane were just a few of the luminaries who joined in.

Singer Sugar Pie DeSanto told Pepin: "I'd go to Bop City a lot. Thelonious Monk, Nancy Wilson, any famous person could walk in and get up on stage and jam, and a lot of people did. It was our hangout. Everyone would get dressed up in those days. We really got sharp. Everyone was nice, and there were no fights. The crowd was mixed, and for a while the police didn't like it. They hassled us for a little while, but it stopped. We told the cops to leave us alone. We didn't care about color, we cared about music."[5]

The club's clientele was eclectic, with working-class fans listening alongside celebrities like Joe Louis, Marilyn Monroe, Sammy Davis Jr., Jack Kerouac, and even young jazz fanatic Clint Eastwood.

Bop City's admission was only a dollar, and musicians were admitted free, but Edwards didn't let just anyone into his club: "We don't allow no squares in Bop City. If you don't understand what we doin', then leave and don't come back."[6]

Bop City closed in 1965.

→ OPPOSITE **Duke Ellington and friends celebrate at Bop City in 1952. While the banner cites the year as his twenty-fifth in music, he'd actually been a professional musician for thirty-five years; 1952 was the twenty-fifth anniversary of his Cotton Club debut.**

A Conversation with

ROBIN GIVHAN

Writer, cultural critic, and author Robin Givhan may be best known as fashion critic for the *Washington Post*, but in 2006, she became the first writer specializing in the genre to win a Pulitzer Prize for Criticism. As the Pulitzer committee praised "her witty, closely observed essays that transform fashion criticism into cultural criticism," likewise the *Washington Post* website notes, "She writes about fashion as a business, as a cultural institution and as pure pleasure." Givhan has written for the *Detroit Free Press, San Francisco Chronicle, Vogue,* the *Daily Beast,* and *Newsweek.* She is also the author of *The Battle of Versailles: The Night American Fashion Stumbled into the Spotlight and Made History.*

Jeff Gold (JG): The fashion we see and the personal style in these images is so strong. I wanted to speak to someone who could look at the images from that perspective. You're such an impressive deconstructor of images; I thought you'd have something to say about this.

Robin Givhan (RG): [*Chuckles.*] Well, I'll give it my best try.

JG: When did you first become aware of musicians as style icons—people like Billie Holiday, Sarah Vaughan, Miles Davis, and Duke Ellington?

RG: Probably just as I began covering the fashion industry and thinking about the way that different styles develop and who various designers looked back on for inspiration. The way that history—pop cultural history, cultural history, social history—always speaks to [and] influences contemporary designers. It was much more so in my professional life that I was sort of thinking about them as style icons.

JG: Because they really were influencers. When you look at somebody like Miles, who was always so sharp . . . as his music evolved, so did his sartorial approach. It was clearly a very important thing for people like him or Duke Ellington or Billie Holiday or Sarah Vaughan. You never saw pictures of them where they weren't really done up, and each of them had a particular point of view.

Are there any designers you can cite who might have been influenced by those people or that scene?

RG: I can't think of a specific collection, but I can think of designers, certainly people like Catherine Malandrino. It's interesting, in an off way, that often it's European designers who have zeroed in on jazz artists too, possibly to a more noticeable degree than American designers. I take some of that to be simply because of the role that jazz and jazz expats played within Europe versus within the United States.

Catherine Malandrino once had one of her shows at the Apollo Theater. And someone like Jean Paul Gaultier, who had a quite famous collection in—I believe it was the mid-1990s—in which he was partially inspired by the women of Harlem. He created this really interesting collection that explored and merged African diaspora style with the jazz style of Harlem. All of it sort of mushed together into this really interesting accessibility that was vaguely from the 1950s meets the 1970s. It was done in that way that designers so often do, where things all come together in this pastiche of notions to create something unique. But Gaultier was clearly trying on the jazz era of Harlem and blending it with the African immigrants that he saw on the streets of Paris.

JG: This music had a fan base here and was important, but when these artists went to Europe in the 1940s and 1950s, they were greeted like conquering heroes. They were so embraced; there wasn't the kind of racism they faced in the United States. Ben Webster and Dexter Gordon eventually moved to Denmark. Kenny Clarke and other people moved to France. I can see why Gaultier had that notion. It almost seems like a romantic notion now, to look at that era and those clothes. Does that resonate for you?

RG: Yes. I think that for a lot of designers, particularly in Europe, the jazz artists did represent a sort of romantic notion, an imagery that they personally loved. There was an element of the exotic to it as well. I think there was also a greater sense of freedom to draw inspiration from that world—that perhaps American designers didn't necessarily feel as comfortable pulling inspiration from that era. I don't think that for American designers, you can divorce it from the political and social aspects of that time, you know, the Jim Crow aspects of that era. Whereas in Europe there was much less of an apparent burden in that respect.

↑ ABOVE **Duke Ellington in his Paramount Theatre dressing room, New York City, September 1946.**

JG: It's almost like a romantic ideal in some ways.

RG: To some degree, yes. But, as with all things in fashion, it's never literal, it's always sort of blended with other ideas and other points of inspiration. Sometimes that's for the best, and sometimes it gets designers into trouble because they will tend to divorce or attempt to divorce an aesthetic from its context. And that can be problematic.

JG: I'd like to get your read on some specific photographs. This picture, from Smalls' Paradise, probably from the 1930s, is most likely the earliest one I have. It was the first Black-owned club in Harlem. Smalls' opened in the 1920s. You can see there are white people in the front, a Black waiter, and then in the upper right corner you can see a Black patron. Integration was really happening on the ground in these clubs. People were mixing, and the jazz musicians don't get credit for it. I can't tease any nuance out of this other than that it exists and it's kind of interesting. Does it at all say anything to you?

RG: Just sort of generally with a lot of these pictures, the thing that I'm struck by is the formality—at least the seeming formality of their attire. The fact that in many instances, it's almost like you could take some of the women and they could just as easily be walking into Sunday church as a nightclub. They're not wearing anything that particularly revealing or glitzy, or I would probably say excessively glitzy. I don't know if that speaks to the esteem in which they held the music, or the sense that—when they were out in public or with a mixed audience—that they always had to sort of be dressed beyond reproach, even when they were at leisure.

There are a couple of photos—and I guess the other one that comes to mind is the one with Dizzy Gillespie—where the women do seem to be in a bit more sort of party clothes. I mean, I have no idea who these people are.

JG: Nobody does.

RG: There does seem to be like a greater intimacy in that picture than in the others. I mean, just from his smile to the way the woman's arm is sort of casually draped around his shoulder. They just seem like they are

something more than just a group of people that he happened to sit down with for a photograph. Or maybe he's just drunk? [*Laughs.*] I don't know.

JG: Here's another one from Smalls' Paradise (see page 242, left), one with two couples. It looks like it could possibly be a white couple and an African American couple? Everybody just looks so happy. And these hats the women have. And those . . . interesting . . . church outfits. It's a kind of Sunday best. Do you have anything to say about that?

RG: If this is a mixed-race group, it's very challenging to be able to discern that. And I think if it is, it speaks to, to some degree, who had the ability to be in these spaces and who felt comfortable there. And . . . I was just thinking, not necessarily just with this one, but with the other images as well, it's striking that regardless of race, everyone is sort of dressed the same. There's not that sense of fashion tribes that you get today. There is

↑ ABOVE Smalls' Paradise souvenir photograph, New York City, circa 1930s.

→ OPPOSITE Birdland souvenir photograph of Dizzy Gillespie (*far right*) with fans, New York City, date unknown.

one style. And everyone plays into that. And everyone accepts that as the standard. You look at the men's attire and it really is . . . the same regardless of the race of the man or his age.

JG: It looks to me like they're wearing the best clothes they own.

RG: Yeah, I mean it's not necessarily the best, but certainly the most dashing, the most elegant. I always have to remind myself that during the heyday of jazz, it was really a popular form of music. Sometimes people would come not just to listen, but also to dance and to enjoy themselves, and to party. And today, so often, particularly among the most serious jazz bands, it's almost this kind of intellectual pursuit. You get shushed if you're talking too loud.

↑ ABOVE, LEFT   **Smalls' Paradise souvenir photograph, New York City, date unknown.**

↗ ABOVE, RIGHT   **Savoy Ballroom souvenir photograph, New York City, date unknown.**

→ OPPOSITE   **Club Baby Grand interior, New York City, 1947.**

JG: The musicians I talked to all said they felt they were communicating with the audience. And what the audience was doing directly influenced the way the performance manifested. So it was kind of a singular organism.

RG: When I look at the pictures, people seem so engaged with each other and seem to be having so much fun. There's a flirtatiousness between the man and the woman. When I think of jazz now—and this is from someone who's not an intense follower, but I admire it, I enjoy it—there's always this element of reserve. You're not going to hoot and holler, like at a rock concert.

JG: It's more cerebral.

RG: Which I think creates this wall between the performer and the audience.

JG: That's a great point. I'd like to ask you about this one from the Savoy Ballroom with this mixed group, with five African American guys and two white women. I love the fact that race just seems like a nonissue for these people. They're just there having fun and that's that. Does that say anything to you?

RG: I think it's interesting that it's five African American men and two white women [*laughs*] as opposed to the reverse.

JG: That's interesting. Do we have the reverse? No. I don't think I have ones with African American women and white men. I feel particularly ill equipped to comment on that. And this shot of the interior of the Club Baby Grand. The men's hats. I love all of that.

RG: It plays on a sense of anonymity to some degree. It's a uniform, and there's probably a certain degree of safety and camouflage in that—you know, a man's suit and tie as a form of armor. I suspect there's probably an element of protection in dressing with the crowd, not standing out. It's probably the person who stands out who's creating trouble, who's finding trouble. It's the whole notion of welcoming the Black musicians but not regular Black folks in its audience—it's the notion of being willing to embrace the exceptional but not the average.

JG: Well, that was only true of one particular club, the Cotton Club. That was the one racist club and it was gone by the late 1930s. We'll get back to that, but every one of these other clubs was integrated. It's interesting, this picture's all men. That strikes me. I wonder what that's about.

Here's one from Murrain's, "Harlem's Gayest Cabaret" (page 244, above left). I love this couple.

RG: Aw, they're sweet.

JG: I love the hats on the women. It seems like, uh . . . maybe is that the one place that they felt kind of liberated to take more chances with their dress? We'll get to some wilder ones.

RG: The hats were always a point of pride and expression of creativity. I suppose it doesn't really necessarily surprise me all that much that I don't sort of see groups of Black women. I suspect that it was probably harder for them to feel that they could go out in that way without the husband or the boyfriend. Like that.

RG: It's quite the flamboyant suit. It looks very much like a stage costume, with the really wide lapels that look much wider than those of the guy that he's with. And the really bold pinstripe. It's an exaggerated suit, meant to be seen from the back corner of the room.

JG: These pictures are kind of primordial selfies. Where somebody's at a club, it costs a dollar to take a picture. I talked to Sonny Rollins about this; he said people were asking him to pose for pictures and for autographs all the time. There are maybe twenty images like this in the collection I have, where artists are posing with fans.

Today people walking down the street will stop and get a picture with a celebrity—or try to. But back then, other than in this situation, when would you be in a situation to pose with a hero of yours? And then from a racial standpoint, where do you see white people just glowing to be meeting their African American heroes? Especially in the 1940s. I can't think of any other situation like that. Jackie Robinson was popular about that time, but it wasn't easy—he had to deal with a lot of resistance. These musicians were embraced. I can't think of any other situation at this time, probably the late 1940s or early 1950s, where you'd see white people so excited to be posing with their African American hero. Can you?

RG: Not off the top of my head. I think that probably the music was the world of the least racial resistance. I'm sure you have a much better sense of this, but my sense is that jazz was always a kind of music that attracted a kind of more daring, open-minded, cosmopolitan fan base. As opposed to, say, the blues, which I'd presume had a much more predominantly Black fan base. Rock and roll was probably another realm in which the whole point was to subvert traditions and was rebellious and all of that. But jazz [at this time] wasn't big band; there was always a bit of recklessness to it. I would think that built into that would be people who were more willing

JG: I do have a few of those. And then there are a number of ones—like the ones with the Harriet Tubman Social Club (page 212) and the other social club—where that seems to be the one sort of exception to what you're talking about, where they do go out in groups.

RG: Right, because it's their space.

JG: This one is from the Royal Chicken Roost (page 2 and top of next column), a fried chicken restaurant that turned into a jazz club that they dubbed the "Metropolitan Bopera House." It was a really important place for bebop people. Here's Charlie Parker looking fantastic with two fans. And I just love the attitude and the way he's dressed in this picture.

↑ ABOVE, LEFT **Murrain's souvenir photograph, New York City, date unknown.**

↗ ABOVE, RIGHT **Charlie Parker at the Royal Chicken Roost, New York City, circa 1948.**

→ OPPOSITE **The Famous Door, New York City, circa 1940s.**

to step outside of tradition, social norms, and expectations and to go into forbidden spaces or so-called forbidden spaces.

JG: I think that's true. New York was where all this was happening. In the 1920s and 1930s, it was about dancing to the big bands. There were spaces that were owned by Black people as well as by white where folks would come to dance. Black bands would play with white bands. As early as the mid-1930s, Benny Goodman integrated his group with Teddy Wilson and Lionel Hampton. So in Jim Crow America, jazz was a real early area where barriers were breaking down. By many accounts, people got along fine. The authorities may not have been into it as much as the people, but people got along. White people went up to Harlem to experience this integration—to some extent because it was exotic. Then when Fifty-Second Street started thriving, these clubs were pretty much integrated. The Cotton Club was really the one exception.

I'm struck by how happy everybody looks in these pictures, which reinforces what Quincy and Sonny told me about how these clubs provided an escape from daily life for them and how people from different races mixed easily at the time when that was extremely unusual. Sonny said, "Jazz was really where the racial barriers broke down heavily." Quincy told me, "Racism would have been over by the 1950s if they'd have listened to the jazz guys." Then I started looking at these pictures and thinking, *Where do you see African Americans and white [fans] posing together and seemingly getting along so well during that era?* So I think what you said is right: jazz drew progressive audiences.

Bebop was music made for listening, not dancing. It's really one of those crazy quirks. Jazz became less ballroom based and more small-club based. And the music itself became more about listening to, rather than dancing to, it. But the fans kept coming. Black fans and white fans. It was really surprising to me that this scene was at the vanguard of . . . "desegregation" seems like the wrong word, but these clubs were very early places where racism was not an issue.

RG: I didn't know that.

JG: This is a favorite picture [of mine] from the Famous Door (page 60 and below)—look at these three, especially the guy on the right with the tipped head. It looks like he's wearing a tuxedo. His expression is just so fantastic.

These really are stolen moments. The people shooting them walked around from table to table, taking a picture that they were hoping they could sell for a dollar at the end of the evening. There wasn't a lot of preparation going into these things.

I can't tell if that's a real carnation on the woman's dress. Do you have anything to say about this picture?

RG: She's really pretty. She also seems to be the only one who realizes the photo's being taken. Seems like she's with the guy in the tuxedo and the other guy joined them or something.

JG: He just looks like he's so in love with her. They're so besotted. Does it look that way to you?

RG: Well, I can't really tell if he's looking at her or he's looking at something at the other end of the table. But yeah, with his little side-parted hair and everything. . . . They look well-to-do.

JG: He's kind of out of the uniform you described, he's got a tuxedo on. It's got studs and satin lapels.

RG: It seems like they've come from elsewhere to end their evening here. They do seem very overdressed. Much more formal than in any of these pictures.

JG: In this one from the Crown Propeller Lounge (page 246), the clothes seem to be a different kind of uniform, a much less formal one. The guy on the left doesn't have on a tie. And the woman looks like she's got on a pullover sweater or something.

RG: It's probably the most casual photograph that I've seen so far.

JG: We've been looking at New York clubs, and this one is in Chicago. The New York clubs, all in all, were much fancier than the clubs in other places.

RG: I suppose even if the New York ones weren't technically fancier, there tends to be an expectation that you dress a little sharper.

JG: People that are there have to be on their A game.

RG: Yeah, for sure.

JG: This is from the Hurricane [Show Club] (page 180 and at right) in Chicago. The guy on the right's got—is this some kind of jacket made out of two different fabrics?

RG: Yeah. It looks like one of those—I don't know, something you'd see on *I Love Lucy.*

↑ ABOVE **Crown Propeller Lounge souvenir photograph, Chicago, 1956.**

↗ ABOVE, RIGHT **Hurricane Show Club, Chicago, date unknown.**

→ OPPOSITE, LEFT **Club Alabam, Los Angeles, date unknown.**

→ OPPOSITE, RIGHT **Zardi's souvenir photograph of fans with Oscar Peterson, Los Angeles, mid-1950s.**

JG: [*Laughs.*] It looks like one of those Nat Nast shirts to me, or something, but as a jacket. I love that guy's kind of attitude, or expression. It looks like those girls might be—they're wearing similar things, it looks like they could be sisters.

RG: Or they could just be really good friends, you know? That is sort of a girl thing.

JG: Dressing the same?

RG: Well, it's that element of "Oh, it's a double date. What are you wearing?" There tends to be a kind of unwritten understanding that you don't want to dress too far afield from what your female friend is wearing.

JG: So as not to upstage her or something?

RG: If your friend is wearing a prim Sunday-morning dress, you don't want to be the friend showing up in the low-cut bright red dress.

JG: That makes all the sense in the world, but I never knew about that. So there's a coordination?

RG: I don't know. It's almost a passive agreement of the tone that's being set by your clothes. And that's not to say that in groups of women there isn't the one who's going to be the more provocative dresser. But there's also—sort of in the worst kind of situation—there's also the understanding that, well, of course, she is the provocative one.

JG: [*Laughs.*] Well, as you can imagine, guys probably didn't spend as much effort coordinating their outfits on double dates.

This is from Club Alabam (page 220 and opposite, left) on Central Avenue, the big jazz street in Los Angeles from the 1930s and 1940s. I love the hat on that woman on the left. It looks like a flying saucer.

RG: The one thing is that the people look really glamorous, really

Hollywood. Look at the poses—the women look very comfortable in front of a camera. Especially this one in the front. She knows her angles. [*Laughs.*]

JG: She's fantastic, isn't she? I read the piece you wrote about "effortless chic,"[7] and I wanted to know, are we seeing effortless chic in these pictures?

RG: I don't know that I would necessarily describe it that way. For me, and perhaps because I know that they're in Los Angeles, it reads very much like they are emulating what Hollywood glamour means, what dramatic glamour means. Just look at the woman with the long gloves on. The woman on the right looks like she's leaning on what is like a fur or something draped over a chair. They have these bold, face-forward, leaning-forward smiles. They're very glossy.

JG: This one's from Zardi's on Hollywood Boulevard. That's Oscar Peterson in the middle. And those people just seem so happy to be posing with their hero.

RG: Absolutely! It's interesting that you refer to him as their hero. I don't know about that. Is he a hero or are people just delighting in celebrity?

JG: I'm guessing that going to see somebody like Oscar Peterson, a serious musician, is not about going dancing or anything like that. You're going to see somebody you know, not just "Let's go out for an evening and see whoever is playing piano at the place." I'm guessing it's a more deliberate decision than that. And the people are not just smiling; they seem to be glowing over the fact they're posing with him. He's not just somebody famous, he's *Oscar Peterson*. Maybe he's just played—and they're just so happy. I love that giant mink coat—which, in my youth, was a way of telegraphing your social status, having a coat like that.

RG: I think that's right. I think that's true.

JG: Especially in Los Angeles, where you would never need a coat like that for warmth. And finally, here's a shot from the Town Casino in Buffalo, dated 1954 (page 248). It says, "Senior girls go to see Eartha Kitt."

RG: They look very young. A fifty-year-old could be wearing any of those clothes. Or have that hair!

JG: Was that typical of the time?

RG: It really wasn't until the late 1960s when adulthood didn't essentially mean dressing like your mother. That's the first time you really see a style of dress that could be called "youthful," which is why that era was known for its "youthquake" in fashion. There was a particular youthful style of dress, as opposed to just adult women's clothing, which was what you stepped into as soon as you technically became an adult.

JG: And is the trigger for that kind of the counterculture and the Beatles and Summer of Love and all that stuff?

↑ ABOVE **Town Casino souvenir photograph, Buffalo, New York, 1954.**

RG: The trend really started in London with [fashion designer] Mary Quant, with the miniskirt, but yes. And the models of the time, like Twiggy, who had a very distinctive youthful kind of look. So it did draw inspiration from that. I think that's why when you look at pictures from the early 1960s, it's very hard to tell the difference between the late 1950s, in terms of the way that the women are dressed. The men too, for that matter. It's really not until you start getting into maybe 1965 and later that you start really seeing a distinctive difference between the way that parents dress versus their kids. The young men have the short-cropped hair just like their fathers'.

JG: I grew up around that time, and for me, the Beatles were the line in the sand, where you wanted to grow your hair longer and you fought with your parents about that. And you wanted to start expressing yourself—I wouldn't have put it this way at the time—but you wanted to start wearing different clothes that you chose yourself. That was kind of the trigger for it in the United States and England at least.

RG: It definitely fed into that. What's curious to me is that in these pictures in the jazz clubs, the music might be more rebellious and subversive than what's happening socially is. But in terms of this cultural custom, it still feels very much rooted in the 1940s and 1950s. The way that people visually express themselves hadn't caught up, perhaps, to the way that they might have been starting to think about themselves.

JG: There were obviously women like Sarah Vaughan and Billie Holiday, who were expressing themselves with fashion—and the men were too—but the men's fashion from these pictures seems pretty much in keeping with what some of the artists were wearing. Do you think that the clubs and what the performers were wearing in the clubs influenced what the patrons were wearing?

RG: My initial thought is probably no, not really. It seems like both what the men and the women were wearing, both onstage and off, was very similar. Maybe the volume was turned up a little bit more in the way that Charlie Parker wore it. His suit was essentially the same style that the men were wearing in the audience, just a bit bolder so that it would stand out. But I don't know that I could fully say that what they were wearing onstage was having that big of an impact on what they were wearing offstage.

JG: Where did people in the 1940s and 1950s buy stylish clothes and hats . . . things like these? Was it a department store thing? Was it a local store thing?

RG: My guess is that most of these people probably went to a mass department store. What they were buying was derivative of what very wealthy women were wearing, and that was based on Paris fashions. We really hadn't gotten to a point where there was very much influential trend-driving ready-to-wear. Probably much of what people were buying in department stores was a knockoff of something that was being dictated by Paris designers.

JG: The people in these pictures seem to be generally dressing very stylishly. Is that your perception?

RG: I think they were dressing by the rules. I don't think that they were necessarily injecting that much individuality into their clothing. There was sort of a set standard of what was appropriate for various occasions, what was fashionable, and pretty much if you wanted to be a fashionable, stylishly relevant woman, that's what you wore.

JG: The people in these pictures seem very stylish, though, to me. Maybe unusually so for pictures from the 1940s and 1950s.

RG: I don't know that I think they're unusually stylish. I think that they're all dressed for the occasion. There were much firmer and closely followed rules about what one wore to an occasion. So if you were going to a cocktail lounge, you wore cocktail attire. If you were having lunch with a friend during the week, you wore a lunch suit. I think in hindsight they looked particularly stylish, but in the time, they looked appropriate. I think the word "appropriate" sounds very old-fashioned now, though.

JG: Any overall thoughts on the pictures?

RG: They are a really wonderful slice of a particular—a rather rarified group of people who were able to comingle at a time when that wasn't the norm. The thing that is the most striking to me is that if you remove the faces from underneath the hats and from wearing the suits and ties, everyone would be exactly the same. They all are wearing versions of a similar kind of dress. The similarities are so striking that the race doesn't really matter. It's not as if you can determine the race of someone by what they were wearing. There was a sort of agreed-upon style of dress and things that the clothing signified, and it seems they signified similar things across the board.

JG: It's so interesting to have different people look at these pictures through different lenses. Thanks so much, Robin. ●

Epilogue

As the 1950s drew to a close, jazz continued to evolve. There was cool jazz, West Coast jazz, modal jazz, and hard bop. Innovators like Ornette Coleman began playing highly improvised free jazz, which was soon picked up by more established musicians, most notably John Coltrane.

External forces continued to weigh heavily upon jazz. Musicians were combining elements from rhythm and blues, gospel, jazz, and country into rock and roll. In 1955, Bill Haley and the Comets' "Rock Around the Clock" became the first rock and roll record to hit number one. Little Richard and Chuck Berry had chart hits as well. In 1956, Elvis Presley's "Heartbreak Hotel" reached number one; by the end of the year, he became the first artist to have nine singles in the Top 100 at the same time. By the end of the decade, 43 percent of all records sold were rock and roll.

Then, in 1964, the Beatles came to America. That year, Louis Armstrong had a fluke number one hit with a version of "Hello, Dolly," which knocked the Beatles out of the top position. But as jazz critic Gary Giddins noted in Ken Burns's *Jazz*, it was "the last gasp of another age."

The enormous success of rock and roll diverted the attention of club owners, concert promoters, record labels, movies, television, and print media to the new music. Jazz musicians, desperate for work, began taking any job they could find—in cocktail lounges, television studios, symphony orchestras, and all manner of recording sessions. Some moved to Europe.

There was still an audience for jazz, and occasionally a performer or an album would capture the public's imagination. But overall the jazz audience was shrinking, and in 1968, the last club on Fifty-Second Street closed.

In 1969, Miles Davis saw Sly and the Family Stone perform at the Newport Jazz Festival. Startled by the ecstatic reaction of the young audience members, both Black and white, he rethought his own music, adding elements of funk, rhythm and blues, and rock, creating jazz fusion. In the 1970s, bands like Return to Forever, Weather Report, and Mahavishnu Orchestra continued to push the boundaries of jazz, and new fans began to emerge. Eclecticism continued in the 1980s and 1990s, with musicians like Keith Jarrett, Pat Metheny, and Bobby McFerrin expanding the definition of jazz. The audience may have shrunk, but innovation continues apace, with new genres like acid jazz, jazz rap, new jazz, and even punk being played alongside more conventional jazz.

Acknowledgments

Supreme gratitude to my family: Jody Uttal, Cleo Gold, and Ella Gold.

Profound thanks to my agent, Jennifer Gates, and my editor, Elizabeth Viscott Sullivan, for making this book possible.

Thank you, Norman Saks, for collecting so many of the extraordinary items pictured here.

Thanks again to Quincy Jones, Sonny Rollins, Jason Moran, Dan Morgenstern, and Robin Givhan for sharing your wisdom and insights.

For invaluable assistance in creating this book, thanks to lead researcher Cleo Gold, map designer Ella Gold, and chief of staff Erin Schneider. For editorial assistance, I'd like to thank Gene Sculatti and Loren Schoenberg, and for their support through the years, Lee and Whitney Kaplan.

Sincerest thanks to Kevin Young and Mary Yearwood of the Schomburg Center for Research in Black Culture at the New York Public Library.

Thank you: Steve Ades, Mark Arevalo, Jeff Ayeroff, Samantha Belmonte, Kent Beyda, Beverly Brown, Zach Cowie, Billy Crystal, Sharif Dumani, Bob Eaton, Zev Feldman, Adam Fell, Parker Fishel, Jim Fishel, Lucy Fisher, Richard Foos, Rick Frystak, Yasuhiro Fujioka, Ken Gold, Mark Goldstein, Niels Hansen, Tad Hershorn, Terri Hinte, Glenn Horowitz, Robin Hurley, Jeff Jampol, Patie Jenater, Gary Johnson, Anastasia Karel, Denise Kaufman, Larry Kopitnik, Howard Kramer, Johan Kugelberg, Andy Leach, Sunny Levine, Bobby Livingston, Marty Longbine, Steve Martin, Andrew Miller, Julie Miller, Glenn Mitchell, Joe Mosbrook, Jeff Rosen, Jacob and Yael Samuel, Jon Savage, Bob Say, Phil Schaap, Elizabeth Pepin Silva, Alyssa Smith, Jai Uttal, Geoffrey Weiss, Lorraine Weiss, Doug Wick, and Laura Woolley.

Rest in peace, Gil Friesen and Robert Matheu.

Thank you to the Ira and Leonore S. Gershwin Fund Collection, Music Division, Library of Congress, for sharing William P. Gottlieb's extraordinary photographs.

Notes

PART ONE: THE EAST COAST

NEW YORK

1 David Freeland, *Automats, Taxi Dances, and Vaudeville: Excavating Manhattan's Lost Places of Leisure* (New York: New York University Press, 2009), 156.

2 Ken Burns, dir., *Jazz* (United States: PBS Home Video, 2001).

3 Steven Watson, *The Harlem Renaissance: Hub of African-American Culture, 1920–1930* (New York: Pantheon Books, 1995), 128.

4 Qtd. in Michael Lasser, *City Songs and American Life, 1900–1950* (Rochester, NY: University of Rochester Press, 2019), 75.

5 Meg Greene, *Billie Holiday: A Biography* (Westport, CT: Greenwood Press, 2006), 18.

6 Barbara Engelbrecht, "Swinging at the Savoy," *Dance Research Journal* 15, no. 2 (Spring 1983): 3–10.

7 "Moe Gale Dies; Impresario, 65; Discoverer of Ink Spots Was a Founder of the Savoy," *New York Times*, September 3, 1964, nytimes.com/1964/09/03 /archives/moe-gale-dies-impresario-65-discoverer -of-ink-spots-was-a-founder.html.

8 Ibid.

9 James F. Wilson, *Bulldaggers, Pansies, and Chocolate Babies* (Ann Arbor: University of Michigan Press, 2011), 178.

10 "Here's What Happens at Harlem's Famous Ubangi Club," *The Afro-American*, February 8, 1936, available at http://www.queermusicheritage.com/BENTLEY /New%20Clippings/1936-bentley-ubangi-020836.jpg.

11 David Hinckley, "Live from the Apollo . . . Porto Rico Chapter 172," *New York Daily News*, September 20, 2002, nydailynews.com/archives/news/live-apollo -porto-rico-chapter-172-article-1.507671.

12 Frank Driggs, liner notes to *Jazz Odyssey*, vol. 3: *The Sound of Harlem* (New York: Columbia, Jazz Archive Series, Mono-C3L 33, 1964), vinyl record.

13 Sondra K. Wilson, *Meet Me at the Theresa: The Story of Harlem's Most Famous Hotel* (New York: Atria Books, 2004), 75.

14 Qtd. in Wil Haygood, *Sweet Thunder: The Life and Times of Sugar Ray Robinson* (Chicago: Lawrence Hill Books, 2011), 100.

15 June Bundy, Vox Jox, *Billboard*, November 12, 1955, 95.

16 "N.Y. Club Sudan Spending $5,000 on Name Talent," *Billboard*, November 24, 1945, 35.

17 David Ritz, *Faith in Time: The Life of Jimmy Scott* (Cambridge, MA: Da Capo Press, 2003), 50.

18 Qtd. in "The Baby Grand, Harlem, 1953," *Harlem World Magazine*, April 22, 2012, harlemworld magazine.com/the-baby-grand-harlem-1953.

19 Arnold Shaw, *52nd Street: The Street of Jazz* (New York: Da Capo Press, 1971), 21.

20 Ibid., 280.

21 Qtd. in Gilbert Sandler, "Webb Won the Battle of the Bands," *Baltimore Sun*, April 28, 1992, baltimoresun.com /news/bs-xpm-1992-04-28-1992119136-story.html.

22 Qtd. in ibid.

23 Shaw, *52nd Street*, 162.

24 James E. Powers, "Tax on Night Clubs Costs 5,000 Job's of Entertainers . . . ," *New York Times*, April 22, 1944, nytimes.com/1944/04/22/archives/tax-on -night-clubs-costs-5000-jobs-of-entertainers-many -places-drop.html.

25 Dizzy Gillespie, *To Be, or Not . . . to Bop* (Minneapolis: University of Minnesota Press, 2009), 232.

26 Martin Torgoff, *Bop Apocalypse: Jazz, Race, the Beats, and Drugs* (Boston: Da Capo Press, 2016), 131.

27 Burns, *Jazz*.

28 Shaw, *52nd Street*, 349.

29 Ibid., 19.

30 Margaret Moos Pick, "52nd Street, NYC: Big City Jazz in the 30s," Jim Cullum Riverwalk Jazz Collection, Stanford Libraries, 1990, riverwalkjazz. stanford.edu/program/52nd-street-nyc-big-city-jazz -30s. Accessed March 9, 2019.

31 John Chilton, *Billie's Blues: A Survey of Billie Holiday's Career, 1933–1959* (London: Quartet Books, 1975), 47.

32 Billy Taylor, *The Jazz Life of Dr. Billy Taylor* (Bloomington: Indiana University Press, 2013), 40.

33 Qtd. in Alyn Shipton, *Groovin' High: The Life of Dizzy Gillespie* (New York: Oxford University Press, 2001), 96.

34 Patrick Burke, *Come In and Hear the Truth: Jazz and Race on 52nd St* (Chicago: University of Chicago Press, 2008), 161.

35 Qtd. ibid., 161.

36 George Shearing, *Lullaby of Birdland: The Autobiography of George Shearing* (New York: Continuum, 2004), 97.

37 Shaw, *52nd Street*, 205–206.

38 Barry Kernfeld, ed., *The New Grove Dictionary of Jazz* (New York: St. Martin's Press, 1994), 896.

39 Burke, *Come In and Hear the Truth*, 171.

40 "Ubangi Club (New York)," *Variety*, April 1937, available at archive.org/stream/variety126-1937-04 /variety126-1937-04_djvu.txt.

41 New York Beat, *Jet*, October 29, 1953, 65.

42 Miles Davis, *Miles: The Autobiography* (New York: Simon & Schuster Paperbacks, 2011), 66–67.

43 Robert W. Dana, "Café Zanzibar," *New York World-Telegram*, October 15, 1945. Available at Tips on Tables, November 28, 2019, tipsontables.com /zanzibar.html.

44 Ibid.

45 Qtd. in Jean-François Pitet, "Zanzibar Cafe, New York: Home of Cab Calloway," *The Hi de Ho Blog*, October 2, 2009, thehidehoblog.com/blog/2009/10 /zanzibar-cafe-new-york-home-of-cab-calloway.

46 Richard Carlin, *Godfather of the Music Business: Morris Levy* (Jackson: University Press of Mississippi, 2016), 10.

47 Ibid., 11.

48 Ibid.

49 Ibid., 12–13.

50 Bill Chase, "Bop City Opening Bopsolutely Mad," *New York Age*, April 23, 1949.

51 Leo T. Sullivan, *Birdland: The Jazz Corner of the World* (Atglen, PA: Schiffer Publishing, 2018), 7.

52 Davis, *Miles*, 238.

53 "Beyond the Cool," *Time* Magazine 75, no. 26 (June 27, 1960): 56.

54 Lorraine Gordon, *Alive at the Village Vanguard: My Life in and out of Jazz Time* (Milwaukee, WI: Hal Leonard, 2006), 99.

55 Ibid., 96.

56 Margaret Pick, "A Night at Nick's: Hot Jazz in the Big Apple," Jim Cullum Riverwalk Jazz Collection, Stanford Libraries, 2011, riverwalkjazz.stanford.edu /program/night-nicks-hot-jazz-big-apple. Accessed May 22, 2019.

57 Diane Fischer, "Changing Times Down Dixie's Last Bastion," *Village Voice*, August 15, 1963, https://www .villagevoice.com/2009/05/18/dixieland-in-the -village-old-nicks-is-nixed.

58 Dorian Lynskey, "Strange Fruit: The First Great Protest Song," *Guardian*, February 16, 2011, theguardian.com/music/2011/feb/16/protest -songs-billie-holiday-strange-fruit.

59 Billie Holiday, *Lady Sings the Blues*, 50th Anniversary Edition (New York, NY, Harlem Moon/Broadway Books, 2006), 94.

60 Michael Riedel, "NYC's First Integrated Nightclub Was a '30s Celeb Magnet," *New York Post*, July 15, 2016, nypost.com/2016/07/15/nycs-first-integrated -nightclub-was-a-30s-celeb-magnet.

61 Scott Yanow, "Eddie Condon: Profiles in Jazz," *Syncopated Times*, January 24, 2019, syncopatedtimes .com/eddie-condon-profiles-in-jazz.

ATLANTIC CITY

1 Brad Parks, "How Atlantic City Has Always Been Full of Last-Chance Losers," *New York Post*, September 7, 2014, nypost.com/2014/09/07/requiem-for-atlantic -city-the-city-built-on-failure.

2 Bryant Simon, *Boardwalk of Dreams: Atlantic City and the Fate of Urban America* (New York: Oxford University Press, 2004), 45.

3 Nick Catalano, *Clifford Brown: The Life and Art of the Legendary Jazz Trumpeter* (New York: Oxford University Press, 2000), 71.

4 Simon, *Boardwalk of Dreams*, 52.

A CONVERSATION WITH SONNY ROLLINS

5 Gillespie, *To Be, or Not . . . to Bop*, 139.

WASHINGTON, D.C.

1 Richard Harrington, "After Years of Singing the Blues, Jazz Is Swinging Again," *Washington Post*, January 13, 1980, washingtonpost.com/archive /lifestyle/1980/01/13/after-years-of-singing-the -blues-jazz-is-swinging-again/2629bbc3-5599-4d09 -8d7f-8990bb60854a.

3 Ahmet M. Ertegun, *"What'd I Say": The Atlantic Story: 50 Years of Music* (New York: Welcome Rain Publishers, 2001), 7.

J. Freedom du Lac, "A Stirring Moment in Jazz History to Echo in Turkish Embassy," *Washington Post*, February 3, 2011, washingtonpost.com/wp-dyn /content/story/2011/02/04/ST2011020400138.html ?sid=ST2011020400138.

BOSTON

1 George Wein, *Myself among Others: A Life in Music* (Cambridge, MA: Da Capo Press, 2003), 97–98.

2 Richard Vacca, "Oct 16, 1951: Vout-O-Reenee! Slim Gaillard at the Hi–Hat," Troy Street, October 17, 2013, troystreet.com/tspots/2013/10/17/oct-16-1951-vout -o-reenee-slim-gaillard-at-the-hi-hat.

PART TWO: THE MIDWEST

CLEVELAND

1 "Jazz Studies History," Oberlin College & Conservatory, 2019, oberlin.edu/conservatory/divisions /jazz-studies/history. Accessed November 28, 2019.

2 Evelyn Theiss, "In Cleveland's 'Second Downtown,' Jazz Once Filled the Air: Elegant Cleveland," Cleveland.com, February 5, 2012, cleveland.com/ arts /2012/02/in_clevelands_second_downtown.html.

3 Updated January 12, 2019.

3 Ibid.

4 Ibid.

DETROIT

1 Holiday, *Lady Sings the Blues*, 68.

2 Ashley Zlatopolsky, "Before Motown: A History of Jazz and Blues in Detroit," Red Bull Music Academy, August 7, 2015, daily.redbullmusicacademy.com /2015/08/detroit-jazz-and-blues.

3 Nat Shapiro and Nat Hentoff, eds., *Hear Me Talkin' to Ya: The Story of Jazz as Told by the Men Who Made It* (New York: Dover Publications, 1966), 356.

4 Lars Bjorn and Jim Gallert, *Before Motown: A History of Jazz in Detroit, 1920–1960* (Ann Arbor: University of Michigan Press, 2001), 65–66.

5 Ibid., 111.

6 Ibid.

7 Tom Moon, "Dorothy Ashby and a Harp That Swings," NPR, November 15, 2006, npr.org /templates/story/story.php?storyId=6488979.

8 Mike McGonigal, "The Legendary Flame Show Bar Opened 66 Years Ago Today," *Detroit Metro Times*, June 24, 2015, metrotimes.com/city-slang /archives/2015/06/24/the-legendary-flame-show -bar-opened-66-years-ago-today.

9 Bjorn and Gallert, *Before Motown*, 72.

CHICAGO

1 Dan Caine, "Blue Note Memories," *Chicago Reader*, August 17, 1989, chicagoreader.com/chicago /blue-note-memories/Content?oid=874300.

2 "Chicago Night Club Era Ends with Closing of Club DeLisa," *Jet*, March 6, 1958, 61.

3 Ron Chepesiuk, "The Chicago Outfit Makes Its Move," *Crime Magazine*, September 7, 2007, crime magazine.com/chicago-outfit-makes-its-move-0.

4 "Queer Bronzeville: Female Impersonators," OutHistory.org, outhistory.org/exhibits/show/queer -bronzeville/part-2/female-impersonators. Accessed July 7, 2019.

[5] Ibid.

[6] "Queer Bronzeville: Queer Business: The Case of Joe Hughes," OutHistory.org, outhistory.org/exhibits /show/queer-bronzeville/part-2/joe-hughes. Accessed July 7, 2019.

[7] "Hot Talent War Brewing on Chicago's South Side," *Billboard*, December 30, 1944.

[8] Gregg Akkerman, *The Last Balladeer: The Johnny Hartman Story* (Lanham, MD: Scarecrow Press, 2012), 23.

[9] Caine, "Blue Note Memories."

[10] Ibid.

KANSAS CITY

[1] Ross Russell, *Bird Lives: The High Life and Hard Times of Charlie (Yardbird) Parker* (New York: Da Capo Press, 1996), 31.

[2] Torgoff, *Bop Apocalypse*, 68.

[3] Shapiro and Hentoff, *Hear Me Talkin' to Ya*, 284.

[4] Qtd. in Martin Chilton, "Jay McShann: Master of Boogie-Woogie Piano," *Telegraph*, January 12, 2016, telegraph.co.uk/music/artists/jay-mcshann-master -of--boogie-woogie-piano.

[5] Qtd. in Robert Gottlieb, ed., *Reading Jazz: A Gathering of Autobiography, Reportage, and Criticism from 1919 to Now* (New York: Vintage Books, 1996), 131.

[6] Qtd. in Nathan W. Pearson, *Goin' to Kansas City* (Urbana: University of Illinois Press, 1994), 206.

[7] Count Basie, *Good Morning Blues: The Autobiography of Count Basie*, 2nd ed. (New York: Da Capo Press, 2002), 145.

[8] Ibid., 148–149.

[9] Frank Driggs and Chuck Haddix, *Kansas City Jazz: From Ragtime to Bebop* (New York: Oxford University Press, 2005), 126.

[10] Chuck Haddix, *Bird: The Life and Music of Charlie Parker* (Urbana: University of Illinois Press, 2013), 134.

ST. LOUIS

[1] Dennis C. Owsley, "City of the Gabriels: The Jazz History of St. Louis," Jazz Saint Louis, jazzstl.org /wp-content/uploads/2018/01/jstl_studyguide _history.pdf. Last modified January 2018.

[2] Qtd. in Kevin Belford, Christian Frommelt, and Michael R. Allen, "The Palladium Made St. Louis Music History; What Will We Make of the Palladium?" Preservation Research Office, December 15, 2011, preservationresearch.com/midtown/the-palladium -made-st-louis-music-history-what-will-we-make-of -the-palladium.

[3] Gillespie, *To Be, or Not . . . to Bop*, 188.

PART THREE: THE WEST COAST

LOS ANGELES

[1] George Spink, "Benny Goodman Launches Swing Era in Chicago," *Chicago Sun-Times*, November 10, 1985. Available at web.archive.org /web/20090209021911/http://tuxjunction.net /bennygoodman.htm.

[2] Ross Firestone, *Swing, Swing, Swing: The Life and Times of Benny Goodman* (New York: W. W. Norton, 1994), 149.

[3] Donald Clarke, "The Rise and Fall of Popular Music: The Swing Era Begins," Music Box, donaldclarkemusicbox.com/rise-and-fall /detail.php?c=10.

[4] Burns, *Jazz*.

[5] Ted Gioia, "Jazz Central," *City Journal*, Summer 2016, city-journal.org/html/jazz-central-14614.html.

[6] Clora Bryant et al., eds., *Central Avenue Sounds: Jazz in Los Angeles* (Berkeley: University of California Press, 1999), 149.

[7] "H'wood Plantation to Relight May 10 with Andy Kirk Ork," *Billboard*, May 12, 1945, 28.

[8] Leonard Feather, *Inside Be-Bop* (New York: J. J. Robins & Sons, 1949), 35.

[9] Ibid.

[10] Ibid.

[11] Toby Gleason, ed., *Conversations in Jazz: The Ralph J. Gleason Interviews* (New Haven, CT: Yale University Press, 2016), 101–102.

[12] Ted Gioia, *West Coast Jazz: Modern Jazz in California, 1945–1960* (Los Angeles: University of California Press, 1992), 373.

SAN FRANCISCO

[1] Elizabeth Pepin, "Swing the Fillmore," PBS, 2000–2001, pbs.org/kqed/fillmore/learning/music /swing.html. Accessed May 8, 2019.

[2] Elizabeth Pepin, "*Harlem of the West: The San Francisco Fillmore Jazz Era* author Elizabeth Pepin," interview by Adrienne Wartts, Jerry Jazz Musician, August 16, 2006, jerryjazzmusician.com/2006/08 /harlem-of-the-west-the-san-francisco-fillmore -jazz-era-author-elizabeth-pepin.

[3] Elizabeth Pepin and Lewis Watts, *Harlem of the West: The San Francisco Fillmore Jazz Era* (San Francisco: Chronicle Books, 2006), 77.

[4] Ibid., 82.

[5] Pepin, "Swing the Fillmore."

[6] Carol Chamberland, "Jimbo Edwards: In Remembrance," *Jazz Now*, May 2000. Available at users .rcn.com/jazzinfo/v10n01May00/FinJimbo.html, accessed October 15, 2019.

A CONVERSATION WITH ROBIN GIVHAN

[7] Robin Givhan, "What We Talk About When We Talk About 'Effortless Chic,'" *Washington Post*, September 28, 2018, washingtonpost.com/news/arts-and -entertainment/wp/2018/09/28/what-we-talk-about -when-we-talk-about-effortless-chic.

Selected Bibliography

BOOKS

Bird, Christiane. *The Da Capo Jazz and Blues Lover's Guide to the U.S.* 3rd ed. Cambridge, MA: Da Capo Press, 2001.

Jackson, Maurice, and Blair A. Ruble, eds. *DC Jazz: Stories of Jazz Music in Washington, DC.* Washington, D.C.: Georgetown University Press, 2018.

Mosbrook, Joe. *Cleveland Jazz History.* 2nd ed. Cleveland: Northeast Ohio Jazz Society, 2003.

O'Connell, Sean J. *Los Angeles's Central Avenue Jazz.* Charleston, SC: Arcadia Publishing, 2014.

Reisner, Robert George, ed. *Bird: The Legend of Charlie Parker.* New York: Da Capo Press, 1975.

Stryker, Mark. *Jazz from Detroit.* Ann Arbor: University of Michigan Press, 2019.

Taylor, Arthur. *Notes and Tones: Musician-to-Musician Interviews.* New York: Coward, McCann & Geoghegan, 1982. First published 1977 by Perigee Books.

ARTICLES

Felten, Eric. "How the Taxman Cleared the Dance Floor." *Wall Street Journal*, March 17, 2013. wsj.com/articles/SB10001424127887323628804578348050712410108 (accessed May 19, 2019).

"Live! From Club Kavakos!" Victorian Secrets of Washington, DC. victoriansecrets.net/kavakos2.html (accessed February 11, 2019).

"The Second Most Historic Jazz Structure in KC." Kcjazzlark, July 19, 2010. kcjazzlark.com/2010/07/second-most-historic-jazz-structure-in.html (accessed February 17, 2019).

Photography and Illustration Credits

Little is known about the photographers of the club souvenir images, who are likely to have been employees of the individual clubs or concessionaires. We will remain forever grateful for their contributions.

All photographs, photo folders, and memorabilia courtesy of Jeff Gold except:

Abbott, John: 120.

Getty Images: 19: Bettmann via Getty Images; 101, Gjon Mili/The LIFE Picture Collection via Getty Images; 106, Bob Parent/Hulton Archive via Getty Images; 206, Hansel Mieth/The LIFE Picture Collection via Getty Images.

Gold, Ella: 51, 94.

Hart, Adam: 90: © Adam Hart.

Hershorn, Tad: 202: Tad Hershorn/Courtesy Dan Morgenstern.

Historical Society of Washington D.C.: 133: Remembering U Street photograph collection, Historical Society of Washington, D.C.

Kramer, Howard: 147 (bottom, left), 150 (right), 151: Collection of Howard Kramer.

Library of Congress: 10–11 (top, center), 13, 26, 35, 49, 53, 62, 63, 71, 92, 123, 125, 138, 139,

239: William P. Gottlieb/Ira and Leonore S. Gershwin Fund Collection, Music Division, Library of Congress. 14: Library of Congress, Geography and Map Division.

Los Angeles Public Library: 217 (bottom); 219: Shades of L.A. Collection/Los Angeles Public Library.

Magnum Photos: 99: © Dennis Stock/Magnum Photos.

McBride, Clay Patrick: 160.

Moran, Jason: 54, 55: Collection of Jason Moran.

Perkins, Marc and Mary: 2: From the collection of Marc and Mary Perkins.

Samuel, Jacob: 260.

Seidman, Helayne: 238.

Smithsonian National Museum of African American History and Culture: 31, Collection of the Smithsonian National Museum of African American History and Culture; 237: Collection of the Smithsonian National Museum of African American History and Culture, Gift of Mary E. Jackson, Posthumously and Linda A. Jackson, © Linda A. Jackson / Estate of Steve Jackson Jr./CTS Images/ NMAAHC.

sittin' in

To Norm + Marg, Jucki Charlie Parker

SITTIN' IN

© 2020 by Jeff Gold

All rights reserved. No part of this book may be
used or reproduced in any manner whatsoever
without written permission except in the case
of brief quotations embodied in critical articles
and reviews. For information address Harper
Design, 195 Broadway, New York, NY 10007.

HarperCollins books may be purchased for educational, business, or sales promotional use. For
information please email the Special Markets
Department at SPsales@harpercollins.com.

First published in 2020 by
Harper Design
An Imprint of HarperCollins*Publishers*
195 Broadway
New York, NY 10007
Tel: (212) 207-7000
Fax: (855) 746-6023
harperdesign@harpercollins.com
www.hc.com

Distributed throughout the world by
HarperCollins*Publishers*
195 Broadway
New York, NY 10007

ISBN 978-0-06-291470-5
Library of Congress Control Number:
2018965720

Book design by Paul Kepple and Alex Bruce
at Headcase Design
www.headcasedesign.com
Printed in Malaysia
Second Printing, 2021

About the Author

← LEFT **Jason Moran**
(left) and Jeff Gold.

Jeff Gold is a Grammy Award–winning music historian, archivist, author, and executive. Profiled by *Rolling Stone* as one of five "top collectors of high-end music memorabilia," he is an internationally recognized expert who has consulted for the Rock & Roll Hall of Fame, the Museum of Pop Culture (formerly the Experience Music Project), record labels, and cultural institutions. A former executive at Warner Bros. Records and A&M Records and a four-time Grammy-nominated art director, he has helped curate exhibitions including EMP's *Beatlemania! America Meets the Beatles, 1964* and *Bob Dylan's American Journey, 1956–1966*. He has also appeared as a music memorabilia expert on PBS's *History Detectives* and VH1's *Rock Collectors*. The author of *101 Essential Rock Records: The Golden Age of Vinyl from the Beatles to the Sex Pistols* and *Total Chaos: The Story of The Stooges/As Told by Iggy Pop*, Gold is the owner of the music collectibles website Recordmecca and writes about topics of interest to collectors on its blog, recordmecca.com /blog. He lives in Venice, California, and you can follow him on Twitter at @recordmecca or Instagram at recordmecca.